Frommer's™

Wales

with your family

From cliff-top castles to sandy coves

by Nick Dalton & Deborah Stone

John Wiley & Sons, Ltd

UK Publisher: Sally Smith
Executive Project Editor: Daniel Mersey (Frommer's UK)
Commissioning Editor: Mark Henshall (Frommer's UK)
Development Editor: Kate Calvert
Project Editor: Hannah Clement (Frommer's UK)
Cartographer: John Tulip
Photo Research: Jill Emeny (Frommer's UK)

Wiley also publishes its books in a variety of electronic formats. Some content that appears in
print may not be available in electronic books.

British Library Cataloguing in Publication Data
A catalogue record for this book is available from the British Library

ISBN: 978-0-470-72320-3

Typeset by Wiley Indianapolis Composition Services
Printed and bound in China by SNP Leefung Printers

5 4 3 2 1

Contents

About the Authors

Nick Dalton is a freelance writer who has written regularly on travel and other subjects for the *Daily Telegraph, Sunday Telegraph, Times* and *Sunday Express.* He also contributes to numerous travel, ski and music magazines and writes regularly on family travel for takethe family.com

Deborah Stone is a freelance writer who works regularly for the *Daily Telegraph* and *Sunday Telegraph,* working on both travel and lifestyle supplements. She has worked for the *Daily Express,* written for *The Times, Daily Mail,* parenting and travel magazines and for takethefamily.com. She writes about gardening as well as travel and family life. She and Nick live together in Wimbledon with children Georgia and Henry.

Acknowledgements

Here's to our children Georgia and Henry – we couldn't have done it without them. Also many thanks to all our friends and relatives who have come up with ideas, suggested favourite places and helped with research – especially Marge and Ken Stone, Jacqueline and Malcolm Ackland and Ken Packer.

Thanks to Glenda Davies and Lowri Jones at Visit Wales, Ed Townsend at Cardiff & Co, Jacquie Knowles and Pat Jones at Star Attractions. Thanks also to Blacks for the use of their top-notch camping gear on our travels.

Dedication

This book is dedicated to our children Georgia and Henry, but also to our own parents, brothers and sisters, and the memories of happy family holidays we shared – many of them in Wales!

An Additional Note

Please be advised that travel information is subject to change at any time and this is especially true of prices. We therefore suggest that you write or call ahead for confirmation when making your travel plans. The authors, editors and publisher cannot be held responsible for experiences of readers while travelling. Your safety is important to us however, so we encourage you to stay alert and be aware of your surroundings.

Star Ratings, Icons & Abbreviations

Hotels, restaurants and attraction listings in this guide have been ranked for quality, value, service, amenities and special features using a star-rating system. Hotels, restaurants, attractions, shopping and nightlife are rated on a scale of zero stars (recommended) to three (exceptional). In addition to the star rating system, we also use 5 feature icons that point you to the great deals, in-the-know advice and unique experiences. Throughout the book, look for:

FIND	Special finds – those places only insiders know about
MOMENT	Special moments – those experiences that memories are made of
VALUE	Great values – where to get the best deals
OVERRATED	Places or experiences not worth your time or money
GREEN	Attractions employing responsible tourism policies

The following **abbreviations** are used for credit cards:

AE	American Express
MC	Mastercard
V	Visa

A Note on Prices

In the Family-friendly Accommodation section of this book we have used a price category system.

An Invitation to the Reader

In researching this book, we discovered many wonderful places – hotels, restaurants, shops and more. We're sure you'll find others. Please tell us about them, so we can share the information with your fellow travellers in upcoming editions. If you were disappointed with a recommendation, we'd love to know that too. Please email: frommers@wiley.co.uk or write to:

Frommer's Wales with Your Family, 1st Edition
John Wiley & Sons, Ltd
The Atrium
Southern Gate
Chichester
West Sussex, PO19 8SQ

Photo Credits

Inside Images

All images © Nick Dalton & Deborah Stone with the following exceptions:

© Catherine Murrison: p91.

Courtesy of Alamy: p77 (© The Photolibrary Wales); p153 (© Realimage); p171 (© Scott Hortop Travel); p175 (© World Pictures); p183 (© Powys Photo); p196 (© David Angel); p205 (© David Noble Photography); p215 (© Coyote-Photography.co.uk); p228 (© Holmes Garden Photos).

Courtesy of FotoLibra: p1, p72, p83 (© Nick Jenkins); p110 (© Mark J Slack).

Courtesy of PCL: p62 (© Nick Dryhurst); p103, p127, p143, (© Chris Warren); p129 (© Edmund Nagele).

Courtesy of TTL: p178 (© Andy Williams).

1 Family Highlights of Wales

Since our childhoods Wales has been the place for classic family holidays, offering windswept beaches and sandy sandwiches, castles and green hillsides. It still offers all those things, but now it's also the home of television's regenerated *Doctor Who*, with youngsters clamouring to see the Daleks in the exhibition at Cardiff's hip new Cardiff Bay development. It is also a place parents will recognise from the dark and decidedly adult alien-fighting TV hit *Torchwood* – a *Doctor Who* spin-off. There are major new attractions, a host of historic rail journeys, and the biggest natural attraction in England or Wales – Mount Snowdon. It's a place we love to take our own children.

Family holidays in Wales have a retro joyfulness, open spaces, mountains, rivers and coastal walks, Thermos flasks and ginger biscuits. But, should you choose to do so, you can stop for a cappuccino, shop for hip surfing gear and visit hi-tech hands-on attractions.

Hopefully, there will always be parts of Wales that are far enough from the crowds to provide a natural antidote to the rigours of a stressful modern life. There's still a delightful *Famous Five* feel to exploring distant bays, climbing sand dunes and poking around in rock pools. Holiday resorts still look like they've been lifted straight from the 1950s. Yet peek behind the lace curtains and discerning parents will find smart and trendy hotels that welcome children with more than a hastily-scrawled sign.

It's not hard to find restaurants that revel in local produce, and take pride in providing youngsters with more than chicken nuggets and ketchup. There are also family pubs that really are family places – smoke-free and cheery without having the feel of a playbarn.

Don't, though, think that Wales is simply a quiet backwater. The holiday resorts of north Wales – Rhyl and Llandudno – are awash with people in high season, and the masses of smart holiday cottages in Pembrokeshire down south generally get booked up months in advance. Lanes leading to picturesque beaches (or at least to the cliff paths to picturesque beaches) reach gridlock – and far too much of the coast is covered in a sea of past-their-sell-by-date caravan parks.

But forget any thoughts that a family holiday here is a poor relation to a week on the Costas. Our children, Georgia and Henry, at the time of writing 10 and 7, have been here more times than they can count and loved every minute – whether staying in the luxury of the Italianate resort Portmeirion or sleeping in the roof of a camper van; in a cosy B&B or in a tent at one of the green and pleasant new breed of camping and caravan sites.

Every day is an adventure, filled with splashing in the surf on a balmy summer's day, eating creamy Welsh-made ice creams, and playing beach cricket, barbecuing juicy local lamb burgers, creeping through the dark tunnels of abandoned mines, climbing mountains and generally enjoying the great outdoors.

It can still be a place for a cheap holiday, and you can have a great time on even the tightest budget if you take a tent (or brave the bleak regimentation of a caravan park). But it is also a place to splash out on smart accommodation and fun

Wales has all the attractions of Europe's lakes and mountains destinations, places that families cheerfully get on a plane to visit at great expense – so why not stay in Wales?

WALES FAMILY HIGHLIGHTS

Best Experiences We love the variety of experiences that Wales has to offer, from the city life of Cardiff (p 21), to the wonderful beaches of the west coast (p 120), to the awesome splendour of Snowdon and the Brecon Beacons (p 219 and p 91).

Best Man-made Attractions

Dr Who Up Close (p 31) in Cardiff's Bay is a favourite of children and adults alike, with an ever-updated, changing collection of memorabilia, from outfits to full-size talking Daleks and Cybermen. The Big Pit (p 66), in the valleys north of Cardiff, is the essence of Wales, coal-mining-turned-tourism, man-made in the very biggest sense, with the chance to go underground wearing helmet lamps.

Best Natural Attractions

Snowdon, obviously, but the Brecon Beacons and the Black Mountains are also a treat. On a more focused level, Henrhyd Falls (p 98) and other waterfalls in the Beacons are stunning, and the National Showcaves (p 97) are eerily beautiful.

Best Beaches Where do you start? Almost any beach on the Gower Peninsula – especially Three Cliffs Bay – although Pembrokeshire is our family's favourite part of Wales with the

View over Cardiff Bay

wildly beautiful Marloes Sands (p 137), the desert island feel of Barafundle Bay (p 132), or the miles of wide open sand at Newgale (p 138), and the seaside resort sands of Tenby (p 128). Neighbouring Cardiganshire (Ceredigion) is also a delight, especially Mwnt, near Cardigan (p 161) or the sands and dunes at Ynyslas north of Borth, just across the river from Aberdyfi, which itself has an unusually lovely estuary beach. Then there's the crescent beach at Abersoch (p 00) on the Llyn Peninsula, and uncrowded sandy coves further west.

Best Resorts Tenby (p 128) is the main resort town in the south, which along with its villagey-harbour neighbour Saundersfoot offers a near-perfect blend of beaches and town life. New Quay (p 164) on the west coast is smaller, combining seaside fun with sea-faring adventures. And Barmouth (p 228), on the edge of

Seaside spades, New Quay

the Snowdonia National Park, has quietly become a favourite of ours. The small but lively town has a long beach and a backdrop of mountains.

Best Outdoor Activities
Walking stretches of the Pembrokeshire Coastal Path (p 123) can be fun for parents with teenagers or energetic youngsters – try heading up on to the cliffs at Stackpole (calling at Barafundle Bay), or walking around Dinas Head, near Fishguard. In fact, just about any seaside spot you visit will have the path meandering through. The National Mountain Centre at Capel Curig (p 00), offers mountain fun of the organised variety, including children's and family taster days – one of dozens of activity centres around the country.

Best Watery Activities
Cardigan Bay Active (p 145) is a loose collective of enthusiastic types who organise everything from delightfully peaceful trips through Cilgerran Gorge, just south of Cardigan, to sea kayaking and coasteering (climbing and splashing your way along the coast).

Best Boat Ride The Dolphin Survey Ship from New Quay (p 164), Cardiganshire, takes you to look for dolphins and other creatures. VentureJet (p 147) operates from outside St David's, Pembrokeshire, with hair-raising jaunts to look for sealife, darting into caves in jet-propelled dinghys.

Pembrokeshire Coastal Path

Best Castles Caerphilly (p 46) is one of Europe's biggest, and is just what every youngster thinks a castle should be – battlements, towers, arrow slits – all that stuff. However, perhaps more fascinating to both young and old are the magical faux castles built on old foundations for coal baron Lord Bute. Cardiff Castle (p 27) in the city centre and Castell Coch (p 41) in the hills outside, are magical fantasy lands of ornately painted rooms, exquisite craftsmanship and extravagant style, like a cross between *Harry Potter* and *The Lord of the Rings*, while Castle Coch – with its circular, roofed towers – has a touch of *Chitty Chitty Bang Bang* thrown in.

Best Museums The National Museum of Wales (p 30) in Cardiff is of international quality with art, dinosaurs and much more. The National Slate Museum (p 221) in old slate quarry buildings in Llanberis was a surprising hit with us, and St Fagans: National History Museum (p 42) near Cardiff, is superb, too.

Best Family Events Cardiff has regular events in Roald Dahl Plass, outside the Millennium Centre on the Bay, such as Cardiff Harbour Festival in August. Food festivals also abound, with Abergavenny one of the biggest (p 95). All – including Cardigan (p 158) with its riverside setting – include family entertainment.

THE BEST ACCOMMODATION

Most Family-friendly Option
The Porth Tocyn Country Hotel on the cliffs above Abersoch (p 211) on the Llyn Peninsula does it with style. Family-run, you feel like you're part of a big country house party, children running around the meadows outside then sitting down to their own dinner, with adults dining later (along with outsiders in the

know) in a restaurant that's been in the Good Food Guide for years.

Best City Hotel We stayed at the cool, modern Hilton (p 47) opposite Cardiff Castle and now the children whoop the name and want to stay whenever we pass a Hilton sign. The stylish rooms, stainless steel swimming pool and Razzi restaurant (with activity sets and free quality meals for youngsters eating with hotel guests) went down a storm. It has a perfect position, too.

Best Grand Hotel Portmeirion is an Italianate folly (star of TV's *The Prisoner*) just outside Porthmadog. There's the hotel itself and a number of rooms and apartments in fantastical buildings around the 'village', which is enclosed, safe, and somewhere our children adored for simply being a brilliant place to stay.

Best Self-catering These are the places that companies such as English Country Cottages offer – not just cottages but historic farmhouses and country piles, sleeping anything from parents with a baby to a multi-generation family get-together.

Best Setting It has to be Portmeirion again.

Best Camp Site It's difficult to choose the best camp site because much depends on how full it is – particularly at weekends. But, during the week, Hillend Camp Site on the Gower Peninsula (p 89) is as close to the beach at Rhossili Bay as you can get – yet sheltered by huge sand dunes and with family-only fields, play area and café.

Best Boutique Hotel Escape in Llandudno looks as trad as its surroundings, yet beyond the gardens and white façade is a deliciously-modern B&B. There are PlayStations in rooms along with posh TVs (and sea and mountain views) They take children from age 10.

Portmeirion

Best Budget Accommodation
We really are fans of Youth Hostels. They're often in spots that money couldn't buy and we (and the children) love the freedom they offer. Port Eynon YH, a former lifeboat station on the Gower Peninsula (p 89), is quite sensational.

Best Extended Family Accommodation Feel like lords of the manor at Tros Yr Afon, a stone manor house near the rocky shoreline of the Menai Strait in Anglesey. The main building sleeps 16, plus two. Then converted cottages and stables in the courtyard take another nine. Beaches abound and the charms of the town of Beaumaris are just a stroll away.

THE BEST EATING

Most Child-friendly Restaurant Castle Deudraeth at Portmeirion. The brasserie-style restaurant is big and airy, with lots of youngsters wandering about. The picture windows open on to a large lawn with views of the sea where they played happily. Children's food was both tasty and attractive – Georgia's grilled chicken with chips was something we'd have gladly eaten ourselves.

Best Seafood Hive on the Quay in Aberaeron serves crab, lobster, grilled mackerel and other delights from Cardigan Bay in an old wharf building in one of the coast's most delightful towns.

Best Budget Nosh Pete's Eats, a kind of hippy hikers cafe in Llanberis, where those who've walked Snowdon have tucked into huge meals for 30 years. It's where mixed grill eaters meet brown rice lovers – and children's meals cost less than £2.50. Open for dinner – and wine's £6.70 a bottle.

Best Ice Cream There are any number of swish ice cream makers in Wales, but we all love Cadwalader's, available at the maker's growing chain of cafes where you can also get sandwiches, coffee – and alcoholic ice cream cocktails. Ices come in everything from chocolate to dragon's breath (don't ask!) and, should you visit at the right time, Christmas pudding. The one at Cardiff Bay is great for grabbing a cornet, the one in Portmeirion fun for people-watching, and the brand new one at the original 1927 shop in Criccieth best for sea views, across Tremadog Bay.

CYCLING

This is the place. There are more than 1,000 miles of cycle trails in Wales that are part of the 10,000-mile National Cycle Network throughout the UK. Whether you want to cruise with tots along the Promenade at Rhyl or put in serious training on the slopes of Snowdon, there's something to suit every family. About a third of the trails are off-road – more generally meaning that they're on paths or old railway tracks rather than being serious mountain biking for experts. And despite the mountains, many are flat and safe for even the youngest cyclist, deep in the country and returning softly to their starting point.

For the more fit and adventurous there's the 377-mile Celtic Trail from Chepstow on the English border to Fishguard on the Pembrokeshire coast. Well, perhaps more realistically you could try part of it, which is how it's designed. The Millennium Coastal Path near Llanelli, on the south coast, translates into a 12-mile seaview dream loop. To the west, the Camarthen–Fishguard loop is 146 miles of spectacular – but hilly – scenery.

Bike hire shops are susprisingly in evidence in most areas of Wales. For full details visit the National Cycle Network sites *www.sustrans.org.uk*, or *www. cycling.visitwales.com*.

GOLF

Wales has gone golf mad since winning the right to host the 2010 Ryder Cup, at the Celtic Manor Resort near Newport, Gwent. Its 200 courses are experiencing a boom, which might mean crowds but also means top facilities, as well as a drive to encourage youngsters to take up the game. The Golf Foundation works towards improving standards in schools, and attitudes are more relaxed towards children at many clubs. The Celtic Manor, a luxury resort for all the family, offers junior golf tuition, including coaching weeks during school holidays. If it's just dad or mum who wants to play, there are courses across the country that are ideal for slipping off for a few hours while the rest of the family hits the beach or a range of other attractions. Visit *www.golfasitshouldbe.com*.

FISHING

Nowhere is better for a bit of father and son (or daughter) bonding than Wales, where you've got an unrivalled collection of rivers, reservoirs, lakes and sea. You can fish for huge pike in the ancient waters of Lake Bala in Snowdonia National Park, or huge sea bass at many locations around the coast. Charter boats take you off Pembrokeshire where you can bag a shark, or you can find trout in the River Usk in the Black Mountains. There are more than 500 lakes in Wales with dozens of rivers and charter boats in almost every port. See *www.fishing.visitwales.com*.

2 Planning a Family Trip to Wales

WALES

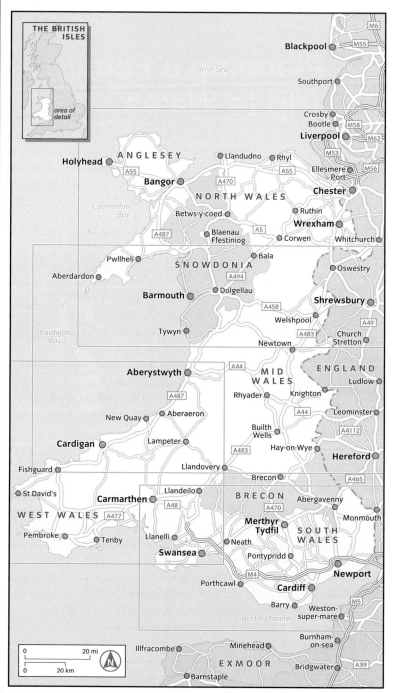

Wales, for many, is a holiday destination for a summer get-away. We – and the children – would happily spend a week or even longer here, enjoying the great outdoors in the same way as we would in somewhere like Brittany.

For many more it's somewhere you can get to for a long weekend, or even a short one. You can be across the Severn Bridge in a couple of hours from west London, or across the border in far less from cities like Birmingham, Manchester and Liverpool. That means it's increasingly a place where you can easily find a decent family retreat for a couple of nights. And the ever-increasing number of adventure specialists also means that more and more people expect to come outside high season (and expect to get wet). The great thing about Wales is that you are going to a completely different country, with different attitudes, yet you don't have to worry about passports and airports, foreign baby foods and strange electricity sockets. Wherever you go you'll find recognisable high street shops and food that's as reassuring as you want it to be. When we first took the children they didn't know what to expect, but quickly became attuned to the fact that they might be on a beach one day and up a mountain the next, in a theme park or in a water park. Our trip to Cardiff was one of the biggest hits (they're usually quickly bored walking along streets), and they rarely objected to getting into the car, knowing that there was going to be somewhere and something interesting at the other end. Don't worry too much about where you'll end up – just go!

WHERE TO GO & WHY

Cardiff City life with hands-on museums, sports stadiums, waterfront, culture, great restaurants, plenty of shops, parks ... and the *Doctor Who* exhibition. And Cardiff is a perfect base for exploring the seaside (Penarth), and the interior where there's a wealth of countryside along with industrial heritage (particularly coal mines), which has been turned into child-friendly attractions.

The South You couldn't wish for a more varied landscape and region. There's the tranquillity of the Welsh Wye Valley towns, the surprisingly pretty Vale of Glamorgan and its Heritage Coastline, the fascination of the Welsh Valleys' industrial heritage, and the new visitor attractions of Swansea – plus the world-class beauty of the Gower Peninsula's beaches.

The West Tenby is one of the biggest, busiest seaside resorts and yet it just about maintains the feel of a moderate-sized fishing town. There are dozens of beautiful beaches to discover in the Pembrokeshire Coast National Park – most of them sandy. Manorbier, Barafundle, Broad Haven South and Marloes are among the best. Go further and you find the delights of the St David's Peninsula, a place of crashing waves and beaches, wedged between cliffs or stretching for miles. The coast becomes wilder and the cliff tops more beautiful as they skirt past Fishguard northwards to the sandy estuary beaches of Newport and Poppet Sands, where Teifi estuary heralds the start of mid Wales.

The Middle This green heaven tumbles down on either side of the Cambrian Mountains where you'll find isolated gold mines, the pretty university town of Lampeter, reservoirs and more mountains. The Brecon Beacons and the Black Mountains both have their lofty, away-from-it-all charms, but are in easy reach of civilisation.

The North One of the biggest, boldest places in the UK, this is where you find Snowdon, the highest mountain in Wales, and a bewildering mix of hard-core outdoor activities and tourist attractions centred on the village of Llanberis, set among the most stunning scenery in the country. In one direction you find sparsely-populated Anglesey, in the other the bucket and spade seaside frenzy of Rhyl and Llandudno. It's yet another region of extraordinary contrasts, typical of Wales.

WHEN TO GO

Whenever you can. The weather is always going to be unpredictable (in the north we've sunbathed on the beach one summer's day, and been drenched in the most insidious mountain mist the next) but it's probably better than you think. So while the hills can be cloudier – and especially in Snowdonia rainier – than England, the coasts, and particularly the southwestern one, can be at least as sunny as the English south coast, and the western coast warm too, though sometimes windy – generally from the west.

Wild daffodils, bluebells and masses of other spring and early summer flowers make Wales a delight before the main summer months. Autumn is wonderful for walking – the russet tones of bracken colouring the cliff tops just as much as the Brecons and other mountain areas. Winter snow on the mountains is also a wonderful sight, with many holiday homes, B&Bs and small hotels offering crackling log fires to ensure a cosy, restful experience once you're back indoors.

GETTING THEM INTERESTED

How can any child not be interested in a country whose national emblem is a giant red dragon? A country where Merlin the magician grew up – you can visit his birthplace near Carmarthen – and where King Arthur himself is said to be buried? The legends of Wales may have striking similarities with those of other Celtic strongholds (south west England and north west France spring to mind), but after climbing the mysterious Black Mountain near the Brecon Beacons National Park, who could doubt that the tarn here was the very spot that The Lady of The Lake of Arthurian legend appeared?

There are many websites that children could look at to find out more about Welsh legends before you travel. A good starting place is *www.bbc.co.uk/wales/history* which covers several aspects of Welsh history, with links to other sites. Wales is also one of the few places in Britain where tourists can take a trip down a real coal mine – and wear a proper miner's hat at the same time. The Big Pit is the Welsh National Coal Museum and only a short diversion off the M4 just outside Cardiff. Tales of child labour down the pits are sure to get them interested – and if that doesn't do it they can't fail to be drawn to the plight of pit ponies. To find out more about The Big Pit and other Welsh National Museums – all with the added bonus of free entry – go to *www.museumwales.ac.uk*.

Of course, not all children will be turned on by history and Arthurian legends – even though Wales has some of the most impressive castles in the world to visit. Perhaps yours are more outdoors children. If that's the case, you couldn't find a better place to take them – practically all of Wales is outdoors. You could easily base your holiday around one of their favourite activities. There's plenty of scope for mountain biking or just plain old fashioned cycling, for instance, and they can download information on traffic-free cycle routes from *www.sustrans.org.uk* so they can help you plan where to go. You might want to base yourself near outdoor activity centres if you have older children who want to get into canoeing, climbing, abseiling or windsurfing – and that's just for starters. They are bound to have an opinion on what they want to do, and you'll find some useful information in our Active Families sections. If they just want to go to a different outstandingly beautiful beach every day, you're home and dry in West Wales (weather permitting). And if all else fails just remind them that Wales is where the BBC makes Dr Who. The iconic TV series is filmed in and around Cardiff, with lots of sights showing up in classic episodes, many of which you can visit yourself. You could even try to interest them in that other Welsh television icon Ivor the Engine – although that particular 1960s children's TV gem may not have the pull that it used to (even though BBC2 Wales has used Ivor in adverts to promote its digital service).

Understanding the Lingo

To the novice holidaymaker, it's quite extraordinary just how *Welsh* Wales is. Signs, addresses, place names, menus are mostly in both Welsh and English, which can be baffling in itself. The road signs are in dual language, which leads the unwary to suspect there are two different towns ahead. And then sometimes there's a lone sign that's just Welsh, making you think you've missed the road to Cardiff. Because, unlike many other languages, there's rarely a translation obvious to the untrained eye, Pembrokeshire becomes Dyfed while Cardigan comes in slightly closer as Cerdigion. *Llan* (which seems to be the start of half the place names) means *church*, while *aber* (which seems to start the other half) is river mouth.

Several words it is handy to know are *gwesty* (hotel), *siôp* (shop), *gorsaf* (station), *traeth* (beach), *ffordd* (no, it's road) and *cawl cennin* (well, you never know when you might fancy leek soup).

And while we're on the subject we shouldn't forget the classic Llanfairpwllgwyngyllgogerychwyrndrobwllllantysiliogogogoch, the village in Anglesey, which (roughly) is *The Church of St Mary by the pool with the white hazel near the rapid whirlpool by St Tysilio's church and the red cave.* Although on road signs you'll see it as Llanfair PG, which isn't half as much fun. See p 00 for a more extensive list of Welsh words.

GETTING THERE

By car The M4 runs from the south-west of London across the Severn Bridge and two-thirds the length of south Wales. Access couldn't be easier from the south and south-east, and even from areas north of the capital. The M4 Severn Bridge crossing costs €6.40for cars, but you only pay west-bound. Connections with M50 and M5 provide links to the Midlands and South West. On a good day you can make it from London to Cardiff, just off the M4 (J29–33) in less than three hours, and you can sail serenely on to Swansea and almost to Pembrokeshire before things slow down.

That's the easy bit. Once you go across country, it's like driving through treacle. There are few straight roads let alone main ones, and you have to be prepared for a long, scenic drive. (Portable DVD players are handy distractions for small passengers.)

If you're heading from the Midlands towards North Wales, the A5 turns north-west before reaching the border and makes something of a beeline for Bangor, then Anglesey. The fact that it goes across Snowdonia slows things down somewhat. From the A5 the A494 heads south-west across the mountains to the seaside resort of Barmouth. All manner of roads cross from Shropshire and Herefordshire but none get you anywhere fast. If, however, you are travelling from the north of England or Scotland there's excellent access to the holiday spots of the north coast. The M56 gets you from Manchester to Chester, and the A55 does a good job of taking you the length of the coast. For more information contact Traveline: ☎ *0870 608 2608; www. traveline.org.uk*.

By coach National Express operates a comprehensive network to more than 80 Welsh destinations from London and many other British towns and cities. Some are direct, some involve changing. National Express: ☎ *0870 580 8080; www.gobycoach. com*.

By air Cardiff International Airport, Rhoose CF 62 3BD: ☎ *01446 711111; www.cwlfly.com*. The airport has direct flights from a number of UK destinations including London (Heathrow, Gatwick, Stansted and Luton), Manchester, East Midlands, Glasgow and Newcastle. It's 19km west of Cardiff and signposted from the M4 at J33. Checker Cars is the airport's official taxi service: ☎ *01446 711747; www.checkercars.com; E: Cardiff@ checkercars.com*. A free shuttle bus runs to the airport railway station where you can catch a train to Cardiff Central and onward services to the west and the north. Cardiff Bus service X91 and EST Transport's 95 bus runs between the airport and Cardiff Central railway station. Hire car firms operating from

the airport include Avis (☎ *0870 608 6328*), Europcar (☎ *01446 711924*) and Hertz (☎ *01446 711722*).

By train There are direct connections from London, Manchester, Liverpool, Bristol, Portsmouth and other UK cities to Cardiff Central Station (Central Square, Cardiff, CF10). Call ☎ *0845 606 1660* or contact National Rail Enquiries (☎ *08457 484950*) or First Great Western (*www.firstgreatwestern.co.uk;* ☎ *0845 700 0125*). The journey from London Paddington takes about two hours. Deals and tickets: *www.thetrainline.com*. Arriva (*www.arrivatrainswales.co.uk*) runs services within Wales, including connections from Cardiff to Swansea and Pembrokeshire (Tenby, Pembroke, Milford Haven, Fishguard and Haverfordwest) and up to Merthyr Tydfil and as far north as Rymney. Virgin Trains (☎ *08457 222333; www. virgintrains.com*) runs services from London Euston to Chester, and across North Wales including Llandudno, Rhyl, Colwyn Bay, Bangor and Holyhead. From other areas of England or Scotland you have to change at Crewe.

There are trains across country from Shrewsbury to Welshpool and all the way to Aberystwyth and Barmouth on the mid-west coast, and a line that heads south-west from the Midlands through Llandrindod to near Swansea.

The Freedom of Wales Flexi Rover pass gives unlimited rail

Welsh Cakes & Other 'Food'

The children are obsessed by them, and once we're across the border a supermarket stop is demanded to stock up. Welsh cakes are flat, soft, floury things, a bit like a thin, bendy scone dusted with sugar, and they are very moreish. You can buy home-made versions (there's a stall at Cardiff indoor market that's piled high) but mostly they come in supermarket packets.

Ice cream is another delight. Their eyes light up at the sight of a Cadwalader's Ice Cream Café, a new Welsh Institution – places where you can have wonderful ices along with sundaes, milk shakes and even a sandwich while adults might fancy an alchoholic ice-cream delight. Other names spring to mind, such as Gianni's (made with organic milk from Caerfai Farm near St David's in Pembrokeshire), and Joe's, a Swansea favourite since 1922 which now has three local parlours. Heavenly have their own shop in their west Wales hometown of Llandeilo, and use bananas, oranges and lavender from historic Aberglasney Gardens as flavourings.

The latter suggests the inventiveness and flair that now infuses traditional favourites across the country. Most evenings we cook on the barbecue at camp sites and, while the children are in heaven with a simple sausage or burger, we want something more. Like the enormous lamb sausages we found at Hancocks of Monmouth (34 Monnow Street), a fine award-winning traditional butcher, and the pork and caramelised onion sausages from an altogether more modern concern in Aberystwyth.

Cawl is an historic Welsh dish, a soupy stew of mutton with lots of vegetables, and deserves its place alongside more eclectic use of favourite ingredients in the new (and in most cases family-friendly) restaurants that are springing up.

Wales is at the forefront of the trendy (and worthwhile) movement that demands local and organic produce. And so it should be. The hills are alive with Welsh lamb and Welsh black cattle, the seas full of everything from lobster to simpler, everyday fish. Vegetables thrive in the balmy (and sometimes wet) climes of the south west. The livestock help create creamy local cheeses, all manner of sausages and other products that might at first seem like adults-only fare yet which end up being wolfed down by excitable children ravenous after another day on the go before another ice cream, perhaps on top of a Welsh cake.

travel for four or eight days, and the freedom of most bus services throughout (adults £65, children 5–15 £32.50, under 5s free).

There are two other passes, for South Wales and North and Mid Wales.

Welsh Whales & Other Wildlife

The west coast of Wales, all around Pembrokeshire, up along Cardiganshire (Ceredigion) and even into Snowdonia, is a special place for marine wildlife. The wild seas and the wild coastline combine to be home to a huge collection of creatures. Off the coast, particularly in Cardigan Bay, you can see seals, bottlenose dolphins, harbour porpoises (subtly different) and even minke whales and basking sharks. The Cardigan Bay Marine Wildlife Centre in New Quay runs boat trips out to look for the creatures – the Bay's 150–200 dolphins is the only resident population in Wales and England.

Grey seals are often seen around the Pembrokeshire islands of Skomer, Skokholm and Ramsey. Groups of fin whales, second only in size to blue whales, have been seen off Ramsey. There are also pilot whales and the occasional humpback and killer whale. Further north, the Llyn Peninsula and Lynas Point on Anglesey are good places for whale and seal spotting.

The wild rocky coasts are the haunt of the peregrine and chough. The islands just off the coast are a haven for seabirds. Half the world's population of the orange-chested Manx Shearwater nests on Skokholm and Skomer. On the latter, one of the UK's three Marine Nature Reserves, a truly stunning sight is the Wick, a sheer cliff with ledges packed tight with nesting seabirds. Guillemots, puffins and razorbills soar colourfully while circling kittiwakes look like a snowstorm – although with their loud cries it's nowhere near as peaceful.

There are many boat trips on offer, from many spots up and down the coast, some which cruise about looking for mammals, others which head out to islands, combining seal spotting with a look at the astonishing bird colonies – fun for all the family, not just nature-lovers.

Inlets and estuaries like the Dyfi, and the secret creeks round Milford Haven, are full of wildfowl and waders, while you barely have to head inland before you see a red kite circling on the breeze. For many years the only handful of these graceful birds clinging on in Great Britain were in remote Welsh valleys, now they have recovered and can be seen across much of the heartland of Wales, where there are opportunities to see them being fed. Meanwhile, on many streams and rivers kingfishers, grey wagtails and dippers are common, with little ringed plovers nesting on gravel banks.

CARAVAN PARKS

The bane of Wales. And yet so many people go to them. We don't mean the pretty fields where you can pull in for the night, we mean the vast tracts of white, tin mobile homes (mobile only in as much as they arrived on the back of a lorry) that fill unlandscaped

Wales on the Rails

The industrial history of Wales, full of coal, copper, limestone and more coal – all stuff that was heavy – led to a huge number of small railways which wound through the valleys and across mountains in the most unlikely fashion. As the pits closed down, other industry faltered, the train as a tool of passenger transport became regarded as outmoded and lines fell into disuse. Some never returned, their routes and tunnels now paths for cyclists and walkers. Others, however, have risen phoenix-like from the ashes of the millions of tons of coal they shifted and Wales now has more than 20 historic lines, running mostly thanks to enthusiasts and volunteers. They operate among some of the most stunning scenery, from bleak mountaintops to the coast, wooded valleys to pristine lakesides. Youngsters love seeing the gleaming engines and climbing aboard the rickety carriages (even if they maybe don't fully appreciate sitting back and enjoying a leisurely trip). Most have fascinating museums, cafés, gift shops and idyllic places for picnics so make a perfect day out. If you're going to try a steam railway anywhere, Wales probably has the best variety of choice within a small area than anywhere else in the world.

Narrow Gauge Railways

Bala Lake Railway A 6.5km trip along the shores of the North Wales lake. *www.bala-lake-railway.co.uk*

Brecon Mountain Railway Travels through Brecon Beacons National Park along the full length of the Taf Fechan Reservoir. *www.breconmountainrailway.co.uk*

Corris Railway Former slate line links Corris, near Machynlleth, and Maespoeth in Mid Wales. *www.corris.co.uk*

Fairbourne and Barmouth Railway Between Barmouth (where you have to use a small ferry to cross the Mawddach Estuary) along the river to Fairbourne on the north-west coast. *www.fairbournerailway.com*

Ffestiniog Railway Stirring ride from Porthmadog at sea level to 216m Blaenau Ffestiniog, at one point looping above itself to gain height. *www.ffestiniograilway.co.uk*

Llanberis Lake Railway Runs for 3.2km in the shadow of Snowdon along Padarn Lake on the line which served Dinorwic slate quarries. *www.lake-railway.co.uk*

Snowdon Mountain Railway Tiny rack and pinion line has been taking tourists to the 1085m summit since 1896 – where there's a new €11m visitor centre. *www.snowdonrailway.co.uk*

fields and can all but be seen from space. According to Visit Wales there are well over 300

parks around Wales and in 2006, 19% of overnight holiday visits to Wales were in static

Talyllyn Railway Beautiful Mid-Wales scenery between Tywyn and Abergynolwyn and Nant Gwernol, passing the delightful Dolgoch Falls. *www.talyllyn.co.uk*

Teifi Valley Railway Enchanting trip along the River Teifi in West Wales *www.teifivalleyrailway.com*

Vale of Rheidol Railway Rises 180m during its 19kmmile journey between Aberystwyth and Devil's Bridge *www.rheidolrailway.co.uk*

Welsh Highland Railway (Caernarfon) Trains run 19km through Snowdonia National Park from Caernarfon with plans to double the length all the way to Porthmadog, linking with the Ffestiniog Railway, a total journey of 65km. *www.festrail.co.uk*

Welsh Highland Railway (Porthmadog) Short trip, but one which includes a journey through the engine sheds, at what will be the terminus of the Caernarfon extension. *www.whr.co.uk*

Welshpool and Llanfair Railway Nearly 26km through mountainous Mid-Wales scenery along the Banwy Valley. *www.wllr.org.uk*

Great Little Trains of Wales (*www.greatlittletrainsofwales.co.uk*) offers a discount card for Bala Lake, Brecon Mountain, Ffestiniog, Llanberis Lake, Talyllyn, Vale of Rheidol, Welsh Highland, Welsh Highland Railway (Caernarfon) and Welshpool and Llanfair railways.

€12.5 gets you a 20% discount on a return journey on each, within a 12-month period.

Standard Gauge Trains

Barry Island Railway Two short branches along the waterfront just south of Cardiff. *www.valeofglamorganrailway.co.uk*

Gwili Railway Evocative recreation of part of abandoned Great Western Railway's Carmarthen–Aberystwyth line. *www.gwili-railway.co.uk*

Llangollen Railway Enchanting ride alongside the River Dee from Llangollen to Carrog through beautiful scenery. *www.llangollen-railway. co.uk*

Pontypool and Blaenavon Railway Starting beside the Big Pit, from where it used to transport coal, this is Britain's steepest historic line, reaching the highest station in England and Wales at 396m. *www. pontypool-and-blaenavon.co.uk*

The list is growing with lines like the Garw Valley Railway near Bridgend, the Swansea Vale Railway, Llanelli and Mynydd Mawr Railway and others aiming to extend the choices.

caravans – and a truly frightening 15 per cent of ALL overnight visits. Some truly are grim; others are the modern equivalent of holiday camps, which, while the rows of caravans may not be a beautiful sight, offer large and often luxurious accommodation along with water parks, restaurants, extravagant night time entertainment and beachfront access. Needless to say there's no one-stop website, so you're on your own. Parkdean Holidays operate two of the best, in South Wales, while Hoseasons and Blakes offer holidays at a number of options.

YOUTH HOSTELS

We like youth hostels, make no mistake, and the children do too. They've never seen a hosteller wearing a big woolly jumper, even in irony. They associate them with freedom and fun. As the YHA people love to tell you, they've changed. Gone are the bleak, if bargain, lodgings and what replaces them are at best still a bargain but have the style of a simple, modern hotel or historic cottage. At worst

they're the sort of house you'd quite like to live in after you'd stripped the woodchip wallpaper. Breakfasts feature posh sausages and Fairtrade coffee.

Anyway, Wales has about 30 to choose from, plus bunkhouses. There are some real style classics, and locations which boutique hotel owners would die for; like Port Eynon on the Gower Peninsula, an old lifeboat station; and Manorbier, on a cliff above the splendid Pembrokeshire beach in a futuristic MoD building. Dolgellau's hostel is a riverside country house, while Ffynnon Wen on the edge of Snowdonia National Park is a stone farmhouse in eight acres of grounds, one of a handful that surround Snowdon.

Families are an important clientele, and rooms that used to be full of bunks now sleep four or six, and are often en-suite, all for a nightly cost of about £14, less for children.

Caravanning through Brecon Beacons

3 Cardiff & the Surrounding Area

Cardiff is the capital of Wales and has been officially since, ooh, 1955. It's Europe's youngest capital city (even though it's long been the country's most important city), and that very recent elevation to greatness is reflected in the youthful feel which makes it ideal for a family visit (even though its roots can be traced back to 600BC when the Celts invaded Europe). At its centre is Cardiff Castle, deep down an ancient monument (a Roman fort) but rebuilt a century ago as the holiday home of the third Marquess of Bute, at the time reputedly the richest man in the world.

The second Marquess of Bute owned Cardiff docks and built the railway that brought coal from the family's mines down to the docks – a neat monopoly which funded his son's extravagant transformation of Cardiff Castle and Castle Coch nearby. However, the docks also brought prosperity to Cardiff, just a small town at the beginning of the 19th century but with full city status by 1905. That prosperity can be seen in the city's impressive civic centre, which incorporates Cathays Park, the National Museum and Gallery and is made of the same elegant Portland stone as Cardiff University next door.

The docks once handled more coal than any other port in the world but after the First World War demand began to fall. The Great Depression of the 1930s badly affected the city's economy and during the Second World War Cardiff was badly bombed.

However, though the docks have largely been decommissioned – in the same way as the Welsh Valleys coal pits – the waterfront has found an exciting new lease of life. A few years back a barrage was built to one side of the remaining docks, creating a vast freshwater lake (with sea locks). Stand amid the stunning new buildings, historic sites, busy attractions and booming restaurants and it's almost like being by the sea.

It's a new nightlife hub but there's plenty for families to do during the day, including exhibitions, concerts and shows at the magnificent Wales Millennium Centre, and there are child-friendly restaurants both during the day and in the evening. With Cardiff Bay only a mile from the city centre by bus, train or boat up the River Taff, it's an unmissable part of the Cardiff experience.

The city itself is also family-friendly with pedestrianised shopping streets, indoor shopping centres, Victorian arcades and an atmospheric indoor market all only a stone's throw from the National Museum and Gallery where dinosaurs all but rub shoulders with the Millennium Stadium's sports heroes.

Further afield are seaside resorts, some of Britain's most impressive castles, industrial heritage centres, Roman ruins, country parks and beautiful countryside.

Yet you can travel the universe without ever leaving the city, which is home to the regenerated TV favourite *Doctor Who* and the scary, alien-hunting spin-off *Torchwood*. The ever-changing Doctor Who Up Close exhibition is a delight – and you can search out real-life sets around the streets.

ESSENTIALS

Visitor Information

Cardiff Gateway Visitor Centre, Old Library, The Hayes
(0870 1211 258, *www.visit cardiff.com*). This is at the heart of the city, next to St David's Hall and near the main shopping centres and central market, where, as well as providing free information leaflets, staff can book accommodation, and there's a left luggage service.

Cardiff Bay Visitor Centre
(02920 463833, *www.cardiff harbour.com*) sits on the promontory between the Bay attractions and the docks; a big, squashed metal cylinder, it's known as The Tube so you can't miss it. Offers plenty of info to pick up and take away, along with interactive exhibitions on the Bay's history and ecology, and a scale model of the city. Further information, including events, can be found on *www. visitcardiffbay.com*

City Layout

The compact layout of Cardiff's city centre makes it an easy place to explore. St David's Shopping Centre and Queens Arcade Shopping Centre are right in the middle of town next to St David's Hall – the National Hall

and Conference Centre of Wales and home to the Welsh Proms among other events. Nearby are the elegant Victorian indoor market and equally intricate Victorian arcades – Morgan Arcade and Royal Arcade.

Walk from here down to the River Taff and you'll find the majestic Millennium Stadium which holds music and sporting events as well as Welsh rugby international matches. North along the river is Bute Park, a haven of peace, with Cardiff Castle nestling in the south east corner of what was once part of the castle's grounds. Five minutes' walk further north is the impressive Civic Centre and the National Museum and Gallery Cardiff, in Cathays Park.

In between all these is a network of interesting streets full of individual shops, restaurants and cafes along with the chain stores and familiar High Street restaurants.

Areas in Brief

The once run-down Cardiff docklands, a mile from the centre, have been transformed into a gleaming example of new Wales. Extravagant buildings on a bustling waterfront and the coffee bars and restaurants of the central Mermaid Quay, combine with historic places to form Cardiff Bay.

This area has always been at the heart of the city's (and the country's) development. It was here that in the 19th century coal from the valleys set sail for the world, powering the industrial revolution.

Coal funded grandiose buildings like City Hall, the Coal Exchange and the New Theatre, and helped coal baron the Third Marquess of Bute (who, handily, also owned the docks) become the richest man in the world.

This was always a multicultural area with almost 50 nationalities passing through and settling in neighbourhoods such as Tiger Bay. After the Second World War the coal fire burned less brightly and the docks gradually fell into disuse.

Regeneration started when the Cardiff Bay Barrage was built in 1999, protecting the coast and transforming a swathe of mucky mudflats into a huge freshwater lake.

The lake is now a sailing and watersports centre (great for teenagers), while the waterfront offers lots of space for youngsters to run around (they love the monolithic stainless steel sculpture with a sheet of water running down), and the chance of boat rides.

Attractions include the Techniquest hands-on science discovery centre, and the Millennium Centre, an architectural icon and performing arts centre rolled into one.

Just across the road is the Red Dragon Centre, an aircraft hanger-like building full of family-friendly restaurants, a multiplex Odeon cinema, 26-lane bowling alley and the Doctor Who Up Close exhibition, celebrating more than 40 years of the sci-fi favourite, now filmed in and around the city.

Regular free festivals and events such as the Caribbean Carnival and the International Food and Drink Festival, take place throughout the year.

Getting Around

By car In the city itself you're best to abandon the car. Street parking is difficult but there are several NCP car parks (☎ 0870 606 7050; www.ncp.co.uk) and year-round weekend park and ride sites (☎ 029 2087 2087/8; www.cardiff.gov.uk;). There is also some parking in Cardiff Bay, but you can get there easily by bus or waterbus – or even catch the train to Cardiff Bay railway terminus.

For out of town destinations though a car is still handy, and there's plenty to see in the surrounding countryside or on the nearby coast – most adventures involving at least one stretch of the M4.

By bus Day tickets on hop-on/hop-off buses make travelling around the city easy. Call ☎ 0870 608 2608 or see www.cardiffbus.com for more details. A South Wales Freedom of Wales Flexipass (☎ 0845 6061 660; www.walesflexipass.co.uk) gives unlimited local bus travel for a week and train rides for four days.

By foot Most city-centre attractions are within easy walking distance of each other, and you can get free city maps from the tourist centre. However, it's probably too far for most children to walk from the centre to Cardiff Bay. Public transport is your best bet but, once you're there the only way to see anything is on foot.

WHAT TO SEE & DO

Top 10 Family Experiences

❶ **Coming face to face** with a real Dalek at the Doctor Who Up Close Exhibition in Cardiff Bay's Red Dragon Centre.

❷ **Hearing the cheers** of the (tape-recorded) crowds as you run down the tunnel to the pitch on a Millennium Stadium tour.

❸ **Finding the invisible man** in the fairytale wall tiles in the nursery at magical Cardiff Castle.

❹ **Stepping back in time** among the picturesque old buildings relocated to St Fagans: National History Museum.

❺ **Pretending to be Rapunzel** at the fantastically-turreted Castle Coch, set in woodlands overlooking a steep gorge.

❻ **Having a picnic** at the ruined Roman amphitheatre at out-of-town Caerleon.

❼ **Playing on the beach** at lovely Penarth before eating fish and chips on the pier.

Cardiff Castle

❽ **Checking out the dinosaurs** at the National Museum and Gallery in Cardiff Civic Centre.

❾ **Eating Cadwalader's ice cream** from the cafe at Cardiff Bay on the Riverbus trip back to the city centre.

❿ **Splashing in the water** at the bottom of the fountain outside Cardiff Bay's Millennium Centre.

Family-friendly Festivals

National St David's Day Parade

City centre, www.stdavidsday.org

Bands, choirs and musical groups in national or historical dress are all part of this colourful event, which also includes dance troupes, mediaeval re-enactment groups and community clubs.

There will be other events in the afternoon and late into the evening, but the main parade starts some time after 1pm at Sophia Close and goes down Cathedral Road heading for Westgate Street and the High Street before finishing at the National Museum Wales.

March

WOW Festival – Wales One World Film Festival

www.wowfilmfestival.org; www.chapter.org

This film festival takes place in several venues throughout Wales including Cardiff's Chapter Arts Centre. Some of the films are aimed at family viewing – but think international art film genre rather than Disney.

March

RHS Spring Flower Show Cardiff

02920 872087; www.rhs.org.uk

The RHS show season gets under way at Bute Park, with designer gardens specially created to exhibit spring flowers at their most beautiful, and leading nurseries displaying some of the very best plants you can buy in the UK – all under one roof. This is a great RHS show for the family to enjoy – far more child-friendly than the Chelsea experience.

April

Cardiff Outdoor Action Show

02020 872087; www.cardiff-festivals.com; www.cardiffharbour.com

Take part in a range of land and water sports and activities at Cardiff Bay's Roald Dahl Plass – and watch some spectacular exhibition performances.

June

Cardiff International Food & Drink Festival

02020 872087; www.cardiff-festivals.com; www.cardiffharbour.com

Get a taste of Wales with some of the country's finest home-produced specialities. There will also be an international flavour to the food on offer at this festival, which stretches right around Cardiff Bay.

July

Welsh Proms

02020 872087; www.cardiff-festivals.com

This series of concerts at St David's Hall in central Cardiff always includes several performances aimed at younger audiences.

July

Children's Festival

02020 872087; www.cardiff-festivals.com

There's sport, music, theatre, circus shows and workshops at this popular festival on Cooper's Field in Bute Park, just behind Cardiff Castle.

July

Cardiff Big Weekend

☎ 02020 872087; www.cardiff-festivals.com; www.cardiffharbour.com

The UK's biggest free outdoor music festival is combined with the Cardiff MAS Carnival and a traditional family funfair to create the city's biggest free event of the year. The music festival and funfair is held at Cardiff Civic Centre over three days, with the Caribbean-style carnival parade winding its way around the city centre on the Saturday afternoon.

August

Mermaid Quay Cardiff Harbour Festival

☎ 02020 872087; www.cardiff-festivals.com; www.cardiffharbour.com

A weekend of family entertainment with a nautical theme at Roald Dahl Plass, where children can take part in water-based activities and workshops as well as exploring tall ships in the Bay.

August

Calan Gaeaf

☎ 02920 573500; www.museumwales.ac.uk

Celebrate All Hallow's Eve – Calan Gaeaf – with traditional Halloween events such as apple bobbing, ghost stories and burning the Wicker Man at St Fagans: National History Museum.

October

Cardiff's Winter Wonderland

☎ 02920 871847; www.cardiff.gov.uk; www.visitcardiff.com

Cardiff's Christmas lights are switched on in November and the winter wonderland continues until New Year with an ice rink, craft stalls, fairground rides and Santa's Grotto on the lawn outside City Hall.

December

The Magic of Christmas Bay

☎ 02020 872087; www.cardiff-festivals.com; www.cardiffharbour.com

Carol concerts, Christmas workshops and the Christmas market at the Norwegian Church, Cardiff Bay.

Throughout December

Calennig

☎ 02920 871847; www.cardiff.gov.uk; www.visitcardiff.com

New Year's Eve celebrated outside Cardiff Civic Centre, includes live music and a family fireworks show.

December 31

City Centre

Cardiff Castle ★ ★ ★ ALL AGES

Castle Street, CF10 3RB, ☎ 029 2087 8100; www.cardiffcastle.com

If you only have time to do one thing in Cardiff city centre, take a guided tour around this castle-come-fantasyland. There's been a fort on the site since Roman times, and the 12th century Norman keep is still intact with

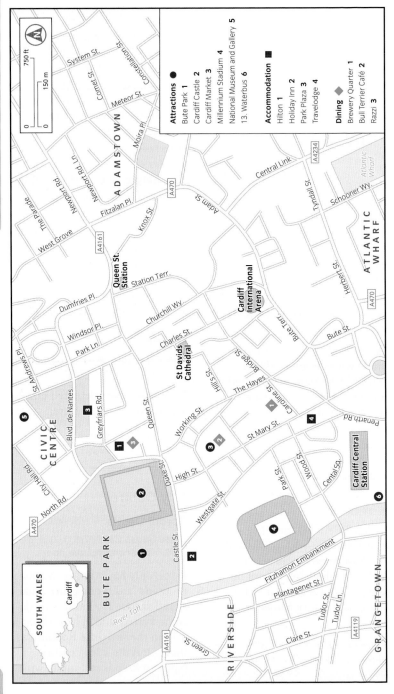

Attractions ●
Bute Park **1**
Cardiff Castle **2**
Cardiff Market **3**
Millennium Stadium **4**
National Museum and Gallery **5**
13. Waterbus **6**

Accommodation ■
Hilton **1**
Holiday Inn **2**
Park Plaza **3**
Travelodge **4**

Dining ◆
Brewery Quarter **1**
Bull Terrier Café **2**
Razzi **3**

fabulous views from its tower. But the building now known as Cardiff Castle was rebuilt in Gothic style by the Third Marquess of Bute – reputedly the richest man in the world as owner of the coal mines, the railway which took the coal to Cardiff docks, and the docks themselves.

Although the family only lived here six weeks a year, the castle was decorated in sumptuous style. Exquisite wall paintings depict fables, fairytales and Biblical stories. Among the highlights is the Banqueting Hall with a minstrels' gallery – where both the Queen and Prince Charles have dined; the ladies' sitting room, cheekily decorated like a harem; the library – Lord Bute's favourite room; and the rooftop garden, which is simply beautiful. But best of all is the day nursery with a series of painted wall tiles depicting nursery rhymes and fairy stories. Children love the combination of the film set extravagance inside, and the large grass area outside.

The last tour starts an hour before closing time but although you need a guide for the castle itself, you can wander freely round the grounds, the walls, the keep and military museum – or go down to the atmospheric restaurant. On the menu is Carmarthen ham, Welsh rarebit and cawl – broth made from lamb and vegetables.

Open daily, March–Oct, 9.30am–6pm; Nov–Feb 9.30am–5pm. **Closed** Dec 25 & 26, Jan 1 **Admission** grounds & tour, adults £7.50, children £4.50, OAPs/students £5.95. Grounds only, £3.75/£2.25/£3/€3.50/€3.75. Credit V, MC. Senior Citizens: £3 **Amenities** grounds and tea room accessible to wheelchairs, but not the castle or keep. Disabled toilets.

INSIDER TIP

The castle's timed tours, every half an hour, fill up early so don't turn up for the last one (an hour before closing) and expect to get in. Book at least an hour before then either pop back to the shops or wander the grounds and grab a coffee – but be careful as innocent-looking chocolate cake can actually be pricey 'gateau'.

Millennium Stadium ★★
ALL AGES

Westgate Street, CF10 1NS, ☎ 029 2082 2228 (tours); ☎ 08705 582582 (tickets); **www.millenniumstadium. com**

You don't have to be a rugby or football fan to appreciate the magnificence of this world-class stadium with its truly impressive retractable roof. Just walking down the players' tunnel as the emerald green grass and thousands of seats come into view is enough to bring a lump to anybody's throat. You can also enjoy the experience of sitting in the royal box, where little princesses can try the Queen's seat. Boys will be happy just getting their hands on the silverware which the guide brings along for photo opportunities, or wandering around the changing room (away team only) where international sports stars have trodden before them.

Holding the trophies at the Millennium Stadium

Open Mon–Sat 10am–5pm; Sun & Bank Holidays 10am–4pm. *Closed* Dec 25 & 31, Jan 1 *Admission* adults £5.50, children £3 (under 5s free), concessions £3.50. Book in advance to avoid match days and Christmas closing. *Amenities* souvenir shop, toilets

National Museum and Gallery Cardiff ⭐ ALL AGES

Cathays Park, CF10 3NP, 📞 *029 2039 7951; www.museumwales.ac.uk*

Cardiff owns one of the largest collections of Impressionist paintings outside Paris, thanks to an incredible bequest by the wealthy Davies sisters of Gregynog Hall, in Powys. Gwendoline and Margaret were granddaughters of 19th century coal and shipping magnate David Davies, who built the docks at nearby Barry. The sisters' art collection was given to the nation in the 1950s and 1960s, and now works by Renoir, Monet, Manet, Van Gogh and Cezanne are on permanent display in this magnificent domed building of white Portland stone,

next to City Hall. You might need more than a day to see everything here, but children should like the Evolution of Wales section which takes you from the Big Bang to life-size woolly mammoths and dinosaur skeletons. There are also the interactive, hands-on Glanely Gallery, activity bags, and school holiday events.

Open Tues–Sun and Bank Holidays, 10am–5pm. *Closed* Dec 24, 25, 26, Jan .1 *Admission* free. *Amenities* restaurant, coffee shop, souvenir shop, baby changing, disabled access, Highlight Audio Tour.

Cathays Park ALL AGES

Civic Centre 📞 *029 2087 1847, www. cardiff.ac.uk*

Behind National Museum Cardiff and City Hall is a small oasis of calm, home to the Temple of Peace, which houses the first Welsh Book of Remembrance. Nearby is Alexandra Gardens, where you will find the Welsh National War Memorial, a sunken courtyard with Corinthian columns. The park also includes Gorsedd Gardens which has the Gorsedd Circle – a stone circle dating back to 1899, site of national Eisteddfod events – and Friary Gardens, another secret garden escape perfect for quiet picnics.

Open daily. *Admission* free.

Bute Park ALL AGES VALUE

Castle Street; North Road (car park), 📞 *029 2068 4000*

Once the playground of the fabulously rich Bute family, this

Capability Brown-designed park extends from the back of their former family home – Cardiff Castle. There are recreation grounds and plenty of space for children to run around and play games. There are also flower gardens and an arboretum for more peaceful pursuits. The River Taff runs through the park, and on the other side is Sophia Gardens, home to Glamorgan County Cricket Club – one of Great Britain's cricket institutions (📞 0871 282 3401).

Open *daily, dawn until dusk.* ***Admission*** *free.* ***Amenities*** *horse riding, the Welsh Institute of Sport.*

Cardiff City Football Club
OLDER CHILDREN

Ninian Park, Sloper Road, CF11 8SX, 📞 *029 2034 1148, **www.cardiffcity fc.co.net***

Cardiff's football team play in the English league and now attract big players such as Jimmy Floyd Hasselbaink.

Admission *Tickets vary depending on opposition, but from £22.50 adult, discounts for children/OAPs.* ***Amenities*** *fast food outlets.*

Cardiff Bay

All Cardiff Bay attractions are clustered together round the water's edge, with regular free festivals and entertainment in Roald Dahl Plass, the big open space outside the Millennium Centre. The Bay is signposted at several M4 turn-offs, and from the city centre, a mile away. There's a pay car park outside the Red Dragon Centre.

However, with luxury flats going up all over, parking is getting more difficult and it's best to come without a car as you can spend the entire day here wandering from one place to another. Cardiff Bay rail station has regular shuttles from Cardiff Central, there's a bendybus service every 15 minutes until late, while the Waterbus is another option.

Doctor Who Up Close ★ ★ ★
ALL AGES **FIND** **VALUE**

Red Dragon Centre, CF10 4JY 📞 *07818 083 843, **www.doctorwho exhibitions.com***

The barrage of noise from restaurants, bowling alley and the regular live music and dance events that take place in the Red Dragon Centre is nothing to the frenzy once you make your way into the ticket office and gift shop of this homage to the reborn sci-fi TV series. It was a temporary affair when it opened several years ago – and the black, windowless space shows it – but it's great fun and just keeps on setting records for attendance. An opening exhibit informs young fans of the old doctors, but you're quickly into a cacophony of sound and light that's right up to date. The exhibition works closely with the BBC and costumes and artefacts appear on show sometimes within days of being seen on TV – some then vanishing again to be used in a later episode. The joy is that it's ever-changing.

Of course, there's always a Dalek screaming 'Exterminate!' and a Cyberman, along with

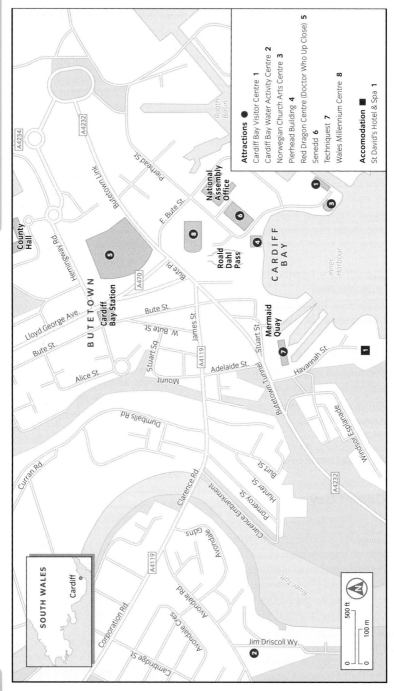

Attractions ●
Cardiff Bay Visitor Centre 1
Cardiff Bay Water Activity Centre 2
Norwegian Church Arts Centre 3
Pierhead Building 4
Red Dragon Centre (Doctor Who Up Close) 5
Senedd 6
Techniquest 7
Wales Millennium Centre 8

Accomodation ■
St David's Hotel & Spa 1

SOUTH WALES
Cardiff

clothes worn by the Doctor and his trusty sidekicks Rose, Martha and Donna. An interactive screen tells you some of the places used as backdrops in the series that you can visit, before spewing you out into the shop, piled high with must-have *Doctor Who* toys, books and clothes, along with interlopers like *Red Dwarf* spaceships and pricey silver *Clangers* cruet sets.

A wristband ticket gets you in and out as many times as you want during the day. Try to get out and see some of the filming locations, then do a walk through to pacify the children before heading home. Entry gives you free parking at the car park outside.

A must – but don't be surprised if by the time you get there it's disappeared, Tardis-like, to a larger location.

Open *daily 11am–8pm (last entry 7.45pm).* **Closed** *Christmas Day, Boxing Day, New Year's Day.* **Admission** *adults £5, children/concessions £3.30, family £14; Credit MC, V.* **Amenities** *sci-fi shop.*

Wales Millennium Centre ☆
ALL AGES

Bute Place, CF10 5AL, ☎ *08700 40 2000,* ***www.wmc.org.uk***

This is the building that everybody can picture when they think of Cardiff Bay – an iconic arts centre with giant lines of poetry cut into its copper roof. The auditorium, like some jagged red rock canyon from the American West, is even more stunning. The Centre was built as a 'stage for the nation' and it fulfils its role magnificently, presenting opera, musicals, ballet and more at very reasonable prices. Welsh stone, wood, metal and glass have been used in its construction, with Welsh artists commissioned to produce its internal fixtures, fittings and public art. There are free foyer performances, and sometimes free exhibitions. Families with older, possibly star-struck children will also enjoy a behind the scenes tour of Britain's second largest stage with its massive backstage areas. You'll see giant

Wales Millennium Centre, Cardiff Bay

sets stored away, racks of costumes, rehearsal studios and dressing rooms, as well as being able to take a seat in the gorgeous auditorium with its solid wood floors and terracotta-like walls – built to maximise acoustics for this multi-function theatre. Our children enjoyed peeking out of the roof windows through the poetry, and playing with the touchy-feely surfaces (don't worry, the guide suggested it). Alternatively, just drop in to relax. There's an ice cream parlour, a couple of trendy café-bars, plus the cosmopolitan brasserie, which is open until midnight.

Open daily from 10am. **Closed** Dec 25. **Admission** free entry to lobby; backstage tours (book in advance) adult £5, concessions £4; show tickets £5.35. Credit V, MC. **Amenities** gift shop, baby changing, disabled access.

Techniquest YOUNG CHILDREN

Stuart St, CF10 5BW, ☏ 029 2047 5475, www.techniquest.org

You're either going to love this interactive science playground or find the noise and random nature of a room full of brightly-coloured plastic just a bit tedious. Techniquest has apparently been voted the UK's best science centre and there were certainly lots of children running from one exhibit to the next, banging things together when we went. But within 20 minutes our pair were bored trying to work out what their 'experiments' were all about, or totally unimpressed with their results.

The 150 interactive exhibits are best suited to small children who enjoy hitting things without the risk of being told off. Certainly the tiny 'planetarium' (extra charge) is little more than a series of slides featuring cartoon characters and a few fairy lights. The chap in charge did his best with little material, but we all felt cheated at having extended our visit by nearly an hour to get one of the few seats.

Open Mon–Fri 9.30am–4.30pm; Sat, Sun & Bank Holidays 10.30am–5pm; school holiday weekends 9.30am–5pm. **Closed** Christmas, a week in September. Call for exact dates. **Admission** adults £6.90, children £4.80, concessions £4.80, family £20; **Credit** MC, V. **Amenities** café, souvenir shop, toilets, disabled access.

INSIDER TIP ▷

Parking is free at Cardiff Bay's Red Dragon Centre if you get your parking ticket validated when you eat at one of the restaurants or visit the Odeon cinema, Hollywood Bowl or Doctor Who Up Close exhibition.

Norwegian Church ALL AGES

Harbour Drive, CF10 4PA, ☏ 029 2045 4899

This pretty white clapboard church, gazing out over the sea, was built to serve the Norwegian seamen at the old docks. It's where *Charlie and the Chocolate Factory* author Roald Dahl was christened, but nowadays is a small arts centre and café. You can sit inside, outside at picnic tables, or along the low wall that winds around the bay and doubles as a seat, with fossils and sea

Norwegian Church

creatures carved into the surface. Play area nearby.

Open *daily 9am–5pm.* ***Admission*** *free.*

Cardiff Bay Visitor Centre
ALL AGES

Harbour Drive, CF10 4PA, 📞 *029 2046 3833, www.visitcardiff.info*

It looks like an aircraft fuselage that's been sat on by a Roald Dahl troll – a white, shiny, flattened tube. This is the Bay's main info centre and an attraction in its own right. Films on the area are shown in the big, open-plan space, there are exhibits and wall-mounted history lessons, windows overlooking the water, and an architect-style model of the city and the bay, so children can have fun working out where they've been, and adults can get their bearings.

The place is a haven for leaflet collectors, and those seeking souvenirs bearing Welsh dragons.

Open *Mon–Fri 9.30am–6pm, Sat–Sun 10.30am–6pm (April–Sept); Mon–Fri 9.30am–5pm, Sat–Sun 10.30am–5pm (Oct–March).* ***Admission*** *free.*

The Senedd **OLDER CHILDREN**
VALUE

Cardiff Bay CF10 4PZ 📞 *029 2045 4899* 📞 *029 2089 8477 for tours, www.wales.gov.uk*

This is the Welsh Assembly's debating chamber, opened by the Queen in 2006. Visitors can take a free tour of the eco-friendly building – after airport-style security screening – and watch debates from the public viewing gallery, or simply have coffee and Welsh cakes in the café, gawping at the wonderful, rolling wooden ceiling.

Open Mon&Fri 8am–6pm, Tue–Thur
8am–8pm, Sat, Sun & Bank Hols
10.30am–4.30pm (Oct-Easter)
10.30am–6pm (Easter–Sept)
Admission free

Pierhead Building ALL AGES

Maritime Road, CF10 4PZ, ☎ 029
20487609, www.lightship2000.co.uk

Next door to the Senedd is the
Grade One listed Pierhead
Building, once HQ of the
Cardiff Railway Company
(previously the Bute Dock
Company). It was built in 1897
and is a complete contrast to the
Senedd, with carved friezes, gar-
goyles and ornamental clock
tower. The National Assembly
now uses the building for func-
tions, and there are sometimes
exhibitions – but even if there's
nothing going on it's worth a
quick look around for a glimpse
of more traditional Cardiff.

Open Mon–Sat 9.30am–4.30pm, Sat,
Sun and Bank Hols 10.30am–4.30pm
(Oct-Easter), 10.30am–6pm
(Easter–Sept). *Admission* free.

Cardiff Bay Water Activity Centre AGES 8 AND UP

Cardiff Bay, ☎ 029 2035 3912, www.
cardiffharbour.com

At this centre run by Cardiff
Harbour Authority on the freshwater lake inside the Barrage,
youngsters from age eight can
take part in courses throughout
the year, especially during
school holidays (all must be pre-
booked). Sailing, rowing, kayaking and canoeing as well as rock
climbing are on offer. You can
get a sampler at Come And Try

It sessions for £5 half day, £10
full day (adults too) which are a
great family affair. There are
introductory days (£35) and specialist days (£65).

Llanishen Sailing Centre is a
Royal Yachting Association place
(also run by CHA) for serious
sailing courses.

The centre also organises
events such as powerboat racing,
sailing, rowing and canoeing
championships.

Goleulong 200 Lightship
OLDER CHILDREN

Harbour Drive, CF10 4PA, ☎ 029
2048 7609, www.lightship2000.
co.uk

The Church of Wales runs this
lightship as a focus for its work,
but everybody is welcome to
look over the light tower, engine
room, cabins, conference room
and galley cafe. The ship is also
near the children's playground.

Open Mon–Sat 10am–5pm; Sun
2–5pm. *Admission* free.

Butetown History & Arts Centre OLDER CHILDREN

Bute Street, CF10 5AG, ☎ 029
20487609, www.bhac.org

Set back from the rest of Cardiff
Bay's attractions, this is easy to
miss, but anybody interested in
the history of Cardiff Bay will be
fascinated by the centre's collection of vintage photographs and
documents. There are regular
exhibitions, and a shop selling
local history books.

Open Tue–Fri 10am–5pm; Sat, Sun &
Bank Hols 11am–4.30pm. *Admission*
free.

Cardiff Bay Barrage ★★
ALL AGES

☎ 029 2087 7900; *Barrage control:* ☎ 029 2070 0234, *www.cardiff harbour.com*

An extraordinary feat of engineering has transformed Cardiff Bay into a haven for sailing and other water sports. The Barrage consists of locks, sluice gates and places for fish to pass through. A visit can be a bit wild and windy, but there's a café and nautically-themed children's play area, plus decking where you can sit and enjoy the views back towards the Millennium Centre. Further, it's a photographer's dream.

Open daily. *Admission* free, but car park is pay and display.

Waterbus ★ ALL AGES

☎ 07940 142409, *www.cardiffcats. com*

Somewhere between a cruise and a shuttle, the yellow Waterbus gives an enjoyable 30-minute spin around the Bay, with the opportunity to land at Cardiff Bay Barrage and then walk into Penarth. It leaves the city from Taff Mead Embankment on the River Taff near the Millennium Stadium, or from Mermaid Quay at the Cardiff Bay attractions.

Runs daily. Tickets £5 return, £3 single, children £2.50 return, £1.50 single.

> **INSIDER TIP ≫**
>
> Spillers Records claims to be the world's oldest record shop and is a Cardiff institution. Spillers has been selling records since 1894, now supplemented by CDs. The Hayes shop, in the heart of Cardiff, has been under threat of closure in recent years causing so much uproar that half the members of the Welsh Assembly are said to have signed a statement supporting the shop.

Shopping with Children

Children and shopping don't mix well, but at least in Cardiff there is plenty of car-free room for them to wander. Queen's Arcade

Cardiff Market

Doctor Who

The Tardis, Cybermen and Daleks and the regenerated Time Lord's adventures are filmed in and around Cardiff so if you can't excite the children with the prospect of beaches, ice creams, castles and the countryside, this will do it. Heart of the *Doctor Who* universe is the Doctor Who Up Close exhibition in the Red Dragon Centre at Cardiff Bay (see p 50). It's here that you can see a rolling collection of monsters, props and costumes. It's so up to date that at the start of a series costumes and props can show up here before they've even made it onto screen.

But it's not just the exhibition. *Doctor Who* fever has taken over the city and wherever you visit, there's a tale about the filming there, although buildings rarely appear as anything resembling themselves.

The Tardis has been seen materialising outside the Millennium Centre (which also doubled as a hospital on Nu Earth), and the Daleks rolled down the concrete passageways beneath the Millennium Stadium. Tredegar House, down the road in Newport, features as the mansion where Queen Victoria was threatened by the werewolf. Rose's south London is mostly Cardiff's backstreets. Second World War scenes in *The Faceless Child* – a scary two-parter about the 'Are you my mummy?' boy in the gasmask – were set around the nearby coastal resort of Barry, using the station of the historic railway. Your children will love recognising the locations.

The settings are also used for spin-off shows *The Sarah Jane Adventures* (look for the ornate interior of Cardiff castle) and *Torchwood*. The latter started out as adults-only but since an edited version hit the screens, youngsters can see outrageous alien hunter Captain Jack Harkness and his team disappearing into their HQ beneath the stainless steel water wall of Roald Dahl Plass.

A number of *Doctor Who* settings are featured on a picture map available from the exhibition while the BBC's own website (***www.bbc.co. uk/wales/southeast/sites/doctorwho/locationsguide.shtml***) is full of fascinating and useful info. The Cardiff website even has its own *Doctor Who* section (***www.visitcardiff.com/doctor-who.html***).

---

in Queen's Street has all the usual fashion shops, although children might prefer the Disney Store. Nearby is St David's Centre, Cardiff's largest shopping complex – although St David's 2 is currently being built. The city's energetic mix of old and new is on show in the refurbished Victorian shops like those in The Royal Arcade – which dates back to 1858 – and the nearby Morgan Arcade, from 1896.

The James Howell department store in St Mary's Street sells designer fashion but is also an impressive building, with Corinthian and Ionic columns.

David Morgan in The Hayes is another splendid old department store, with arched pediments, bay windows, black marble columns and an atrium centre.

But probably the most interesting place to shop is Cardiff Central Market, on Trinity Street and High Street. Local produce includes meat, cheese, laverbread and baked goodies such as home-made Welsh cakes.

Family Entertainment

Chapter Arts Centre

Market Road, Canton, Cardiff, CF5 1QE, 📞 *0292 031 1050, www. chapter.org*

Arts centre with a theatre, gallery and cinema which is also a venue for Cardiff film festivals.

***Open** most days. **Admission** prices vary. **Amenities** café, bar, shop.*

St David's Hall

The Hayes, CF10 1SH, 📞 *029 2087 8444, www.stdavidshallcardiff. co.uk*

The national concert hall, offering a wide range of concerts and shows, some aimed at children and families. Also free exhibitions.

***Open** most days. **Admission** prices vary. **Amenities** Art Café Celf for snacks; Celebrity Restaurant and Gallery for lunch and evening menus. Bars with monthly jazz nights; shop sells arts, crafts and souvenirs.*

New Theatre

Park Place, CF10 3LN, 📞 *029 2087 8787, www.newtheatrecardiff.co.uk*

Traditional theatre with musicals, drama, dance, pantomime, family and children's shows.

***Open** most days. **Admission** prices vary. **Amenities** bar, coffee shop, restaurant.*

Sherman Theatre

Alexandra Industrial Estate, Rumney CF24 4YE, 📞 *029 2064 6900, www. shermantheatre.co.uk*

Music, comedy, dance and theatre, including family and children's shows.

***Open** most days. **Admission** prices vary.*

Wales Millennium Centre

Bute Place, CF10 5AL, 📞 *08700 402000, www.wmc.org.uk*

Musicals, ballet, theatre, dance and shows often aimed at families and children.

***Open** most days. **Admission** prices vary. **Amenities** restaurant, cafes, bars, ice-cream parlour, gift shop and behind the scenes tours.*

Millennium Stadium

Westgate Street, CF10 1NS, 📞 *08705 582582, www.millenniumstadium. com*

Rock concerts and sports events as well as international rugby and football.

***Open** Selected days for shows and sport. **Admission** prices vary. **Amenities** food and drink kiosks, souvenir shop.*

Out of Town

It doesn't take long to get out of Cardiff and into the greenery that surrounds it.

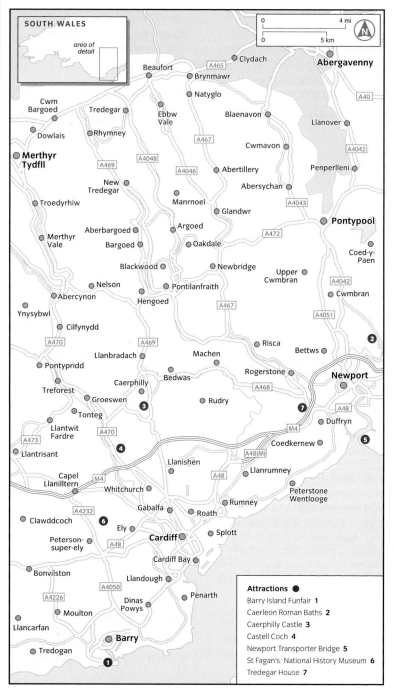

SOUTH WALES

area of detail

0   4 mi
0   5 km

Clydach

Beaufort

A465

Abergavenny

Brynmawr

Natyglo

A40

Cwm Bargoed

Tredegar

Ebbw Vale

Blaenavon

Llanover

Dowlais

Rhymney

A467

Cwmavon

A4042

Merthyr Tydfll

A469

A4048

A4046

Abertillery

Penperlleni

New Tredegar

Abersychan

Troedyrhiw

Manrnoel

Glandwr

A4043

Pontypool

Aberbargoed

Argoed

Merthyr Vale

Bargoed

Oakdale

A472

Blackwood

Newbridge

Coed-y-Paen

Upper Cwmbran

A4042

Nelson

Pontilanfraith

Cwmbran

Abercynon

Hengoed

A467

Ynysybwl

A4051

Cilfynydd

A470

A469

Risca

Bettws

❷

Llanbradach

Machen

Pontypridd

Rogerstone

Newport

Treforest

Caerphilly

Bedwas

A468

Groeswen

❸

Rudry

❼

A48

Tonteg

Duffryn

Llantwit Fardre

A470

M4

❺

A473

Coedkernew

Llantrisant

A48(M)

❹

Llanishen

Capel Llanilltern

M4

A48

Llanrumney

Whitchurch

Rumney

Peterstone Wentlooge

Clawddcoch

Gabalfa

❻

Roath

A4232

Ely

Cardiff

Splott

Peterson-super-ely

A48

Bonvilston

Cardiff Bay

Llandough

A4050

Penarth

A4226

Dinas Powys

Moulton

Llancarfan

Barry

Tredogan

❶

Attractions ●
Barry Island Funfair **1**
Caerleon Roman Baths **2**
Caerphilly Castle **3**
Castell Coch **4**
Newport Transporter Bridge **5**
St Fagan's: National History Museum **6**
Tredegar House **7**

Castell Coch ★ ★ ★ ALL AGES
FIND **VALUE**

Tongwynlais 📞 *029 2081 0101,*
www.cadw.cymru.gov.uk. On the
A470, just off M4, exit J32.

You can see the most beautiful castle in Wales nestling in the tree-covered hillside as you drive along the M4. It looks like the sort of fairytale tower Rapunzel might have been locked up in, or the Bavarian-style castle in *Chitty Chitty Bang Bang*. You can even see it from the ramparts of Cardiff Castle, which is fitting as both were holiday homes of the fabulously wealthy third Marquess of Bute. In both cases he took ancient ruins and had them rebuilt into ornate story-book fantasies which combined historic craftsmanship with a Victorian tilt at medieval decoration.

But whereas Cardiff Castle is a big, rectangular place with an imposing city setting, Coch is more of a *Harry Potter*esque fantasy clinging to the mountainside and approached through thick forest overlooking a gorge in the Taff Valley. The castle is named after the original 13th century Castell Coch – Red Castle – and like its big brother in Cardiff the interior is a sumptuous Arts and Crafts-style interpretation of medieval décor. Scenes from *Aesop's Fables* decorate the walls and ceilings of the living rooms, and the bedrooms are equally impressive, with original furniture on show designed especially for the rooms. Our children loved the spiral staircases and choosing which of the fantasy bedrooms they would like to have themselves. There's also a working portcullis and drawbridge – and a cosy café on the ground floor selling home-made cakes.

The beautiful Castell Coch

Open daily, 9.30am–5pm (April 1–May 31); 9.30am–6pm (June 1–Sept 30); 9.30am–5pm (Oct 1–31); 9.30–4pm (Nov 1–March 31); *Closed* Dec 24, 25, 26 & Jan 1. *Admission* £3.50, reduced rate £3, family ticket £10 (two adults and all children); free to Cadw members.

St Fagans: National History Museum ⋆⋆ ALL AGES MOMENT VALUE

St Fagans, CF5 6XB, ☏ 029 2057 3500, *www.museumwales.ac.uk*. On A4232, just off M4 at J33.

We all adored this open air museum, which has more than 40 old Welsh buildings rebuilt in the 100-acre grounds of St Fagans castle to illustrate the Welsh way of life since the Middle Ages. It's so beautifully laid out that you really do feel you're skipping down country lanes or walking down the high street of an ancient village. The buildings include a farm, school, chapel, bakery, post office, ironmonger's, grocery and workman's institute. The children particularly enjoyed

the Celtic huts with a central fire burning in the main hut and Celtic shields and swords to hold under the watchful eye of a real-life Celtic warrior. There are also traditional craftsmen in work-shops, including a pottery where children can go potty with clay (for a small fee), and play areas where they can just go potty. It's a place you could return to several times to see the buildings, the native breeds of farm animals in the fields, and the indoor History Gallery, Textile Gallery and Agricultural & Costume Gallery, which are brought to life by films, photographs and old docu-ments. If you need a break from history there's also a restaurant, tea room, picnic areas and good museum shop, and there are also regular events at the museum.

Open daily, 10am–5pm, including Bank Hols. *Closed* Dec 25, 26 & Jan 1. *Admission* free; parking £2.50.

A display in the St Fagans National History Museum

Newport

Once a thriving port and indus-trial centre, this historic city is transforming itself into a mod-ern visitor attraction with its Riverfront Theatre and Art Centre and other 21st-century developments. Evidence of Newport's role in the history of both Wales and Britain is all around the city, however. Just 3.2km away is the Roman garri-son of Caerleon, and inside the city is the remains of its Norman castle. Newport Museum's local history displays include the city's crucial part in the 19th-century Chartist Movement – which helped to shape Britain's democratic heritage. Similarly, Streets, the former Pillgwenlly Heritage in the heart of Newport's old docklands, gives an insight into Victorian and wartime experience.

Newport Transporter Bridge

★ OLDER CHILDREN

☎ 01633 250322, *www.newport.gov.uk*. *On the A4042, off the M4 at J28.*

One of the great sights of Newport is its Transporter Bridge, a century-old monument to steel and industry. The enormous gantry suspends a road-high platform that carries cars serenely across the River Usk for £0.50 a go. In the car park is a free, open-air exhibit about the bridge, which was built in 1906 and is now a Grade I listed structure. It was only closed to traffic for a few years before being restored in the 1990s.

Open *Mon–Fri from early morning until evening, Sun until 1pm. Cars £0.50, bicycles/pedestrians free.*

Tredegar House ★ ALL AGES
VALUE

Tredegar House, Coedkemew, NP10 8TW, ☎ *01633 815880, www.newport.gov.uk. On the A48, two miles from Newport town centre, just off the M4, at J28.*

An impressive 17th-century mansion, which was once home to the colourful Morgan family (and their supposed links with the famous real-life pirate of the Caribbean, Sir Henry Morgan, who ended up as deputy governor of Jamaica). The house has

also featured in *Doctor Who*, and there's a 75-minute tour (engaging, if rather too complete even for adults). However, this fine example of a Restoration stately home – one of the best in Britain – sits in 90 acres of parkland with plenty of space for football and running around, a children's play area, toilets, a pretty lake and walled gardens. There are regular events held in the grounds, which include the estate's Home Farm buildings. Some of these are now used as workshops for traditional crafts with shops attached to them. There's also a small pub/restaurant, the Brewhouse Tearooms, and the ticket office features a wall-mounted history of the Morgan dynasty along with area tourist information, ice creams and souvenirs. Tucked away on the estate is a superb Caravan Club camp site (see p 48).

Open *park: daily 9am–dusk; house: Wed–Sun and Bank Hols 11.30am–4pm; craft shops Wed–Sun and Bank Hols 10.30am–5.30pm; Brewhouse Tearooms Wed–Fri 10.30am–5pm, Sat, Sun and Bank Hols 10.30am–4.30pm, (5pm at weekends).* **Admission** *park: free, House: £5.60 adults, concessions £4.10, children under 15 free.*

Cefn Mably Farm
YOUNG CHILDREN

Began Road, Cefn Mably, CF3 6XL, ☎ *01633 680312, www.cefnmablyfarmpark.com. On the A48 north, just off the M4, at J28.*

This offers indoor and outdoor play areas, for tots and the under-fives along with pony rides, touch-and-hold areas with animals, conservation and pond areas. With its pretty picnic area as well as coffee shop and bistro it's a nice relaxed place.

Open *daily 10am–5pm.* **Admission** *adults £4, children £3.50, family £15 (weekends and school holidays); adults and children £3 (term time).*

Fourteen Locks ★ ALL AGES
FIND VALUE

Fourteen Locks Canal Centre, High Cross, Newport, NP10 9GN, ☎ 01633 656656, or 01633 894802 (visitor centre), www.newport.gov.uk; www.mon-brec-canal-trust.org.uk. On the B4591 to Risca, just off the M4, at J27.

This remarkable flight of locks rises nearly 49m in just under a kilometre and you can find out how they work in a virtual journey along the canal at the visitor centre. You'll also find out about the canal's role in transporting coal, iron, limestone and bricks from the South Wales valleys to Newport and Cardiff docks. There are monthly boat trips, a lovely picnic area and marked paths to explore the area.

Open *Daily, dawn to dusk; Visitor Centre: Easter to late September, closed Mon and Tue.* **Admission** *free.*

Caerleon Roman Baths & Amphitheatre OLDER CHILDREN

High Street, Caerleon, Newport, NP18 1AE 4PZ, ☎ 01633 422518, www.cadw.cymru.gov.uk. Just off M4, J25 (westbound) or J26 (eastbound).

One of the most important Roman sites in Britain, this is where the Second Augustan Legion – 5,500 men – built a township fortress, which not only included a barracks but also a huge bath house and large amphitheatre. What's left of the baths are now in the middle of Caerleon, preserved in a stylish wooden building (hidden away at the back of a tiny public car park). Wooden walkways overlook the excavated hot, warm and cold baths, and panels of interesting facts (even to children, as they mostly do the Romans at school early on) line the walls. It's a very atmospheric place, although our pair preferred to explore the remains of the amphitheatre, around the corner in the middle of a field. Stone banks surround the arena, once alive with pageantry and bloodthirsty sports. It's the most complete Roman amphitheatre in Britain, and a great spot for a picnic – as well as somewhere children can safely run, climb and explore. The amphitheatre is also the site of summer events including plays and living history demonstrations (separate charge).

Open *baths, daily, 9.30am–5pm (April 1–Oct 31), Mon–Sat 9.30am–5pm, Sun 11am–4pm (Nov 1–March 31).* **Closed** *24th, 25th, 26th Dec and 1st Jan.* **Admission** *baths: £2.90 adults, £2.50 children, family ticket £8.30. Amphitheatre: free, accessible all year.*

National Roman Legion Museum OLDER CHILDREN VALUE

High Street, Caerleon, Newport, NP18 1AE 4PZ, ☎ 01633 423134, www.museumwales.ac.uk/en/caerleon. As Caerleon Roman Baths.

Just along from Caerleon's Roman baths, this small but lovely museum is on the site of

Penarth's seafront and Victorian pier

the Roman fortress, housing many of the clues to the Legion's life which have been dug up over the years. You'll find all the usual pottery, coins and jewellery, but this place has the knack of bringing them to life for children while retaining the air of a proper museum. Possibly it's the full-size reconstructed Barrack Room, where children can try on replica armour at weekends and during school holidays. Or perhaps the little gift shop with its child-friendly Roman souvenirs. It's certainly well worth visiting either before or after your picnic in the nearby amphitheatre – or after you've tramped around the only remains of a Roman legionary barracks on view in Europe, a few minutes further on.

Open daily, 10am–5pm Mon–Sat, 2–5pm, Sun. **Admission** free. Amphitheatre and barracks open at any reasonable time, admission free.

Penarth

In this delightful timewarp Victorian seaside resort across Cardiff Bay the road from the pretty High Street dives down the hill to a mostly elegant promenade, rocky and partly sandy beach, and a small pier, where the paddle cruisers MV Balmoral and PS Waverley call in the warmer months. On the pier we loved Decks, a chippie selling chips with gravy, along with Joe's ice cream from Swansea. **The Pierson Hotel** is a charming old-style seafront hotel with a modern flourish, while the **Mediterraneo** – in an old boathouse – has seafood specials on its Italian menu. The front garden dining area with views out to sea is particularly alluring, but the place might be a bit sophisticated for younger children. On the edge of town is **Penarth Marina**, a truly massive, posh, complex of waterfront(ish) homes all struggling for a view across Cardiff Bay. At the end is Cardiff Barrage (p 37), which you can stroll across.

Barry Island

This is a seaside resort just the other side of Penarth, and they don't make them like this any more. Dingy amusement arcade, dilapidated buildings, kebab shops and ice cream – and yet it has a stunning Blue Flag beach. The **Barry Island Funfair** was a bit of a legend way back when but now looks tired. On a visit in May it was not only shut but the sign saying when it would open was non-committal. Even the children couldn't think of a reason to stay despite the smooth, golden beach. Having said that, the **Barry Island Railway Heritage Centre** is fun, with restored locomotives and railway memorabilia, and the **Knoll**, a hill promontory, is a great place to walk.

Caerphilly

Caerphilly, 16km north of Cardiff and on the edge of the Brecon Beacons, is dominated by its majestic medieval castle. There are several country parks around town where you can walk or cycle, while horse riding, fishing and quad biking are on the doorstep. But the town's newest attraction is its statue of Caerphilly-born comedian Tommy Cooper and the nearby **Tommy Cooper Walk of Fame**. The children might not be interested, but are we worried?

Caerphilly Castle ★ ★ ALL AGES
VALUE

Caerphilly, CF83 1JD, ☎ *029 2088 3143, www.cadw.gov.uk. On the A470 or A469 (M4, J32) from Cardiff, A468 from Newport.*

Crossing the bridge over the moat around the biggest medieval castle in Wales, you are left breathless at the sheer size of this 30-acre fortress. It even makes the children look up, or perhaps that was being told that the BBC children's show *Young Dracula* was filmed here. Although one tower leans at what looks like a dangerously drunken angle, it only adds to the impressiveness of this 13th-century wonder, built on three man-made islands and surrounded by artificial lakes, created by damming the Nant y Gledr stream. It still looks as impregnable now as it did when it was built by the Anglo-Norman lord Gilbert de Clare in a concentric walls-within-walls design. It comes as no real surprise that it was the wealthy Third Marquess of Bute who restored much of this castle in the early 19th century, with his work continued by the Fourth Marquess. Plenty of places to stroll, run, hide and picnic. Events include theatre, military re-enactments and medieval shows.

Open daily April 1–May 31, Oct 1–31, 9.30am–5pm; June 1–Sept 30, 9.30am–6pm; Nov 1–Mar 31, 9.30am–4pm (Sun, 11am–4pm); Closed Dec 24, 25, 26, Jan 1. Admission adults £3.50, concessions £3, family £10. Amenities gift shop, baby changing, toilets, pay parking nearby.

FAMILY-FRIENDLY ACCOMMODATION

There are plenty of options, from hip new places to good solid names, lots in the city centre but new places are also popping up around the Bay.

EXPENSIVE

Hilton ★★★

Kingsway, Cardiff, CF10 3HH, ☎ 029 2064 6300,
www.hilton.co.uk/cardiff

This is a delightful, friendly modern place in a perfect position across the road from the castle and museum (fantastic views from many of the rooms), and around the corner from the shops. Our children loved the glass lifts that overlook the atrium, the large, sleek-but-comfy rooms, and the stainless steel swimming pool (open to youngsters until 7.30pm, often not the case in hotels with a business clientele). Children stay free in adults' room, or a second room can be booked at 50% of adult rate. The Razzi restaurant, serving modern British and Welsh cuisine, spills out into a glass extension opposite the castle and serves children's meals that appeal to more than tots – properly cooked fish and chips, for instance. The adult menu, two courses for £20+, features the likes of saltmarsh lamb with bubble and squeak. And children under 10 eat free if they're with an adult who's staying at the hotel.

A hot and cold breakfast buffet is included in room rate – our children delighted in chocolate croissants washed down by creamy hot chocolate.

197 rooms. From £92 double. Extra beds and cots free of charge.

Amenities restaurant, two bars, pool, gym, sauna, shop, valet parking. In room A/C, TV, internet access, mini-bar, tea maker.

Park Plaza ★★

Greyfriars Road, Cardiff, CF10 3AL, ☎ 02920 111111, **www.parkplaza. com/cardiffuk**

This stylishly contemporary four-star affair was winner of the AA Hotel of the Year for Wales 2006–07 and has really been getting into the swing of the *Doctor Who* thing, with packages that include a remote-controlled Dalek and entry to the Doctor Who Up Close exhibition (£170 per night for family of four sharing a room). Handily placed for the city centre attractions, there's a smart pool and the Laguna restaurant combines local and international flavours, adult main courses £8–19.50, children's menu £6 for three courses.

129 rooms. From £130 double; children free, but only space in executive rooms (an extra £25). Extra beds and cots free. Amenities restaurant (Mon–Sat noon–2.30pm, 5.30–10.30pm; Sun noon–9pm), bar, pool, spa, Jacuzzi, gym, beauty treatment rooms, shop, valet parking. In room A/C, TV, free WIFI, mini-bar, tea maker.

St David's Hotel and Spa ★

Havannah Street, CF105SD, ☎ 0870 042 4168, **www.thestdavidshotel. com**

Iconic new face of Cardiff Bay, this is a stylish landmark on a promontory offering watery views from every room. The glass atrium is as impressive as the sail-like roof. And there's five-star service to match, whether in the Tides Bar & Grill or the Marine Spa. It might be the place to come for a romantic weekend, but it's an experience for children too.

132 rooms. From £260 double. Extra beds and cots free of charge. **Amenities** *restaurant, bar, pool, gym, spa, shop, valet parking.* **In room** *A/C, TV, internet access, mini-bar, tea maker.*

Holiday Inn Newport ★

The Coldra, Newport, NP18 2YG, ☎ 0163 341 2777, **www.holiday-inn. com**

Set in 14 acres of woodland just off the M4 (J24), this is an ideal spot for exploring both the city and the hinterland. The woods are great for walking, and children love the away-from-it-all feel. Apart from the massive Celtic Manor Golf and Country Club, there's nothing else within walking distance but there's a decent pool, children generally get a goodie bag linked to the latest hit movie, and eat free in Harper's restaurant. There's a hot buffet as well as an a la carte menu for adults.

119 rooms (some connecting). From £80 double (£90 with breakfast). Extra beds and cots free of charge. **Amenities:** *Restaurant, bar, pool, gym, sauna, steam room, shop, baby sitting.* **In room:** *A/C, TV, internet access/WIFI (£5), tea maker.*

Holiday Inn Cardiff City Centre

Castle Street, CF10 1XD, ☎ 0870 400 8140, **www.holiday-inn.com**

On the River Taff, between the Millennium Stadium and Cardiff Castle, the Junction Restaurant and Bar is low-key and friendly – posh bar food rather than restaurant fare – and children eat free. Goodie bags for children.

157 rooms. From £85 double (£95 with breakfast). Extra beds and cots free of charge. **Amenities** *restaurant, two bars, shop, free parking.* **In room** *A/C, TV, internet access/WIFI, mini-bar, tea maker.*

Travelodge

Imperial Gate, St Mary Street, CF10 1FA, ☎ 0870 191 1723, **www. travelodge.co.uk**

A simple, budget option right in the city centre, though as there are noisy bars below and along the street, try not to get a first-floor room at the front. No toiletries, so pack well. The bar/café serves evening meals, from panini £4.95) to steak (£7.95) and up to two children 10 and under eat free with each adult. Breakfast buffet £7.50, children free.

100 rooms. Family room (2 children) from £26. Free cots (limited number). **Amenities** *Bar/cafe, snack machine.* **In room** *TV, tea maker.*

Tredegar House Country Park Caravan Club Site ★

Coedkernew, Newport, NP10 8TW, ☎ 01633 815600, **www.caravanclub. co.uk***. On the A48, just off the M4, at J28*

A delightfully grassy and well-landscaped place in the peaceful setting of one of the area's great parks. Parents enjoy walking among the mature avenues of trees planted decades ago by Tredegar House's teeming staff, while children can run around playing football, cricket or rounders in the park adjoining the site. Every pitch has an electric hook-up and there are modern, spotless toilets, showers and washing-up facilities as well as a laundry. There's a little store selling most things you need (mostly Welsh cakes and wine, it seemed) just outside the back gate, a supermarket 800m away and a farmers' market every other Friday in Newport, 6.5km away. You can also spend a pleasant evening at the pub-restaurant in one of the house's outbuildings and enjoy one of the many free events. We were there during a folk festival so the children also had the benefit of a chip van. The site is only 13km from Cardiff and just off the M4 so you're also within easy reach of the Wye Valley and Brecon Beacons. A great site with, unusually for Caravan Club sites, space for tents.

80 caravan pitches plus camping field. Peak season per night: £7.10 for pitch, £5.40 for adults, £2.10 for children. **Amenities** *hardstanding pitches, showers, toilets, laundry, waste disposal points, small site shop.*

Cwmcarn Forest Drive Campsite

Nantcarn Road, Cwmcarn, Crosskeys, nr Newport, NP11 7FAW, 01495 272001, www.caerphilly. gov.uk

Three small fields provide 40 pitches with hook-ups for tents, caravans and camper vans in this stunning location at the end of 16km Cwmcarn Forest Drive. It's a breathtaking diversion through forests and valleys, with seven car parks at the start of sign-posted walks or cycle ways – each with picnic and barbecue areas. One of the car parks is the start of a woodland walk where magical carvings of Celtic stories are hidden among the trees. There's a visitor centre with café (and registration desk), but it's best to book ahead. Around the forest is one of the best mountain bike trails in Wales, and the camp site itself is beside a river and lake.

40 pitches. price per night £6–9. **Amenities** *electric hook-ups, showers, toilets, waste disposal points.*

FAMILY-FRIENDLY DINING

There are restaurants aplenty, with clusters of the usual chains around the tourist hot-spots along with individual places to eat, whether you want a snack and an excuse to sit down for a few minutes, or a smart night-time experience that the whole family will enjoy. There are three main food areas.

Old Brewery Quarter

This is a cheerful, echoey court-yard off which spills a cluster of mostly chain restaurants filling the space in and outside the old

Brains brewery site. Here, amid a mix of modern fittings and historic surroundings (original vaults and clocktower), you can eat without spending too much, or taking more than a couple of steps off the city centre St Mary's Street. There's a Nando's (its chicken dishes a half-way house between fast food and a restaurant), a Hard Rock Café (big burgers), a Chiquito (Mexican, with children's funpacks, and entertainment such as face painting Sunday 1–3pm), La Tasca (tapas), and Brains's own Yard Bar & Kitchen, a posh pub. A good family spot during the day, it can become busy and noisy in the evening.

Mermaid Quay

It's a bit confusing given that once you're at Cardiff Bay it all seems like one waterside whirl, but Mermaid Quay (*www.mermaidquay.co.uk*) is the name given to the spot with all the restaurants, bars and cafes – 25 at last count. There's Nando's and Pizza Express, plus all manner of places serving Italian, tapas, oriental, American but not, seemingly, English. There's Fabulous Welshcakes (serving the sugary scone-like treats) plus Harry Ramsden's chippie, which, being a few yards to one side, is not technically Mermaid Quay. The place is awash with families, and there are plenty of outside tables so you'll always find something, even if simply a muffin from Starbucks.

Red Dragon Centre

Hemingway Road, Cardiff Bay, CF10 4JY, 📞 029 2025 6260, www.thered dragoncentre.co.uk

The noise from the dance and music performances on the stage combined with that from the restaurants mean you are likely to want to leave this frenetic, aircraft hanger-like complex as quickly as possible – despite the presence of the *Doctor Who* exhibition and assuming you've not come on holiday to see a film or go bowling. But the fact that it's all enclosed can be a boon in poor weather, when you might appreciate the attractions of the mega Old Orleans (typical children's meals £4.95, slightly more sophisticated junior dishes £5.95, all with ice cream) rubbing shoulders with Bella Italia (£4.50 for children's pizza or pasta plus drink and dessert) and Oriental Garden (Mon–Thurs lunch buffet £5.95).

EXPENSIVE

Razzi ★★

Kingsway, Cardiff, CF10 3HH, 📞 029 2064 6300, www.hilton.co.uk/cardiff

Delightful, friendly modern place that neither looks nor feels like a hotel restaurant (it's in the Hilton), in a perfect position across the road from the castle. If you're staying here, children eat free. If not, it's still a decent deal. For adults, two courses from the inventive menu are £23.50, three courses £26.50 (although a number of dishes involve surcharges). Children's three-course meals cost £7.75 for proper food – garlic bread, fish and chips, chicken and the like. Free goodie bags with colouring and crayons.

Open noon–10pm (10.30pm Fri–Sat). **Main courses** £15–25. **Credit** AE, MC, V, DC. **Amenities** crayons and colouring books.

MODERATE

Mediterraneo at the Boat House

10 The Esplanade, Penarth, CF64 3AU, 029 2070 3428, www. mediterraneopenarth.com

Sited in a century-old Admiralty boathouse, this Italian/seafood restaurant on the seafront has the views you might expect. It's charming indoors, there's a great patio along the front, and older children can nip down the steps to the beach when they're done. Central to things are pasta and pizza, albeit a step up from the average, and they're available in children's portions. You've then got delights like fish stew or grilled red snapper and starters like scallops in Pernod sauce, and grilled sardines.

Open Mon–Fri 12 noon–3pm, 5pm–close, Sat, Sun – all day. **Main courses** £8.25–16.95. 2-course lunch special £8.50. **Credit** AE, MC, V.

Bosphorus

31 Mermaid Quay, Cardiff Bay CF10 5BW, 029 2048 747, www. bosphorus.co.uk

Situated on its own little pier, this is a smart modern Turkish restaurant with floor-to-ceiling glass walls, as well as outside tables, giving great views of the action on land and sea. Fine if your children enjoy pitta bread and hummus. Set lunch £7.95

Open daily. **Main courses** £9–15. **Credit** AE, MC, V.

INEXPENSIVE

Demiro's ★

Mermaid Quay, Cardiff Bay, CF10 5BZ, 029 2049 1882, www.demiros.com

This looks like an Italian restaurant of old, all deep red with classical statues and big mirrors, but is actually something more, with side-by-side Italian, Spanish and Welsh menus. Will it be pan-fried lobster tails or home-made faggots with peas and mash? At a basic level they do great thin-crust pizzas, but you can also get tapas or local lamb. Friendly waiters and big windows looking out on to the bay make it great for children, while adults can eat and drink (decent house red, £11.95) well.

Open noon–10pm (10.30pm Fri–Sat). **Main courses** £6.95–17.95. **Credit** AE, MC, V, DC.

Eddie's Diner

Mermaid Quay, Cardiff Bay, CF10 5BZ, 029 2048 4020, www. eddiesdiner.com

Children will enjoy this fun American-style spot even if they've no idea what the place – all black and white tiles, red vinyl booths, neon and statues of Marilyn and Elvis – is pretending to be. A quarter-pounder with fries is £5, but there's a special

Find the Bull Terrier Café in Cardiff Market

Cadwalader's Ice-Cream Cafe ☆

Mermaid Quay, Cardiff Bay CF10 5BZ, ☏ *029 2049 7598, www. cadwaladersicecream.co.uk*

This family ice-cream company started in Criccieth, north Wales, in 1927. The bright, jolly place is full of dreamy ices, whether traditional flavours or outrageous ones like Dragon's Breath and Chocolate Porridge, enormous sundaes with fresh fruit, and children's specials such as Wibbly Wobbly Jelly and Ice cream Sandwiches. Those along with cakes, coffee, rich hot chocolate and ice cream cocktails (an indulgent mixture with your choice of spirit) make this a Willy Wonka experience for young and old.

Open *daily except Christmas Day.* **Credit** *AE, MC, V.*

Bull Terrier Cafe

Cardiff Market, St Mary Street, CF1 2AU

This great little place is on the upstairs balcony of the historic indoor market (open Mon–Sat), between the second hand vinyl, pet supplies and cheap toys. The menu is as timeless as the surroundings – full English breakfast £2.75, egg on toast £1 – offering adults and children alike real fast food above the hurly-burly of the food stalls.

children's mini-burger or hotdog meal with drink for £3.30. There are also half-pounders, hotdogs, chicken and nachos, many involving melted cheese, along with huge, teeth-numbing desserts.

Open *noon–10pm (10.30pm Fri–Sat).* **Main courses** *£5–8.* **Credit** *AE, MC, V, DC.*

INSIDER TIP »

Stop for an alfresco bite at Bywty Hayes Island Snack Bar, a Cardiff institution. This wooden, chalet-like café was once a parcels office for Cardiff Corporation Tramways, but now it provides pavement café-style tea and sandwiches in Victoria Square – right next to St David's Hall.

4 South Wales

SOUTH WALES

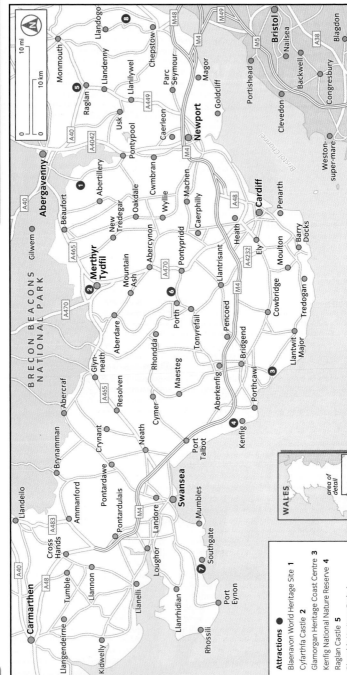

Attractions ●
Blaenavon World Heritage Site **1**
Cyfarthfa Castle **2**
Glamorgan Heritage Coast Centre **3**
Kenfig National Nature Reserve **4**
Raglan Castle **5**
Rhondda Heritage Park **6**
Three Cliffs Bay **7**
Tintern Abbey **8**

This is the country's most populated area, with the most diverse countryside. There's the coastline: the gorgeous Gower Peninsula has fantastic family beaches on its south-east shores, plus breathtaking beaches further west where adventure sports take precedence over sandcastles – and all glorious for walking. The Vale of Glamorgan's coastline is also packed with stunning beaches, dominated by distinctly layered cliffs. These are beaches for water sports fans, walkers and nature lovers as well as traditional holidaymakers. Ogmore-by-Sea is probably the prettiest along this section, although some might vote for Dunraven Bay a few miles east. Between Ogmore-by-Sea and Porthcawl there is also the spectacularly sandy Merthyr Mawr beach, backed by huge dunes.

Then there are the cities of Cardiff (see separate section) and Swansea, dominating south Wales and providing first-class culture and heritage attractions. Swansea is increasingly becoming a tourist destination in its own right, thanks to the Maritime Quarter and its new National Waterfront Museum, the Dylan Thomas Centre and annual festival, along with the sheer beauty of Swansea Bay. But the industrial heritage of The Valleys is also carving out its own niche.

As South Wales comes to terms with the loss of all but a fraction of its coal, iron and steel industries, it is being reborn. Although some parts remain grim and oppressive, defunct coal mines and iron works, still central to the local community spirit, have been turned into attractions where youngsters can get grubby, explore old tunnels, and gaze in awe from under the lights on their helmets. Meanwhile, the mountain railways and the canals that took coal and other goods down to the ports are now places of fun and adventure. So the next time you're planning a mad dash to the West, turn off the M4 for a while and sample some extraordinary natural and man-made attractions that you won't find anywhere else in the world.

ESSENTIALS

Visitor Information

Tourist Information Centres

Visit Carmarthenshire Tourist Board
www.visitcarmarthenshire.co.uk

Aberdulais Falls, Aberdulais Falls National Trust property, Aberdulais, Neath, SA10 8EU, 01639 636674, E: aberdulaistic@nationaltrust.org.uk

Blaenavon, (seasonal opening) Blaenavon Ironworks, North Street, Blaenavon, Torfaen, NP4 9RQ, 01495 792615, www.blaenavontic.com

Bridgend, McArthurGlen Designer Outlet Village, The Drewen, Bridgend, CF32 9SU, 01656 654906, www.visitbridgend.com, E: bridgendtic@bridgend.gov.uk

Chepstow, Castle Car Park, Bridge Street, Chepstow, NP16

5EY, 01291 623772, *www.visit wyevalley.com*, *E: chepstowtic@ monmouthshire.gov.uk*

Llanelli, Millennium Coastal Park Visitor Centre, North Dock, Llanelli, SA15 2LF, 01554 777744, *E: Discovery Centre@carmarthenshire.gov.uk*

Merthyr Tydfil, 14a Glebeland Street, Merthyr Tydfil, CF47 8AU, 01685 379884, *www.merthyrtydfil.gov.uk*; *E: tic@merthyr.gov.uk*

Monmouth, Shire Hall, Agincourt Square, Monmouth, NP5 3DY 01600 713899, *www.visitwyevalley.com*, *E: mon mouth.tic@monmouthshire.gov.uk*

Mumbles, Mumbles Road, Mumbles, Swansea, SA3 4BU, 01792 361302, *www.mumblestic. co.uk*, *E: info@mumblestic.co.uk*

Pontypridd, Pontypridd Museum, Bridge Street, Pontypridd, CF37 4PE, 01443 490748, *E: tourism@pontypridd museum.gov.uk*

Monmouth

Porthcawl, (seasonal opening) Old Police Station, John Street, Porthcawl, Bridgend, CF36 3DT, 01656 786639, *www.visit bridgend.com*, *E: porthcawltic@ bridgend.gov.uk*

Swansea, Plymouth Street, Swansea, SA1 3QG, 01792 468321, *E: tourism@swansea.gov.uk*

Areas in Brief

South Wales is a region of contrasts. Moving from the lazy, leisurely Wye Valley and neighbouring Usk Valley, you find yourself catapulted into a more man-made environment in the former industrial South Wales Valleys. But as nature gradually claims back what is hers, the Valleys are becoming green again, while industrial heritage sites remind us of Wales's importance in British and global industrial history. There's the unexpected tranquility and beauty of the Vale of Glamorgan, and the increasing sophistication of Swansea – gateway to the beautiful Gower Peninsula – before South Wales merges with the tourist magnet that is West Wales.

Getting Around

By car Thanks to its economic importance, South Wales is well-served with good roads, at least in comparison with the rest of the country. The M4 cuts a path through the middle, with a network of A-roads shooting off to either side. All you need is a good map, and you can't go wrong.

By bus There are frequent buses between central Cardiff and Swansea Quadrant Bus Station, where you can catch Gower Explorer and First Cymru buses to outlying districts. ☎ *0871 200 2233, www. traveline-cymru.org.uk*

By foot The beauty of south Wales is that you don't have to go far to find somewhere to walk – and you don't have to walk for miles to enjoy it. To download a brochure on walks published by VisitWales – the Welsh Tourist Board – go to *www.wisdomand walks.co.uk.*

WHAT TO SEE & DO

Top 10 Family Experiences

❶ **Hearing the sound of the sea** at Port Eynon Youth Hostel, a former lifeboat station, where at high tide the water is within feet of the back door.

❷ **Running through the arch** at Three Cliffs Bay on the Gower Peninsula and splashing in the pools near the rocks.

❸ **Going down the mine** at Big Pit, with a hard hat and miner's lamp.

❹ **Rolling down sand dunes** at incredible Merthyr Mawr.

❺ **Jumping on stepping stones** before picnicking near the river next to the ruins of Ogmore castle.

❻ **Playing football** on the firm sands at Ogmore-by-Sea, watching horse riders trekking.

❼ **Pressing buttons** at the inspirational National Waterfront Museum in Swansea.

❽ **Buying fresh Welsh cakes** at Swansea market – the largest covered market in Wales.

❾ **Feeding baby goats** at picturesque Greenmeadow Community Farm, near Cwmbran.

❿ **Walking by the river** at magnificent Tintern Abbey.

Family-friendly Festivals

Monmouth Festival

Agincourt Square and various venues, Monmouth, ☎ *07756 974092, www.monmouthfestival.co.uk*

Eight days of music where there's everything from rock (like '60s stars the Yardbirds, who our Georgia enjoys) to traditional Welsh tunes, plus a carnival on the Sunday of the first weekend when there's also the Kymin Dash – an 11km run up Kymin hill and back. The first Sunday is aimed at families, when there are bands playing during the afternoon as well as a Sing-a-long in the evening. The other days, bands start at the less family-friendly 8pm. Fireworks late on the second Saturday finish things off brilliantly.

Late July–early August.

Vale of Glamorgan Agricultural Show

Fonmon Castle Park, Rhoose, www. valeofglamorganshow.co.uk

See champion cattle, horse jumping and dressage, as well as dog shows, home-produce marquees and woodcraft. The Food Hall is packed with Welsh producers.

Mid August.

Cowbridge Food and Drink Festival

Various venues, Cowbridge, Vale of Glamorgan ☎ 07875 290428, www. cowbridgefoodanddrink.org.uk

As well as the many stalls offering local produce there's music, street entertainers, real ale, crafts and health stalls – and a programme of children's activities.

October.

Margam Kite Festival

Margam Country Park, Port Talbot, SA13 2TJ ☎ 01639 881635, www. neath-porttalbot.gov.uk

Spectacular sight on the lawns of Margam Castle, which you can take part in or simply watch. This historic country estate has plenty of other attractions, including an adventure playground and numerous picnic spots. (Margam Country Show takes place in August when there's an Open Class Dog Show and Model Boat Show).

June.

Two Rivers Folk Festival

OLDER CHILDREN

Chepstow Castle, ☎ 07870 611979, www.tworiversfolkfestival.com

Three evenings of music in the castle grounds at this lively get together, which includes a beer and cider festival, ceilidhs, plenty of stalls, and hundreds of Morris Dancers. A well-organised camp site is set up at Chepstow Racecourse £5 per pitch, £2 weekend shuttle ticket), where other leading artists also play, and there are many smaller concerts around town. A weekend wristband costs £50, but accompanied children under 12 are free.

Early July

Midsummer Madness

Bridgend, ☎ 01656 661338, www bridgend-events.co.uk

Loud, colourful Mardi Gras parade on Saturday along with a three-day market.

First weekend in June.

Gower Folk Festival

Gower Heritage Centre, Parkmill, ☎ 01792 850803, www.halfpenny folkclub.com

Friday night then two full days of traditional folk – weekend tickets are from £35 adults, £10 children, under 5s free. There are special rates for weekend ticket holders at nearby Three Cliffs Bay camp site, on North Hills Farm – £20 for a family tent with free transfer buses. Plenty for children including story telling, magic and shanty workshops along with the centre's attractions which include a play area, sandpit and small animal farm. Lots of food, from burgers to veggie delights and, of course, the beer tent.

Mid- June

Swansea MAS Carnival

*Walter Road to National Waterfront Museum, Swansea, **www.swansea bayfestival.net***

Flamboyant, multi-cultural carnival with a calypso feel as a thousand participants put on outrageous costumes and masks to celebrate the city's colourful history.

Early Aug

Wye Valley & Vale of Usk

The River Wye emerges from Plynlimon Mountain in mid Wales and meanders into England just after Hay-on-Wye. It returns to Wales just outside Monmouth, where the Welsh section of the Wye Valley – an

Medieval Bridge on the river Monnow, Monmouth

Area of Outstanding Natural Beauty – starts. From here it stretches south through Tintern to Chepstow and the Severn Estuary. It's no surprise, then, that the Wye Valley has a unique blend of Welsh and English heritage. Further west the River Usk runs a similar course to the Severn Estuary, creating a valley of patchwork fields and pretty villages before the once-industrialised Welsh valleys start.

Monmouth

Like the rest of the Welsh borders, the Wye Valley was fought over for centuries. The debate over whether Monmouth should be English or Welsh – King Henry V was born at Monmouth Castle – continues to this day. Some claim Monmouth only officially became part of Wales in 1974, others claim it was centuries before. Whatever, it's a lovely market town, with medieval fortified bridge and – as a Fairtrade town – great little independent shops and cafes. There's only a tiny fragment of the castle remaining, but nearby is the **Castle and Regimental Museum**. The **Nelson Museum and Local History Centre** highlights the town's interesting history, which included the 1840 trial of three Chartists – the group which campaigned for workers' rights. The men were sentenced to be hanged and quartered at the court in the town's Shire Hall. You can walk along the banks of the River

Monnow to Vauxhall fields by heading down the lane and steep steps next to the Castle and Regimental Museum.

Castle and Regimental Museum ALL AGES

The Castle, Monmouth, NP25 3BS.
📞 *01600 772175, wwwmonmouth-castlemuseum.org.uk*

Only parts of the Great Hall and Great Tower of this once-important castle survive. It's the birthplace of King Henry V, though it wasn't his home – his family were only visiting. The castle was later abandoned in favour of nearby Raglan Castle and Great Castle House was built with stone from the Great Tower after it was demolished by Cromwell's soldiers. Now Great Castle House is the Royal Monmouthshire Royal Engineers headquarters and the regimental museum is in the stables. There are also the King's Garden, a medieval herb garden, and views over the Monnow Valley – a thoroughly nice place for a family walk.

Open Easter–Oct, daily, 2–5pm; Sat 10am–5pm; Nov–March, Sat and Sun, 2–4pm. Admission free, donations welcome. Amenities shop.

Nelson Museum and Local History Centre ALL AGES VALUE

The Castle, Monmouth, NP25 3BS,
📞 *01600 710630, www.nelson museum.gov.uk*

Admiral Horatio Nelson – hero of the Battle of Trafalgar – visited Monmouth twice in 1802, and impressed the people of Monmouth greatly. Now it has one of the finest collections of Nelson memorabilia in the UK, thanks to Lady Llangattock whose family was one of the most important in Monmouth in the early 20th century. Children will love some of the more bizarre exhibits – such as Nelson's glass eye. There are also local history displays, with a section on Charles Stuart Rolls (as in Rolls-Royce), who lived near Monmouth. There are worksheets and quizzes for children.

Open All year, Mon–Sat, 11am–1pm and 2–4pm; Sun 2–4pm. Admission free. Amenities shop.

The Kymin ALL AGES

Monmouth, NP25 3SE, 📞 *01600 719241, www.nelsonmuseum. gov.uk. Take the A4136 off the A40.*

This charming little round house was built in 1793 as a gentleman's dining room – and Nelson was a guest in 1802. Now it is owned by the National Trust who provide children's quizzes to make the two-room tower more interesting for them. There's also a temple dedicated to the British Navy. The drive from Monmouth is along a heart-stoppingly steep and narrow road with vicious hairpin bends. We were praying nobody was driving down on our way up. But once there it's a great place for a picnic with spectacular views of Monmouth and the surrounding countryside. There's enough space for ball games too, and in late spring the woods are carpeted with bluebells. You can also walk up to Kymin on the

Offa's Dyke Path, which runs through the grounds. A popular route from Monmouth is to walk over the medieval bridge on the River Wye and follow the A4136 where Offa's Dyke is signposted after the first bend. It's a steep hike though, so not suitable for very young children.

Open grounds: daily; Round House: Late March–Late Oct, Sat–Mon, 11am–4pm. **Admission** grounds: free; Round House: adults £2.20, children £1.10, family £5.50. **Amenities** nine acres of woods and pleasure grounds.

White Castle ALL AGES

Llantilio Crossney, Monmouthshire, NP7 8UD, ☎ 01600 780380, www.cadw.wales.gov.uk

Prepare to be impressed as you walk over the bridge of this romantic, moated castle. From outside, it looks like a ruined castle should do, with huge round towers each side of the entrance and more massive round towers connected by high walls. White Castle was one of three locally built to control the borders. Skenfrith and Grosmont are the others but neither is as impressive as this well-preserved, powerful build-ing. Children enjoy climbing the tower, crossing the moat, and generally running free.

Open April–Sept, Wed–Sun and Bank Hol Mon, 10am–5pm. All other days, including Oct–May, castle open but unmanned. **Admission** adults £2.50, concessions £2, family £7, under 5s free. When unmanned, entrance free. **Amenities** gift shop, car park.

INSIDER TIP ≫

Whitestone Picnic and Play Area in Bargain Wood – part of the Wye Valley forest – is a fabulous place to get away from the tourist trail. There's a car park, picnic benches and barbecue facilities as well as good wooden play equipment, although the acres of woodland are as good a play area as any child needs. You can also get to Bargain Wood on the Wye Valley Walk. Park at Tintern Old Station on the A466 and take the path north a little way up across the road.

Tintern

A small but lovely village with interesting antique and book shops, pubs and cafes, its major attraction, **Tintern Abbey**, is a little further down the hill and takes your breath away when it suddenly looms into view. There's a **Tintern Trail** walk which starts at the Abbey and continues along pushchair-friendly surfaces along the river-side to the old chapel, **Abbey Mill** craft and gift shops and a café overlooking the trout pond. The sign-posted walk then takes you through the village up to **Parva Vineyard**, where vines grow on the south-facing slopes above Tintern open for tours and sales.

Tintern Abbey ★ ALL AGES

Tintern, ☎ 01291 689251, www.cadw.wales.gov.uk. On A4666 between Chepstow and Newport.

This has to be the most spine-tinglingly-beautiful ruin in Wales – especially when all the tourist buses have left and taken the hordes of day trippers with them. At the height of the season it can be difficult to find a space in the car park, so try to go out of season or early/late in the day. If you like exploring ruined abbeys then you'll love this one: it's the best-preserved medieval one in Wales, founded by Cistercians in 1131. The tracery of its huge Gothic windows give its over-powering presence a delicate touch. But it's the abbey's posi-tion by the river and with wood-land climbing above it on both sides of the valley that is really magical – especially when the sun is sparkling. In fact, children will enjoy the abbey just as much walking along the river or in the hills around it, seeing it in all its glory. That's what Wordsworth did when he wrote the poem *Composed A Few Miles Above Tintern Abbey* – and he knew a few things about glorious views.

Open *April–May, daily, 9.30am–5pm; June–Sept, daily, 9.30am–6pm; Oct, daily, 9.30am–5pm; Nov–March, Mon–Sat, 9.30am–4pm, Sun,*

11am–4pm. **Admission** *adults £3.50, concessions £3, family £10, under 5s free.* **Amenities** *free parking, toilets, giftshop, exhibition, audio tour.*

INSIDER TIP ››

Tintern Old Station is a great place to stop for a picnic or to get an ice cream from the café housed in this lovely old railway station. The Wye Valley line was torn up years ago, but the station has been preserved and, as well as the café there's a crafts and gift shop, with leaflets on local walks and attractions. The picnic area has wooden carvings of leg-endary heroes such as King Arthur and Saint Tewdrig, and there's a play area and lawn. There's also a very basic camp-site (01291 689566).

Chepstow

This is another gateway to Wales and one of the most impressive with its magnificent castle on the River Wye, guarding the bound-ary. The town's name is old English for market place, and Chepstow still has several: the

Tintern Abbey, one of the best-preserved medieval ruins in Wales

farmers' market at Cormeilles Square every second and fourth Saturday; Women's Institute Country Produce Market at Cormeilles Square every Friday and every first and third Saturday, and the Sunday market at **Chepstow Racecourse**. There are still parts of the old town wall, known as **The Portwall**. Similarly there's **The Gatehouse**, rebuilt in 1609 but dating back to 1067, which straddles the main street and, like the castle, was built by the Norman invaders to keep undesirables out. There are leaflets detailing walks around the town and along the Wye available from the Tourist Centre in the castle car park, where the walks begin. Opposite is **Chepstow Museum**, in a Georgian townhouse.

Chepstow castle ☆ ALL AGES
VALUE

Bridge Street, Chepstow, NP6 5EY, 📞 *01291 624065, www.cadw.wales. gov.uk*

One of the most interesting castles in Britain, because it was one of the first to be built of stone – a reflection of its importance in the Norman conquest of Wales after their invasion of England just a year before, in 1066. The Norman keep is still there but was added to over 600 years, making Chepstow Castle a complete history lesson in medieval military building. The children may look on blankly but they appreciate the towers, walls, gatehouses and barbicans perched in a formidable wedge on the cliffs overlooking the

River Wye. It's a peaceful place for a few hours, with grassy areas for picnics and playing, and occasional medieval entertainment and displays.

Open April–May, daily, 9.30am–5pm; June–Sept, daily, 9.30am–6pm; Oct, daily, 9.30am–5pm; Nov–Mar, Mon–Sat, 9.30am–4pm, Sun, 11am–4pm. Admission adults £3.50, concessions £3, family £10, under 5s free. Amenities gift shop. Pay and display car park and tourist information centre nearby.

Chepstow Museum ALL AGES
Gwy House, Bridge Street, NP6 5EZ, 📞 *01291 625981, www.caldicot. com;www.gtj.org.uk*

Chepstow was once an important port, with shipbuilding and the wine trade among its more colourful industries – as this great little museum reveals. Children may be more interested in the schoolroom which has been reconstructed in the museum, as well as the many old photos and the quizzes and worksheets.

Open July–Sept, Mon–Sat, 10.30am–5.30pm, Sun 2–5pm; Oct–June, Mon–Sat, 11am–1pm and 2–5pm, Sun, 2–5pm. Admission free. Amenities shop. Pay and display car park and tourist information centre nearby.

Caldicot Castle ALL AGES
Church Road, Caldicot, NP26 4HU, 📞 *01291 420241, www.caldicotcastle.co.uk. From M4 J23a take B4245 to Caldicot.*

There are 55 acres of country park here, with woodlands, pasture and the River Neddern to explore – as well as the castle. Caldicot Castle was built by the

Normans then strengthened during the Middle Ages, finally becoming a family home in Victorian times. Now it combines the usual castle experience with loads of children's activities and special events such as military re-enactments, theatre and seasonal celebrations.

Open *castle: Easter/April–Oct, daily, 11am–4pm; country park:open all year.* **Admission** *castle: adults £3.75, concessions £2.50, family £12, under 5s free. Country park: free.* **Amenities** *shop, tea room, free parking.*

Usk

The River Usk runs through this pretty little town, which is full of antique and craft shops, restaurants, cafes, pubs and fishermen. The anglers come for the river's fabulous salmon, and permits are available from the town's fishing tackle shops. Among the town's other attractions is **Usk Castle**, a romantic ruin with a pretty garden in the centre and benches for you to relax on while the children play hide and seek. Entrance is by an honesty box donation and there's an unmanned stall with postcards and leaflets. The castle was built in the 11th century by the Normans. Henry VIII gave it to his sixth wife, Catherine Parr.

Usk Rural Life Museum
ALL AGES

Malt Barn, New Market Street, Usk, NP15 1AU, ☎ *01291 673777, www.uskmuseum.org.uk*

You really do step back in time here – from between 1850 and the end of the Second World War to be exact. This collection of agricultural and domestic equipment was donated by locals and saved for posterity by a group of enthusiasts who now run this museum in its wonderful barn setting. You can see a typical farmhouse kitchen, dairy and laundry from all those years ago, and children love climbing on old tractors and inspecting a collection of Riley model vehicles. They learn how blacksmiths, cobblers and wheelwrights once worked and see a huge range of old farming equipment. There's also a model railway which depicts the coming of steam trains to the area, and a penny farthing bicycle.

Open *Easter–Oct, Mon–Fri, 10am–5pm, Sat–Sun, 2–5pm.* **Admission** *adult £2, OAP £1.50, child £1.*

Raglan Castle   ALL AGES

Raglan, Usk, NP15 2BT, ☎ *01291 690228, www.cadw.wales.gov.uk*

This is a truly lovely castle, with dressed sandstone walls and decorative details in contrast to the rather grim functional designs of many of the castles in Wales. That's because Raglan Castle was built in more peaceful times. It was started in 1435, 200 years after most of the fortresses built to keep the Welsh under control, and it was still being added to in the mid 16th century. There are many distinctly Tudor-style touches, fitting for a castle which was the boyhood home of Henry Tudor, who became King Henry VII. Raglan is still reasonably intact, considering the damage done during one of the longest sieges in the Civil War during the 1640s, and its grassy grounds make it a great place for children to let off steam. Special events include medieval entertainment, weaponry demonstrations by knights and theatrical productions.

Open April–May, daily, 9.30am–5pm; June–Sept, daily, 9.30am–6pm; Oct, daily, 9.30am–5pm; Nov–March, Mon–Sat, 9.30am–4pm, Sun 11am–4pm. **Closed** Dec 24–26 and Jan 1 **Admission** adults £2.90, children £2.50, under 5s free, family £8.30. **Amenities** shop, free parking.

The Welsh Valleys

The old mining towns here are still a little grim – even with the growth of industrial heritage tourism. But don't let that put you off. There's always a welcome in the hillsides – and plenty to see and do.

Pontypool

This is probably not a town you would naturally head for. However, if you are in the area it's interesting to note that Pontypool is one of the oldest industrial towns in Wales; Pontypool Rugby Football Club is one of the most successful in the Welsh Rugby Union, and Richey Edwards and Sean Moore, of hit makers Manic Street Preachers, were born here. There is also the most interesting

industrial heritage site in Wales virtually on Pontypool's doorstep. Just along the A465 is Blaenavon World Heritage Site and Big Pit. Both need to be seen for you to start understanding south Wales and its people.

Blaenavon World Heritage Site ★ ★ ★ ALL AGES

North Street, Blaenavon, NP4 9RQ, ☎ 01495 792615, www.blaenavontic. com. Follow signs from the A465.

Blaenavon is home to the best-preserved 18th-century ironworks in Europe. When you see what's left of the huge structure, it is hard not to feel humbled. This wasn't even the biggest in Wales – but it was the most advanced in the world in 1789. The ironworks is at the heart of the Blaenavon Industrial Landscape which was awarded World Heritage Status in 2000. You have to pre-book for a tour, but there are plenty of other things to see. The most interesting part for our children was seeing the restored workers' cottages and imagining the way in which they lived. But this is by no means a grim place. Blaenavon town is fast becoming a second-hand book Mecca – although not quite in the Hay-on-Wye league yet. There's a picnic spot with panoramic views at Keepers Pond, on the B4246. There are marked walks, including the Iron Mountain Trails which start from Keepers Pond. Choose from the serious 11.25km walk up Blorenge Mountain, or the family-friendly stroll along the river – Afon Lwyd – where there's a section of the National Cycle Route from Newport. The World Heritage Site also includes Pontypool and Blaenavon Railway and – our favourite by a long way – Big Pit.

Open April–Oct, Mon–Fri 9.30am–4.30pm; Sat 10am–5pm; Sun 10am–4.30pm. Admission adults £2.50, children £2, family £7, under 5s free. Amenities free parking, gift shop, tourist information centre.

Big Pit ★★★ ALL AGES FIND
VALUE

National Coal Museum, Blaenavon, NP4 9XP, ☏ 01495 790311, www. museumwales.ac.uk

Quite honestly we were surprised to see a framed photo of Margaret Thatcher, the prime minister whose stand-off with the National Union of Miners in the 1980s effectively finished the Welsh coal industry. But we put it down to the Welsh sense of humour. It's offbeat to say the least, and in plentiful supply at this utterly brilliant museum. Don't be put off by the word museum, because Big Pit is more an experience than anything else – and it's free – even though it first appears big, bleak and grey. Going underground was hell for the miners, but for us it was the highlight: you get a hard hat with lamp then you are taken 92m down a mineshaft in a real pit cage. It's all authentic and your guide is a real miner. Ours, Mike, explained how the pit ponies were treated better than the miners in the early days. At least when a pit pony died there

was an inquiry, he said. As we walked through, helmets hitting the roof, Mike continually saw the funny side, and we hardly blinked at the sight of a rocking horse in one of the ponies' stables. Above ground there are colliery buildings to explore, including the brilliantly laid-out museum in the pithead baths. The Big Pit is top of our list to return to, as exhibitions are updated regularly.

Open daily, 9.30am–5pm, underground tours Feb–Nov, 10am–3.30pm at frequent intervals. Call for opening times and availability of underground tours Dec–Jan. Closed Dec 24, 25, 26, Jan 1. Admission free. Amenities cafe, coffee shop, gift shop, free parking.

Pontypool and Blaenavon Railway ★ ALL AGES

Blaenavon, NP4 9PT, ☏ 01495 792263, www.pontypool-and-blaenavon.co.uk

Built to transport coal from the Big Pit, this is the highest and steepest railway in Wales, reaching the highest station in England and Wales (400m). It's not very long but there's plenty to see: mountain horses, peregrine falcons, red kites – and loads of sheep. Five minutes from Furnace Sidings are Garn Lakes, a lovely spot for picnics. The Whistle Stop Inn is at the other end, with beer garden and play area.

Open Easter to Sept, Sat, Sun and Bank Hol Mons, departures from about 11.30am–4.30pm. Special events throughout the year, including prolonged summer opening and

Santa Specials in December. Tickets: adults (from 14 years) £2.50, children £1.50, family £6.50, under 3s free. Prices vary for special events. Single tickets also available. **Amenities** buffet car on train, restaurant at Whistle Stop Inn, free parking.

Rhondda Heritage Park ★
ALL AGES

Lewis Merthyr Colliery, Coed Cae Road, Trehafed, Pontypridd, CF37 2NP, ☎ 01443 682036, *www.rhondda heritagepark.com*

Where else would you go to experience Welsh coal mining heritage but the Rhondda Valley? The former Lewis Merthyr Colliery, at Trehafod, has been transformed into an historic experience, starting with a reconstructed village street including shops and homes, which you can explore to see how life was lived from the Victorian era up to the 1950s. Admission is free, but you pay for the Black Gold Tour. This is an audio/video presentation and tour of pit head buildings followed by an underground trip. You get a helmet lamp but only actually go down a few metres, and the train ride finale is more a Disneyesque vibrating 'carriage' in the dark with a runaway train film. Curiously, the children liked the last bit best... There's also Energy Zone, a giant adventure playground, open April–September.

Open Daily, April–Sept, 10am–6pm (last tour 4pm); **Closed** Mon Oct–Easter, Dec 25–Jan 2 inclusive. No underground tours mid-Nov–Jan. **Admission** adults £5.60, children £4.30, family £16.50–21, OAPs

£4.95. , Energy Zone play area £3 children, £1.50 children. Free for restaurant, art gallery and visitor centre. **Amenities** free car park, shop, restaurant, art gallery.

Pontypool Park and Museum
ALL AGES

Trosnant Street, Pontypool, NP4 8AT ☎ 01495 752036, *www.pontypool-museum.org.uk*

Pontypool Park is part of the former estate of John Hanbury, father of the Welsh tinplate industry. The museum is in the estate's Georgian stable block (the house is now a school) and brings to life the social history and industrial domination of Pontypool right up to the 20th-century. Star attraction is the display of Japanware – a 17th–18th century version of Japanese lacquered furniture and accessories – developed in Pontypool and hugely popular in America. Pontypool Park is famed for its shell grotto and folly tower. The grotto was built for Hanbury in about 1784, and used for family picnics. The tower, from 1770, was used as a summerhouse. It was demolished during the Second World War to prevent bombers using it as a landmark, but rebuilt, and opened by the Prince of Wales in 1994.

Open museum: Mon–Fri, 10am–5pm; Sat and Sun, 2–5pm. Grotto and tower: Sat, Sun and Bank Hols, 2–5pm. **Admission** adults £2, children £1. Free Wed and Sun. Grotto and tower: free. **Amenities** free car park, shop, café, leisure centre, tennis courts, skate park, adventure playground, walks.

Cwmbran

The New Town has good shopping facilities claimed to be the best in Wales. Not necessarily a big tourist draw, but it's nice to know they are there.

Greenmeadow Community Farm ALL AGES

Green Forge Way, Cwbran, NP44 5AJ, ☏ 01633 862202, www. abergavenny.co.uk

What is it about children and animals? Ours were transfixed by this lovely old farm's kid goats, and utterly delighted with the rare breed sheep – just because they were allowed to feed them. We thoroughly enjoyed our visit to this farm – even the grown ups. The trailer ride was great fun, with the tractor driver pointing out kestrels (we think) which were circling overhead. The children never allow us to miss out on an adventure playground and the one here came up to their fairly high standards, thankfully. They also loved the huge model dragon, even though it was too cold for it to be spurting water as it does in the summer, when there are also milking demonstrations and events. If we had had longer we might have tried one of the woodland walks, but we did make time for the rabbits and tortoises in pets corner. Lovely place with a very welcoming atmosphere.

Open daily, 10am–6pm, summer; 10am–4.30pm, winter. **Admission** *adults £4.50, children £3.50, family £16.* **Amenities** *café, shop, sand pit.*

Ebbw Vale

Once an iron and steel town, Ebbw Vale has few obvious tourist draws. However, not far from town (on the A4048) is the former site of the 1992 Garden Festival of Wales. Much of its 70 acres is still nicely landscaped managing to combine **Festival Park** (a factory shopping village with 40-plus outlets) with parkland, woodland, lakes, Japanese tea pavilion,

Feed the animals at Greenmeadow Community Farm

woodland craft centre and owl sanctuary. If that's not for you there's **Drenewydd Museum** in Bute Town, near Rhymney, just off the A465. Bute Town was a model village for iron workers, built by the Marquess of Bute who owned the land on which the works stood. Many are still lived in, although two are now a museum. Children will enjoy playing with replica Victorian toys and finding out about organic gardening – Victorian-style.

Bryn Bach Country Park near Tredegar is also worth visiting. It is 340 acres of grass and woodland with a 36-acre fishing lake to cycle around, plus picnic and barbecue areas, visitor centre and restaurant, adventure playground and instructor-led activities such as mountain biking, climbing and kayaking. There is even an 18-bed bunkhouse and campsite for tents and caravans (01495 711 816).

Merthyr Tydfil

It's difficult to believe this town has one of the most amazing histories in Britain. But if you are interested in finding out what made Britain Great, start here. In 1750 Merthyr was a village, but by 1759 an ironworks had opened using local coal and iron ore. By 1784 there were four ironworks and by 1801 Merthyr was the largest town in Wales with a population of 8,000. Dowlais Ironworks became the world's largest by 1830, and by 1845 the population had grown to 40,000. Merthyr's iron and steel was exported across the world as the town played out dramatic moments of the British labour movement. The 1831 Merthyr Rising of 10,000 ironworkers protesting against pay cuts was one of Britain's most violent uprisings. A century later the boom was over and the ironworks closed one by one. A Royal Commission in 1939 said the whole town should be abandoned. The pit closures of the 1980s were the final nail. But things are looking up. The town centre is being regenerated and a café quarter has already been developed. There are heritage walks leaflets available from the tourist office – and youngsters find a strange attraction in the bleak history.

Cyfarthfa Castle Museum and Art Gallery ALL AGES VALUE

Cyfarthfa Park, 01685 723112, *www.museums.merthyr.gov.uk. Take A470 from Merthyr towards Pentrebach, then follow signs.*

Merthyr Tydfil may not be on everybody's tourist trail, but Cyfarthfa Castle – its monument to the industrial revolution – is a great place for a few hours of free entertainment if the weather turns miserable. This castellated mansion was commissioned in 1824 by the town's leading ironmaster, Richard Crawshaw II. It represents the extraordinary wealth created during the iron- and steel-making heyday. The rooms are full of relics, and the art collection includes paintings by Rolf Harris's grandfather, who had a portrait studio in Merthyr. We liked the basement local

Cyfartha Castle, Merthyr Tydfil

pool, adventure playground, band-stand, woodland park and cafe, angling lake, parkland walks.

Joseph Parry's Cottage
ALL AGES

4 Chapel Row, Merthyr Tydfil, ☎ 01685 723112, www.museums.merthyr. gov.uk. Just off the A470 (signposted).

Number 4 Chapel Row is birth-place of composer Dr Joseph Parry. The cottage has been refurbished to reflect life in the 1840s, when Dr Parry lived here as a child. There's an exhibition of Parry's work – he wrote Welsh male choir favourite Myfanwy, an opera and several hymns.

Open *Thur–Sun, 2–5pm, Apr–Sept.* ***Admission*** *free.*

Vale of Glamorgan

Most holidaymakers completely miss this under-rated area as they speed along the M4 towards the Gower or Pembrokeshire. But the gentle, rolling agricultural land and the Heritage Coast beaches are a treat for families. It has the nearest sandy Welsh beaches to England, as well as great walking and several historic towns and villages.

Bridgend

This town played its part in the industrialisation of south Wales as a distribution point for coal. But it was always a market town and still has a covered market daily except Sunday. There's plenty of other shopping in the pedestri-anised centre, though many shoppers are lured out to

history exhibits best, where the children enjoyed pushing the but-tons on the interactive displays.

The children were stunned by pictures of the 1966 Aberfan dis-aster, when 20 houses and a school were buried in a slag heap slide killing 144 people, mostly children. Not typical holiday fare, but it's gratifying to hear our chil-dren asking questions about other people's lives instead of just won-dering where the next ice cream is coming from. Speaking of which, you can get them at the castle's café, and if the weather's fine you can walk around the landscaped grounds and feed the ducks in the pond, or invade the adven-ture playground.

Open *April–Sept, 10am–5.30pm daily; Oct–March, 10am–4pm, Tues–Fri; 12–4pm, Sat and Sun. Park open daily, 7am–dusk.* ***Admission*** *free.* ***Amenities*** *free parking, shop, tearoom, tennis courts, bowling green, model steam railway, paddling*

Bridgend Designer Outlet, which also features a multi-screen Odeon cinema, play area, and children's entertainers such as clowns and face-painting. Oldest part of town is **Newcastle**, where pilgrims used to stop at St John's Hospice on their way west to St David's. There are the remains of an early Norman castle and self-guided walking trails are available from tourist centres. Two miles north-east of town is the much more impressive **Coity Castle** ruins, near the village of Coity. The castle is open most days, unmanned but under Cadw stewardship, and is free – so a good place to break your motorway journey.

> **INSIDER TIP**
>
> Bryngarw Country Park, 3.2km north of Bridgend, is the ideal place to break your journey west and allow children to let off steam. It is just off the M4 at J36, and has 113 acres of gardens and woodlands, lakes, rivers and – of course – picnic areas. There's also an adventure playground, free summer events and a restaurant next to the pay car park. Entrance is free.

Bedford Park & Ironworks
ALL AGES

Cefn Cribbwr, Kenfig Hill, CF32 0BW, 📞 *01656 725155, www.bridgend. gov.uk. North of Junction 37 of the M4, off the A48.*

One of the best preserved 18th-century ironworks in Wales and Britain, but most people will be drawn to Bedford Park for its natural splendour. There are

walking trails, picnic sites and a playground. There are also several cycleways, including the Celtic Trail and National Cycle Route.

Open *daily, dawn until dusk; iron-works: daily, 10am–5.30pm, April–Sept; 10am–4.30pm, Oct–March.* **Admission** *free.* **Amenities** *free parking.*

Wildlife Trust of South and West Wales ALL AGES

Coed y Bwl, Castle upon Alun, 📞 *01656 724100, www.welsh wildlife.org. Just south of Bridgend, on a minor road into the Alun Valley off the B426.*

Coed y Bwl is an ancient ash woodland on the northwest side of Alun Valley, and will enchant most children. It is best known as a wild daffodil wood in the early spring and bluebell wood in late spring, and there are loads of birds to look out for such as buzzard, sparrowhawk and kestrel. This is one of 37 nature reserves in Glamorgan under Wildlife Trust control. For full details see the website.

Open *daily.* **Admission** *free.*

Porthcawl

This rather tired-looking seaside resort features several wonderful sandy beaches and a fast-growing reputation for being a surfer's paradise. Porthcawl was more important as a port until after the First World War, when it was reinvented as a holiday centre, taking advantage of its sand and mixed sand and rock beaches. Among them, **Coney Beach**, **Rest Bay** and **Trecco Bay** have a Blue Flag.

Porthcawl

Kenfig National Nature Reserve ★ ALL AGES

Ton Kenfig, Pyle, CF33 4PT ℓ 01656 743386, www.bridgend.gov.uk

Just north of Porthcawl and one of the most important conservation sites in Europe, this is an ideal place for families to walk and picnic. It is set among the remnants of a huge sand dune system that once stretched along the coast from the River Ogmore to the Gower. There's the 70-acre Kenfig Pool, the largest natural lake in Glamorgan, which is home to thousands of migratory birds in autumn. You'll also find a visitor centre with hands-on exhibition for children, a shop, boardwalk and bird hides, plus miles of walks through the reserve and down to the sandy beach. Of particular interest to imaginative children will be the lost village of Kenfig beneath the sands. Only the top of the castle is still visible.

***Open** daily – no restrictions.*

Coney Beach Pleasure Park
ALL AGES

Coney Beach, Porthcawl, CF36 5BY, ℓ 01656 788911. Take Junction 37 of M4.

On the sandy beachfront of Coney Beach, this old-school amusement park has its roots in the 1920s. There are a variety of rides and amusements including The Megablitz roller-coaster, along with smaller family coasters such as Happy Gater, and a number of fairground-style attractions. The park has become run down over the years and there are constant rumours of redevelopment – don't be surprised to find it gone!

***Open** March–Sept, daily; Oct–Feb, weekends. Hours variable. **Admission** free – pay per ride. **Amenities** cafes, shops, arcades, beach.*

Merthyr Mawr

A pretty little village of thatched cottages, with a lovely church, unusual 15th-century bridge over the River Ogmore, and a huge complex of sand dunes that end at a sandy beach. Merthyr Mawr Warren, as the sand dunes are known, has crept so far inland that parts of the movie *Lawrence of Arabia* were shot here. The dunes cover an ancient burial ground and the lost village of Treganllaw, said to be near to the very spooky ruins of Candleston Castle. But don't let that put you off, this is a spectacular place, fantastic for children to run around. Locals even toboggan down the dunes on bin bags, probably making conservationists wince. You can walk east through the dunes and over stepping stones on the Ewenny Estuary to Ogmore Castle. The area is a National Nature Reserve.

Ogmore-by-Sea

The river and beach are the must-see destinations for Ogmore-by-Sea, although there are some good-looking restaurants and pubs on the road to the beach. Low tide reveals a wide expanse of sand with the River Ogmore, joined by the River Ewenny, flowing fast down into the Bristol Channel. Bathing is restricted on the beach and is forbidden near the river which is far more dangerous than it looks. For all that, this is glorious after the claustrophobia of Porthcawl. Even the car park is pretty, almost randomly organised on common land overlooking the sea, with sheep grazing between the cars and plenty of places for picnics if you don't like sand with your sandwiches. On an autumn visit, when it was sunny but gusty, we watched kite surfers dice with the choppy waves, and horse riders cantering down to the sea on the other side of the river, while we walked over the firm sands and our children poked around the rock pools in their wellies. On the way back we stopped at **Ogmore Castle**, on the B4524, where there's a small car park next to the river. The ruined Norman castle is open

Ogmore Castle is free to explore during daylight hours

Llantwit Major beach has the characteristic cliffs of the Heritage Coast

daily during daylight hours and free to enter, although it is looked after by Cadw. Nearby is **Ogmore Farm**, with farm shop, cafe and riding stables.

Lakeside Farm Park ALL AGES

Hendre-Ifan-Goch Farm, Glynogwr, Blackmill, CF35 6EN ☎ 01443 676805, www.lakesidefarmpark.uk. From M4 Junction 34 take A4119 to Tonyrefail. At 5th roundabout go left (A4093) to Gilfach Goch. Turn left after the fire station.

A splendid working farm in the hills of the Ogmore Valley offers a fishing lake teeming with rainbow trout for adults and a small coarse fishing pond for children. There are lots of places to wander, as well as indoor and outdoor play areas.

Open April–Oct, Fri–Sun, 9am–7pm Admission fishing: 2 fish £10, 3 fish £12.50; play areas and animals £1.50 for children; trailer ride £1. Amenities tearoom, shop, parking.

Southerndown & Dunraven Bay

Most people go to Southerndown to get to Dunraven Bay, at the bottom of dramatic cliffs. It's a beautiful beach, sandy in parts, with stones, rocks and jagged backdrop. Nearby is **Dunraven Park,** and the **Glamorgan Heritage Coast Centre**. Here you can find info about walks, the coast and countryside. On the cliffs are the ruins of **Dunraven Castle** where you can explore the walled garden.

Llantwit Major

The lovely old stone buildings of this pretty little town include the 16th-century **Town Hall**. You'll find the tourist centre here and the Llantwit Major Heritage Centre. The town merits a quick look: the **Old Swan Inn** opposite the Town Hall has a beer garden, does food all day, and welcomes children. US newspaper baron William Randolph Hearst lived at nearby **St Donat's Castle** and entertained British politicians such as David Lloyd George. Neville Chamberlain and Winston Churchill, as well as celebrities like Bob Hope and Charlie Chaplin. The castle is now a college, with a lively arts centre that holds musical and theatrical events featuring household names (℡ *01446 799100, www.stdonats.com*). **Llantwit beach**, a few miles out of town, is a surfers' spot with a café near the car park. It is part sandy, with flat rocks and stones – and the impressive brick wall-like cliffs that characterise this coastline.

Cowbridge

A Roman road runs through the middle of this lovely market town with craft and antique shops, cafes and restaurants, its Norman history also apparent, with the gatehouse of the ruined **St Quentin's Castle** now open to the public. Within the remains of the medieval town walls you will find **Cowbridge Physic Garden**, created in 2004. This herb garden, in the former walled garden of Old Hall, is free to visit. Not far from Cowbridge are two Neolithic burial chambers. The impressive **Tinkinswood Burial Chamber**, near St Nicholas, has one of the largest capstones in Britain. A mile south is the even more mysterious **St Lythans Burial Chamber**. It's in the middle of a field and is said to grant wishes whispered to it on Hallowe'en.

Both are maintained by Cadw, open 10am–4pm, daily, and free.

Dyffryn Gardens ★ ALL AGES

St Nicholas, Vale of Glamorgan, CF5 6SU, ℡ 029 2059 3328, www.diffryn gardens.org.uk. Signposted from St Nicholas, on the A48.

Restoration of these beautiful Grade I listed Edwardian gardens is still continuing, and there are several school holiday events to make family visits even more enjoyable. The tearoom, shop, picnic and play areas can all be used without paying to enter the gardens – so it's a good place to stop for lunch or a cup of tea.

Open *March, daily, 11am–4pm; main season, April–Oct, daily, 10am–6pm; low season, Nov–Feb, Thur–Mon, 11am–4pm.* **Admission**: *main season, adult £6, concessions £4, child £2, family £15, under 5s free. Low season, adult £3, children £1, family £7.* **Amenities** *parking.*

Warren Mill Farm Park
ALL AGES

Pendoylan, near Cowbridge, CF71 7UJ, ℡ 01446 781274, www.warren millfarm.co.uk. Signposted from Bonvilston on the A48.

A picturesque 17th-century farm is home to rare breeds of sheep, miniature cattle, ponies, llamas and red squirrels. The farm was once a mill and the original pond is still there, now stocked with carp, tench, bream, roach, rudd and perch. See the website for tackle and bait rules.

Open *daily, 10.30am–dusk.* **Admission**: *farm, adults £2, children (up to 14) £1; fishing, adults £5, children (up to 15) £3.* **Amenities** *café, picnic and play areas, parking.*

SWANSEA

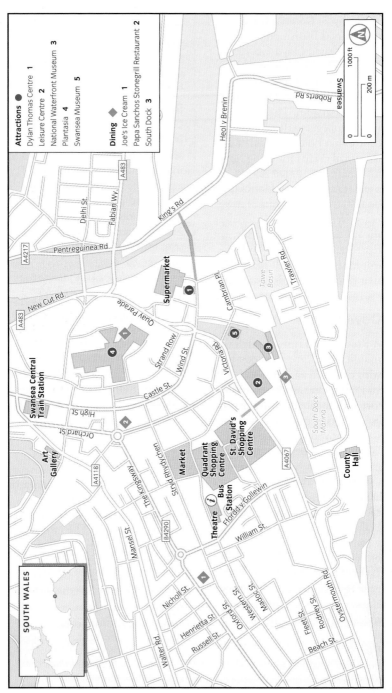

Attractions ●
Dylan Thomas Centre **1**
Leisure Centre **2**
National Waterfront Museum **3**
Plantasia **4**
Swansea Museum **5**

Dining ◆
Joe's Ice Cream **1**
Papa Sanchos Stonegrill Restaurant **2**
South Dock **3**

SOUTH WALES

Gnoll Estate Country Park, is another good stop-off point to break journeys. The 200-acre park has landscaped gardens, an adventure playground and fishing lake as well as a visitor centre and café. Follow signs from the A465 north of J43 of the M4, towards Neath.

Swansea

Walk or cycle around the 8km arch of Swansea Bay on a sunny day and you might think you've been transported to California or Australia it's so beautifully laid back. The sea is central to Wales's second city – from its early shipbuilding history and later prominence as a port to its new-found role as a major tourist centre thanks to its newly-developed and quite superb maritime quarter. That said, stand in Swansea on a murky wet day looking at the rows of terraced housing climbing up its hillside, and you can understand why the nation's greatest poet, Dylan Thomas, described his home as an 'ugly, lovely town'. Whether you get sunshine or rain when you visit, there are a few must-dos. Cycle or walk around Swansea Bay along the **Swansea Bay Promenade,** which follows the old tramway route from the Marina to Mumbles pier. A wide swathe of grass dotted with pine trees makes the views out over the Bristol Channel even more enchanting on a blue-sky sunny day. Visit the free **National Waterfront Museum** in the maritime quarter – a modern glass building that tells the story of Wales's industry and innovation. There's a local produce market here on the first Sunday of every month. Drag the children along to the **Dylan Thomas Centre,** nearby – they'll thank you for it when they're older. Then round it all off with a visit to the country's largest **indoor market,** behind the Quadrant Shopping

National Waterfront Museum, Swansea

Centre. It's the best place in Wales to buy laverbread, the national seaweed dish, and it's also highly regarded for its fresh-baked bread, Welsh cakes, regional cheeses and cockles from nearby Loughor estuary. Also of interest is the **Glynn Vivian Art Gallery**, with work by Welsh artists such as Augustus John and his sister Gwen John. About 1.5km west of the city, at Blackpill, is **Clyne Gardens**, a 50-acre park famous for its rhododendrons, azaleas and other late spring-flowering shrubs. The park was once part of the Vivian family's estate, and is suitably landscaped. Admission free.

National Waterfront Museum, Swansea ★ ★ ALL AGES FIND
VALUE

Oystermouth Road, Maritime Quarter, SA1 3RD, ☎ 01792 638950, www.waterfrontmuseum.co.uk

You could spend hours in this state of the art museum, which explores how the industrialisation of Wales shaped the country and the people who live in it. We went on the perfect day – cold and wet outside – and the time just flew as the children ran from one interactive push button display to another. I'm not sure how much information they took in, but we did enjoy finding out about famous Welsh 'achievers', playing with the huge screens that reveal scenes of the surrounding area and watching video footage of the way of life in Wales over the past century. Downstairs is old industrial equipment, mine trucks,

engines, carriages and cars, and information about the wealth created in Wales and hardships suffered. The museum is a wonderful example of how a listed waterfront warehouse can be transformed into a contemporary treasure house with the imaginative use of glass and slate. At the back is **South Dock** with its historic ships, restaurants, cafes and pubs, and listed late-Georgian, Victorian and Edwardian buildings.

Open daily, 10am–5pm. Admission free. Amenities café, picnic areas. Pay parking nearby.

LC ALL AGES

Oystermouth Road, Maritime Quarter, Swansea, SA1 3ST ☎ 01792 466500, www.thelcswansea.com. Opposite the National Waterfront Museum.

A new multi-purpose centre although for families it's The Edge, Wales' biggest, and certainly most exciting, indoor water park, that's the attraction. There's Surf Rider, a real surf experience, the first of its kind in the world, and Masterblaster, a roller-coaster style ride shoots you uphill on water jets then lets you plunge down. There's the long, windy water flume, the relaxing Lazy River and a wave pool. Youngsters have to be 1.1m for the big stuff, but for young ones there's the interactive pool and lagoon with tipping bucket and fountains

The Core, a massive sports centre, has a four-storey aquatic themed play area, a 30ft climbing wall and other activities. For adults there's The Peak, one of the largest spa and gym areas in

Wales. The centre also has a coffee shop, the Café Lounge restaurant and the family favourite Poolside Bistro.

Open *The Edge: Mon-Fri, 4-9pm (9am-9pm school holidays), weekends, 9am-8pm. Climbing wall, Mon-Fri, 4-9pm, weekends/bank holidays, 10am-6pm. Play area, daily, 10am-6pm.* **Admission** *The Edge: Adults £7, children 3-16 £4, under 3 free. Surf Rider £4.95/45 minutes. Climbing wall, £3.50/30 mins, booking recommended. Play area, £4 (£7 for 2), £2 under 2s. Table tennis £5/hour, badminton £8/hour.* **Amenities** *cafés, shop.*

Swansea Museum ALL AGES
VALUE

Victoria Road, Maritime Quarter, SA1 1SN, ☎ 01792 653763, www.swanseaheritage.net; www.swansea.gov.uk

Irresistibly old fashioned, as you might expect of the oldest public museum in Wales, this is an oasis of peace and somewhere to absorb a real sense of history – ideal for those of us who still like our museums to have glass cabinets and a non-themed, eclectic collection. Children will probably like the Egyptian mummy best and The Tramshed, which is at the back of the museum and right next to the National Waterfront Museum. Here they can climb on to part of the last surviving double-decker Swansea street tram. The Tramshed is only open in the summer (June–August) and on special occasions, as are the museum's historic boats, moored in South Dock. A block of 19th-century streets between museum

and tramshed have been turned into a café-style area.

Open *Tue–-Sun and Bank Hols, 10am–5pm, last admission 4.40pm.* **Admission** *free.* **Amenities** *gift shop.*

Dylan Thomas Centre
OLDER CHILDREN

Somerset Place, SA1 1RRm ☎ 01792 463980, www.dylanthomas.com

Parents owe it to themselves to find out a little about the most important poet and writer Wales has ever produced. Hopefully, older children will also be interested in the recreation of the hut in which he wrote at Laugharne, and the exhibition about his turbulent life and extraordinary work. The complex also includes a theatre, galleries, book shop and restaurant, and is the hub of the annual Dylan Thomas Festival, in October and November.

Open *daily, 10am–4.30pm.* **Admission** *free.* **Amenities** *book shop, restaurant, theatre, galleries.*

Egypt Centre ALL AGES VALUE

Swansea University, Singleton Park, SA2 8PP, ☎ 01792 295960, www.swan.ac.uk

There are 4,500 Egyptian artefacts on display, most from the private collection of American pharmacist Sir Henry Wellcome, who moved to London in 1880. The collection is for academic use, as well as public display, but children with a fascination for mummified crocodiles and hieroglyphics will love it.

Open *Tue–Sat, 10am–4pm.* **Admission** *free.*

Plantasia ALL AGES

Parc Tawe, SA1 2AL, ☎ 01792 474555, www.swansea.gov.uk

A good wet weather option, Plantasia is a giant greenhouse pyramid with a tropical rainforest zone and contrasting arid zone, both filled with plants typical of those climates. The children enjoy the jungle-like feel along with the parakeets, tamarind monkeys, butterflies, aquarium and vivaria – which house a Burmese python and pink toed tarantula.

Open daily, 10am-5pm. Admission adults £3.50, children £2.50, under-4s free. Amenities café, parking nearby.

Swansea Football Club
OLDER CHILDREN

Liberty Stadium, Morfa, SA1 2FA, ☎ 01792 616600, www.swansea city.net. On A4067 towards city from M4 J45.

Former top flight club Swansea are now a respected force again in the English Football League, and this would be a treat for any football-mad youngster. They play at Liberty Stadium, which opened in 2005 (shared with the Ospreys rugby team). It's also used for concerts by the likes of Elton John. The stadium is a short bus ride from the city centre.

Tickets from £16 adults, £10 OAPs, £7 under 16s; if visiting as an away supporter tickets must be bought in advance. Amenities no parking – use park-and-ride M4 J45, £5 a car.

Mumbles

Once a fishing village, then a Victorian seaside resort and increasingly an upmarket haunt of the new breed of wealthy Welsh, Mumbles has half a dozen or more highly-rated restaurants and several designer boutiques, but at heart is still a jolly seaside village at the far end of Swansea Bay. There are the usual gift shops, cafes and pubs, a wonderful sandy beach, and a branch of Swansea's legendary **Joe's Ice Cream**, on Mumbles Road. Near the start of Mumbles you'll find the well-maintained ruins of **Oystermouth Castle**, which stand guard over the Mumbles in beautiful parkland. The park is open year round, the castle only in the summer. It's the best preserved of all the castles in the Gower area and has several summer events. The central **Southend Gardens**, has a play area, tennis courts and crazy golf – although parking can be a problem in high summer. **Mumbles Pier**, at **Bracelet Bay**, the far end of Mumbles, has an all-weather family amusement centre with ten pin bowling, and there's an indoor ice rink at the **Winter Gardens**, next door. Near the car park there's also a good play area, and a grassy headland for picnics with views out to the 200-year-old lighthouse and rocky **Limeslade Beach**. Mumbles is also the gateway to some of the more accessible Gower beaches.

Gower Peninsula

Britain's first Area of Outstanding Natural Beauty,

with a breathtakingly beautiful coastline, is all about beaches, some huge: Rhossili is three miles long. Some are almost exotically picturesque – Three Cliffs Bay is simply magical – others just unspoilt, clean, sandy beaches providing everything you need for a bucket and spade holiday. There is plenty of scope for other outdoor activities here, though. Walking along the coast path is spectacular, or you can walk across the peninsula following the 35-mile **Gower Way**. There's also pony trekking down to the sea, and water sports. Inland there are woods to tramp through, including Forestry Commission land at **Park Wood**, which is near the Gower Heritage Centre at Park Mill, and at **Millwood**, near Penrice, where wild daffodil grow. There's a car park on the A4118 just before Penrice. To the north there's a huge network of sand dunes at Whitford Burrows and Llanrhidian Sands, part of a National Nature Reserve.

www.enjoygower.com
www.the-gower.com
www.welcometogower.co.uk

Langlands Bay

This is a broad, sandy beach with very easy access, so great for families though it can become crowded. This is actually two bays – Langlands and **Rotherslade** – but the latter, to the east, only really exists at high tide. The bay has rock pools to explore, firm sand for castle-making when the tide goes out,

and you can walk along a coastal path east to Limeslade Beach 2.4km or the same distance west to Caswell Bay. There's a row of beach huts along the length of the bay, with Langlands Brasserie at the western end of the beach. It has lovely views and sells everything from hot drinks, beers and snacks to full-blown meals. There's a car park behind the beach huts and there are tennis courts.

Caswell Bay

This is a beautiful sandy beach with rocky cliffs either side, safe swimming and convenient beach shop for ice creams. There are surfers – and a Surfside Café – but it's mostly a family beach and there are life guards in the summer. There's a car park across the road with a wooded valley at the back, which leads to Bishops Wood – a nature reserve with paths up to the cliff top.

Brandy Cove

A secluded beach a 20-minute walk from Bishopston, or walk along the coastal path from Caswell. No facilities.

Pwll Du Bay

Another beach off the beaten track, and a 2.4km walk from Pyle Corner, Bishopston. There are strong currents near Pwll Du Point to the west, and no facilities.

Pobbles Bay

At high tide this is a tiny cove, but at low water you can walk along the sand to glorious Three Cliffs Bay and neighbouring Tor Bay if you time it right. But swimming is only safe at low tide and you have to walk 800m from Southgate to get there. No facilities.

Three Cliffs Bay

Many believe this is the most beautiful beach in Wales, and it certainly has everything: fantastic sand, caves, rock pools, a ruined castle and the unique three pyramid rock formation – with its own natural arch – which gives the beach its name. However, it takes about 20–30 minutes to walk here from the footpath at Southgate car park, and although there are various paths you can scramble down from further west along the cliffs they are hard going with children. Then there's the river (Pennard Pill) to cross at the start of the beach. There are stepping stones but once the tide starts racing in they are of little use, and swimming is too dangerous other than at low tide. But this beach is fine for families with a sense of adventure, who like uncrowded beaches with no garish shops or cafes. You just have to time your visit so the tide is on the way out when you arrive. And if the tide is in, you can explore **Pennard Warren** – the sand dunes leading up the valley to the unmanned ruins of **Pennard Castle**. No facilities.

Tor Bay

Separated from Three Cliffs Bay by the Great Tor headland, this is another picturesque, sandy beach with sand dunes filling the valley behind it. There's always sand, even at high tide, and bathing is relatively safe. The best access is from Penmaen village, where there is parking and a 1.6km footpath to the beach. You can walk (quite a long way) west across the sands to Oxwich, where there are beach shops and cafes, but there are no other facilities.

Oxwich Bay

Plenty of parking near the beach but, consequently, it can become crowded. It lacks the magnificence of other Gower beaches but is great for families. There are beach shops and cafes, 4km of sand, safe swimming, and sand dunes to explore behind the beach-front car park. If you want peace, walk east along the beach to **Nicholaston Burrows**, where the sands are less crowded and the sand dunes extensive. The ruins of **Oxwich Castle** are on Oxwich Point, to the west. It's really a 16th-century mock-fortified manor, and is open all year under the stewardship of Cadw. Family tickets £7 (☏ *01443 336000*).

Port Eynon Bay

Another popular family destination thanks to the ease of access from a car park only minutes from the beach, at Horton.

This was once smugglers' territory, as you might guess from the Smugglers Gift Shop and Smugglers Haunt Restaurant and Coffee Shop. There's also a fish and chip shop and surf shop, but all are open only during summer. The bay is divided into three beaches. **The Sands,** also known as Slade Bay, is furthest east, has firm sand and rock pools and can be reached over the cliffs from Oxwich Bay. You can also walk 15 minutes through a field at the village of Slade, or via the coastal path from Horton. **The Cove,** also a mix of sand and rocks, is nearer the car park. At the far west of the bay the beach becomes rockier. There's a ruined **salt house** a short walk from the excellent beach-front **youth hostel**, which used to be a lifeboat station. East of the salt house is Salt House Mere, a small, stony cove the other side of Port Eynon Point. There are several other rocky coves between here and Mewslade Bay, just before Worms Head.

Mewslade Bay

This is a beautiful, secluded sandy beach, although the sea comes right up to the rocks at high tide so you have to time your visit. It's rarely crowded because you have to walk down Mewslade Valley from the car park at Pitton Farm, in Pitton – a picturesque 20-minute walk which can involve tricky footwork, so avoid taking buggies or too much equipment. There are two natural arches on the beach and a number of caves. The largest is Giant Cave, near neighbouring Fall Bay, which you can only get to across the beach or the National Trust-owned headland. When there's a big surf strong undercurrents make swimming dangerous.

Rhossili Bay

Looking over the cliffs what strikes you is the majesty of this 5km sandy beach. Rhossili Bay faces the powerful Atlantic, which

Rhossili Bay has 5km of sands

comes as no surprise when you contemplate the effect of the sea at **Worms Head** – the kilometre-long islets carved out of the headland. The setting is breathtaking, though the walk down cliff steps to the beach makes access with young children very difficult, and let's not even think about getting back up. But if older children are up for it you'll be rewarded with one of the best beaches in Britain, with good bathing and great cliffs to explore – as well as the skeletons of two shipwrecks. It's also the Gower's best surf beach, though swimming in the big surf here is very dangerous. You can walk the length of the beach to Llangennith Burrows – more huge sand dunes – and at low tide you can walk out to Burry Holms, a tiny island with the ruins of a medieval monastic settlement. An easier walk, without having to go up and down cliff steps, is to walk along the wide, grassy headland towards Worms Head. If the tide's out you can cross the causeway to Worms Head itself, but you need plenty of time to cross back. You should also keep children away from the cliff edges during the walk.

Broughton Bay

Another wide, sandy bay, and good for those seeking a crowd-free space for beach combing, sandcastles and picnics – it's not safe to swim at any time. There's a car park at Broughton, then a 10-minute walk. No facilities.

Whitford Burrows

The National Trust owns this sand dune and pine plantation, now a National Nature Reserve, which includes 3.2km Whitford Sands beach on the edge of the Loughor River Estuary. Swimming is very dangerous, but if your children are happy to tramp through the dunes spotting birds and plants, then you're on to a winner. Nearest parking is at the tiny village of Cwm Ivy. Overlooking Llanrhidian Sands, nearby, is **Weobley Castle**, looked after by Cadw (☎ *01443 336000*, *www.cadw.wales.gov.uk*). Family ticket is £7.

Parkmill

More a wooded valley with the A4118 going through it than a proper village, but home of the Gower Heritage Centre (☎ *01792 371206*, *www.gowerheritage centre.co.uk*). There's a children's farm centred on an old water mill, museum, adventure playground and craft workshops. It's a good alternative to the beach – especially for younger children. The **Gower Inn** is a handsome stone-built pub with large garden; **Parc-Le-Breos Riding Centre** is nearby and there are several waymarked walks and Forestry Commission woods.

For Active Families

Monmouth Canoe and Activity Centre ALL AGES

Castle Yard, Old Dixton Road, NP25 3DP, ☎ 01600 713461/716083,

Keep Walking

Wales is a place for country strolls, from short family walks to long hikes up mountain and down. South Wales has some of the best walks, from coast to peak, with a number of the longer-distance trails passing through. Most stunning is the Heritage Coastal Path, from Aberthaw to Porthcawl, 23 delightful kilometres for both walkers and cyclists who want to get a feel for the Vale of Glamorgan. *www.valeofglamorgan.gov.uk*

The Gower Walk runs the length of the peninsula, from Rhossili to Mynydd y Gwair, but isn't the coastal walk you'd expect, instead taking you cross-country, over fields and moorland and through pretty woodland. It's 56km but can be broken into three shorter legs. Best for families is the 13km Rhossili to Penmaen stretch, which passes the Neolithic burial tomb, Arthur's Stone. *www.walking.visitwales.com*

The Wye Valley Walk starts at Chepstow and meanders north for 219km along the River Wye, in and out of Wales and England, to its source in the Plynlimon Mountains. A few miles can make a pleasing day out. Free guided walks are often available in the summer. *www.wyevalleywalk.org*

Offa's Dyke Path starts in much the same area, about a kilometre south of Chepstow, at Sedbury Cliff on the Severn Estuary. It would take a couple of weeks to complete the full 285km to Prestatyn, up north, but you can dip into the trail at Chepstow, Tintern, Monmouth and Hay-on-Wye for pleasing family strolls. *www.offasdyke.demon.co.uk*; *www. nationaltrail.co.uk*

The Usk Valley Walk starts near Caerleon, just off the M4 near Newport and heads north-west to Brecon. It's a 77km hike but if you just want to get a flavour, then go for a stroll along the riverbank at Usk, about half-way along. *www.uskvalleywalk.org.uk*

The Monnow Valley Walk starts in Monmouth and meanders up to Hay-on-Wye, 64km through farmland and woodland, joining Offa's Dyke Path at Hay Bluff for the final stretch. *www.ramblers.org.uk*

The Taff Trail covers 85km between Cardiff and Brecon Canal Basin and is designed for walkers and cyclists, with some sections suitable for horses. Much of the route is traffic-free, and it can be picked up as it passes through towns such as Penrhos, Pontypridd, Aberfan and Merthyr Tydfil. You can download a leaflet from the Taff Trail website. *wwwtafftrail.org.uk*

www.monmouthcanoe.co.uk.
Follow signs from A40.

You can book instructors, transport and overnight accommodation, but if that sounds a bit ambitious then you can rent a Canadian canoe for a half-day's messing about on the River Wye. These are great for families – once children are past the toddling stage they should be safe with life jacket and proper supervision.

Adventures Outdoor Activity Centre OLDER CHILDREN

Kenfig, Porthcawl, CF33 4PU,
📞 *01656 782300, www.adventures wales.co.uk. From M4 J37 follow Porthcawl signs, turn right at Esso garage, left at bottom of lane, 200m on left.*

Offering all-round adventures, from kayaking to quad-biking, surfing to coasteering, age restrictions differing according to activity. There are quad-biking sessions for children from seven up (£10), a high ropes session (with quad biking thrown in) for £22.50 for 13s and under, and youngsters' surf lessons from £20. Activities vary, with extra options in holidays.

Open *weekends 10am–5pm, weekdays (pre-booking only) 4–8pm, school holidays 10am–5pm.*
Amenities *café, parking.*

Ride On The Beach At Ogmore OLDER CHILDREN MOMENT

Ogmore Farm Riding Centre, Ogmore,
📞 *01656 880856, www.rideonthe beach.com. On the B5424 just before Ogmore-by-Sea.*

The dream of riding a horse on a wide open beach is a reality here. There are two-hour treks at 10.30am and 1.30pm (£30) over the River Ogmore and through the dunes to the beach, and a one-hour trek at 3pm daily (£20) towards the common between St Brides Major and the Ogmore estuary, for young children and less adventurous adults, with long lead reins held by handlers.
Open *daily. Booking advised.*

Parc-Le-Breos Riding and Holiday Centre OLDER CHILDREN

Parc-Le-Breos House, Penmaen, SA3 2HA, 📞 *01792 371636, www.parc-le-breos.co.uk. Turn right off the A4118 at Parkmill and follow 'signs for Parc-Le-Breos'.*

There's more riding on the beach available from this 19th-century hunting lodge set in 70 acres. Weekend and week-long holidays are available plus days and half days, or you can combine riding with golf and pampering. Packages include riding, bed, breakfast and evening meals – family rooms available. High season weeks cost £470, weekends £158. Child discounts.
Open *year round.*

FAMILY-FRIENDLY ACCOMMODATION

From the valleys to the sea to the city, South Wales offers varied places to stay. And it's possible to stay deep in the countryside while being just a few miles from the bright lights of Swansea and the coast of Mumbles or Gower.

EXPENSIVE

The Old Rectory ★★

Rhossilli, Gower Peninsula, 📞 *0870 4584422, www.nationaltrust cottages.co.uk*

The National Trust is heavily involved in the Gower, owning considerable portions of this wild and idyllic peninsula. It also owns and rents out a number of cottages – and the Old Rectory is the Trust's conservation and style at its best. It stands alone on a terrace above the dreamlike expanse of Rhossilli Bay, with uninterrupted views of the white sands and glorious sea all the way to the tidal island of Worm's Head. The main building is from the 1850s with some out-buildings possibly medieval. Inside it is warmly luxurious (thanks to wood-burning stoves) with sitting room, study, dining room and big kitchen and four double bedrooms (one king-sized, one with adult bunks) and a cot. The children can play for hours on the huge, pristine beach and the village is a 10-minute walk. (The NT has two other cottages nearby.)

Sleeps 8 plus cot. From £742 a week; short breaks available within two weeks of start date. **Facilities** *TV and video, radio, washer/drier, highchair, pay phone.*

MODERATE

Bryngwenyn Farm ★

Pontyberem, Llanelli, SA15 5NG, ☎ 01269 843990, www. bryngwenyn farm.co.uk

An organic farm deep in the countryside (yet only several miles from the sea) offers both farmhouse B&B and holiday cottages. On the working side there are rare breed sheep and Welsh Black cattle along with a variety of chickens, goats, minia-ture ponies, floppy-eared bun-nies and quacking ducks. It's an environment of preserved hedgerows, ancient hay mead-ows and a restored lake – all wonderful for the children. A restored flour mill uses local grain and a shop sells the farm's own organic lamb and chicken, preserves, pickles, vegetables, eggs, even goat's milk fudge, along with local pork, sausages and Welsh black beef.

There are two traditional dou-ble rooms in the farmhouse, available with cot and child's camp bed, as well as three cot-tages tastefully-converted from a barn across the farmyard. Each sleeps five in two or three bed-rooms, with free cots and child beds available, and has a fully-fitted kitchen (high chair on request). They share a washer-drier along with a large garden with swings and a living willow wigwam. There are chairs, tables and barbecue area. You can also book the hearty farmhouse break-fasts if staying in the cottages. Evening meals available (from £12.50), as are packed lunches.

Double room B&B from £50. Child bed/cot £5. Cottages from £300 per week, 2-night breaks from £120, inc bed linen. Dogs £10 pw. **In farm-house rooms** *TV with video or DVD, tea maker.* **In cottages** *TV with video or DVD.*

Trecco Bay Holiday Park

Porthcawl, CF36 5NG, ☎ 0871 641 0410, www.parkdeanholidays. co.uk. Turn left at roundabout on entering town, right at next then follow signs.

South and west Wales may be strewn with caravan parks, but when they're done well, they're truly mighty operations which, although they might not suit everyone, are full holiday destinations. Here you've got Splashland, an enormous indoor waterpark with slide, chutes and baby pool, free children's clubs from young children to teenagers (although younger children need parental supervision), play areas and sports activities. That's free, then you pay for bowling, pool, amusements and other attractions. There's a 1,200-seat Showdome where families can watch tribute bands (Abba soundalikes were made for this place) for free, the family-friendly bars have big screen TVs for sports, and there are all manner of restaurants from a fish & chip shop to ice cream parlour. There's also a half-board meals option (min three days) for £13.95 a day adults/£9.95 children.

Oh, and there are caravans aplenty, from moderate affairs to super-wide monsters with more amenities than some people's homes. Some are designated smoke-free, some you can take your dog to, many are double-glazed with central heating.

The park is right by the beach and a stroll away from the lively seaside town of Porthcawl, so plenty of options to explore the outside world.

Prices start at £169 per week for a 2-bedroom caravan sleeping up to six. Park open mid-March–early November. **Amenities** *cafés, bars, restaurants, indoor water park, children's clubs, sports.*

Carmarthen Bay Holiday Park

Kidwelly, 📞 *0845 034 0700, www. camp-sites.co.uk*

Caravan parks might not look so nice if you're cruising past on your yacht, but they have undoubted attractions – like the spectacular views over the Gwendraeth estuary and the south Wales coast. Right by the beach, and handy for attractions such as Folly Farm and Oakwood theme park. There's a heated indoor pool with flume ride along with family food in the Boathouse restaurant and nightly live music and cabaret in the Waterfront Showbar. Clubs for the children to join in, soft play area, adventure playground and amusements.

90 caravans for rent, from around £150 a week, sleeping 6. Also chalets. **Amenities** *café, bar, restaurant, take-away, laundry, indoor pool, snooker, cycle hire.*

INEXPENSIVE

Express by Holiday Inn

Neath Road, Llandarcy Heath, Swansea, SA10 6JQ, 📞 *0870 4425560, www.ichotelsgroup.com. Actually, Junction 43 of the M4.*

Eleven kilometres from Swansea centre, but that can be a boon – you're between the city, the Gower and the Brecon Beacons. Also a good staging point if heading west. Simple but effective, with decent-sized rooms at reasonable rate (children stay free), and free continental breakfast.

91 rooms, all non-smoking. Double room (with sofa bed) from £69.95 with free cot on request. **Facilities** *free breakfast, e-mail, internet, free parking.* **In room** *satellite TV, tea maker.*

Port Eynon Youth Hostel ★★★

Old Lifeboat House, Port Eynon Gower, SA3 1NN, 📞 *0870 770 5998,* **www.yha.org.uk**. *Follow the youth hostel sign at Port Eynon down an unmade road behind the dunes. Park then walk across the field, or around the beach, to the hostel.*

If this were a boutique hotel it would cost a fortune to stay at this cosy beach-side building. But it's not, and it doesn't. Small family rooms and one eight-bed room overlook the sea – when the tide's in it almost licks the back door and when it's out children can jump straight on to the sands while you watch from the lounge's picture window drinking your breakfast tea.

From £14 a night, under 18s £10. **Facilities** *self-catering, BBQ.*

Hillend Camp Site

Llangennith, Gower, SA3 1JD, 📞 *01792 386204. Take the B4295 westward towards Llangennith, the site is just over 1.5km further towards the sea.*

Once a hardcore surfers' camp site thanks to its position right behind the sand dunes at Llangennith beach – the western-most part of Rhossili Bay – this now has two fields set aside for families only and good showers, washing-up and laundry facilities. There's also a play area and family café on site, and a surf school nearby. The downside is that you can't book ahead so summer weekends are a gamble – and it's still popular with young surfers so there's always the threat of noisy neighbours. The upside is that

you can't get any closer to the sea at Rhossili.

£12–18per tent. **Facilities** *shower and toilet block, laundry, café, play area.*

FAMILY-FRIENDLY DINING

There's everything from smart restaurants (particularly on the up-and-up Mumbles) to simple beachfront cafes, and plenty of top-quality fish and chip shops.

EXPENSIVE

Patrick's With Rooms ★★

638 Mumbles Road, Mumbles, SA3 4EA, 📞 *01792 360199,* **www.patrickswithrooms.com**. *On the seafront heading south from Swansea city centre.*

Not a place that markets itself as family-friendly but (like so many of the best ones) it just is. Patrick's is a seriously good restaurant – rated one of Swansea's best – which treats children as, well, valued customers. No special menu, just specially-prepared variations on adult dinners, which include Black Mountain beef, Welsh lamb, fish and various forms of seafood. There are toys to play with, baby-changing room, a play area opposite, and the sea beyond that.

There are also eight swish seaview B&B rooms above the restaurant. A double is £110, a z-bed for children up to 12 is £20, and a cot £5.

Open noon–2.20pm (7 days), 6.30pm–9.50pm Mon–Sat. **Main courses** *£15–21.*

MODERATE

Castellamare Café Bar ★

Bracelet Bay, Mumbles, SA3 4JT,
📞 *01792 369408, www.castellamare.co.uk*

Relaxed and very family-friendly Italian brasserie affair (adjoining the smart à la carte restaurant) with massive views over the bay. For adults there are delights like Gamberetti Vesuvio (spaghetti in a tomato sauce with prawns and chilli) for £6.95, while a simple but effective children's menu offers pasta with Bolognese or tomato sauce, or sausage or nuggets with chips (all £3.75). Large ice creams (knickerbocker glory, £4.25) come with all manner of sauces, syrup and cream. You can also pop in for a snack – baguettes, and the local take on a cream tea (Welsh cakes instead of scones).

Open *daily, hours vary.* **Main courses** *£3.75–6.95.* **Facilities** *big car park, outdoor play area.*

The Bay View

400 Oystermouth Road, Swansea, SA1 3UL, 📞 *01792 652610 www.bayviewbar.co.uk*

This is a pub transformed into a cool Thai restaurant with spectacular views across Swansea Bay. But despite the chillout lounge with big sofas, it's very child-friendly with a children's menu featuring a mix of Oriental and trad favourites, and child minders to help look after the children at certain times, such as Sunday lunchtime. You can eat in the formal restaurant or more relaxed bar area.

Open *Mon–Sat noon–3pm, 6–10pm, Sundays noon–3pm, 6pm–9pm.* **Main courses** *£6.95–10.95; 2-course express lunch menu from £5.95.* **Amenities** *free evening parking in street.*

INEXPENSIVE

Joe's Ice Cream ★★

85 St Helen's Road, Swansea, SA10, 📞 *01792 653880; The Piazza, Par Tawe, Swansea, SA1 2AL,* 📞 *01792 460370 and 524 Mumbles Road, Mumbles, SA3 4DH,* 📞 *01792 368212* **www.joes.webmediaworks.co.uk**

A Swansea institution selling award-winning ice cream in the proper, old-fashioned way. Forget about cornets and flakes, you have to try the sundaes and knickerbocker glories.

Papa Sanchos Stonegrill Restaurant & Café Bar

10 College Street, Swansea, SA1 5AE, 📞 *01792 475767, www.papasanchos.co.uk*

This fun restaurant which specialises in hot stone cooking – meat and fish seared on super hot volcanic stones that are brought to your table. There isn't the most extensive children's menu, but one that would suit most picky children. There's a sizzling (but not on a stone, which would be asking for trouble) 4oz steak with chips for £4.95, a decent margarita pizza (£4.75) or fish fingers (£3.95). Also a selection of pannini, wraps and sandwiches from £3.95.

Open *Mon–Fri 11am–3pm, 6–11pm, Sat 12–4pm, 6–11pm, Sun 12–4pm, 6–10pm.* **Main courses** *£9.75–16.95.*

5 Brecon Beacons

BRECON BEACONS

Attractions ●

Brecon Beacons National Park Mountain Centre **1**	Henrhyd Waterfall **6**
Brecon Mountain Railway **2**	Llangorse Lake **7**
Carreg Cennen Castle **3**	Llanthony Priory **8**
Craig-y-nos Country Park **4**	National Showcaves Centre for Wales **9**
Garwnant Forest Centre **5**	Tretower Court **10**

Brecon Beacons is the only UK National Park to include an area of such geological importance that it has been granted UNESCO Global Geopark status. Fforest Fawr (Welsh for Great Forest) is the range of mountains between the central Beacons and the Black Mountain to the west. The Fforest Fawr Geopark is home to stunning natural attractions such as the National Showcaves Centre for Wales, Craig-y-nos Country Park nearby, spectacular waterfalls and brooding reservoirs, as well as the highest mountain in southern Britain – Pen y Fan – and the wilderness area of the Black Mountain. However, the national park itself extends further to the west, taking in the mountain cliff-top castle of Carreg Cennon, near the market town of Llandeilo, and going as far east as the Black Mountains between Abergavenny and Hay-on-Wye, and as far south as Pontypool, and the outskirts of Merthry Tydfil. There might not be beaches here but we found that our children were entranced by their surroundings – which are totally different from anywhere else – and by the fact that almost anywhere you stop or visit is a place where they can explore, climb or kick a ball.

ESSENTIALS

Visitor Information

Tourist Information Centres

Brecon Beacons National Park Visitor Centre, Libanus, Brecon, Powys, LD3 7DP, 01874 623366, *www.brecon beacons.org*

Abergavenny, Swan Meadow, Monmouth Road, Abergavenny, NP7 5HL, 01873 853254, *E: abergavennyic@breacon beacons.org*

Brecon, Cattle Market Car Park, Brecon, LD3 9DA, 01874 622485, *E: brectic@powys.gov.uk*

Crickhowell, Beaufort Chambers, Beaufort Street, Crickhowell, NP8 1AA, 01873 812105, *E: crictic@powys.gov.uk*

Llandeilo, (seasonal) Car Park, Crescent Road, Llandeilo, SA19 6HN, 01558 824226.

Llandovery, Llandovery Heritage Centre, Kings Road, Llandovery, SA20 0AW, 01550 720693, *E: llandovery.ic@brecon beacons.org*

Talgarth, The Tower Shop, Talgarth, Powys, LD3 0DB, 01874 712226, *www.talgarth. powys.org.uk*

Areas in Brief

The majestic Brecon Beacons National Park incorporates the Black Mountains to the east and a separate Black Mountain to the west of the Brecon Beacons themselves. These mountains and their country towns are a delight in spring, summer, autumn, and even winter when you will see snow on the highest peaks. There are walks to suit all levels of experience, including family treks through bluebell woods, along rivers to spectacu-lar waterfalls, around lakes and in the shadow of ruined castles. The Brecon Beacons are not as high as Snowdonia, but neither are they so crowded – and they still offer an awe-inspiring range of spectacular sights.

Getting Around

By car From the M4 in the south, head north up the A4042 to Abergavenny, or from the North and Midlands you can take the M50 off the M5 and head from Ross on Wye to Abergavenny. Many of the roads that criss-cross the Brecon Beacons National Park are tiny – so you'll need good local maps to find some of the more out-of-the-way attractions – particularly car parks near good walks.

By bus The Beacons Bus provides a fantastic way to explore the area from the end of May until September. You can get dropped off at your chosen starting point then jump back on when you want to return to your digs – or you can leave your car and use it as a park and ride. Most of the buses have bicycle racks. Particularly good for families are the B4 and B8, which run alongside the Monmouthshire and Brecon Canal, so you can catch the bus back from your walk. There are also buses up the mountains and to Offa's Dyke. Family day tickets cost £13. ☎ 01873 853 254, **www.breconbeacons.com**

By foot The Brecon Beacons seem made for exploring on foot. For a great range of guide books,

Ordinance Survey maps and free tourist leaflets visit the National Park's Visitor Centre, also known as the Mountain Centre. You will also be able to speak to staff about walks that are suitable for your family. ☎ 01874 623366, **www.breconbeacons.org**

WHAT TO SEE & DO

Top 10 Family Experiences

❶ **Seeing the stalactites** and the underground waterfalls at the National Showcaves Centre for Wales.

❷ **Walking to Henrhyd Waterfall** and splashing about among the rocks in the river below.

❸ **Running around the ruins** at Llanthony Priory.

❹ **Watching out for kingfishers** while walking along the towpath of the Monmouthshire and Brecon Canal.

❺ **Driving down winding roads** and just seeing where you get to in the Fforest Fawr Geopark.

❻ **Feeling on top of the world** as you look down from the crag where Carreg Cennen Castle is perched.

❼ **Having a picnic in the sun** on the grassy banks of remote Usk reservoir.

❽ **Eating ice cream** by the bridge at pretty Crickhowell.

❾ Buying bargain books in the second-hand shops at Hay on Wye.

❿ Visiting the market at Abergavenny to buy Y-Fenni cheese – which is Welsh for Abergavenny.

Family-friendly Festivals

Talgarth Festival of the Black Mountains

Talgarth Town Square and beyond, 📞 *01570 423981, www.talgarth festival.org.uk*

Anything goes at this free event featuring street entertainers, live music, food fayre (from Black Mountains cheese to homemade Welsh cakes), children's activities, dog show and fireworks.

August Bank Holiday.

Abergavenny Food Festival

Various venues, Abergavenny, 📞 *01873 851643, www.abergavenny foodfestival.com*

One of the biggest and liveliest food festivals in Wales, with celebrity chefs, workshops, master classes, fish market, children's food academy and cheese and wine show alongside music and entertainment.

Mid Sept.

Brecon Jazz Festival

Various venues, Brecon 📞 *01874 611622, www.breconjazz.co.uk*

Since its launch in the 1980s, this festival has grown to become one of the most important cultural events in Wales. It's certainly one of the most fun –

with international jazz stars as well as performers (such as Jools Holland) for those who like the idea of jazz without the full-blown jazziness of it all. There's street music to keep everyone entertained and stroller tickets for the die-hard fans giving them access to every event. Children get half price tickets.

Mid August.

Brecon Beacons Food Festival

Brecon Market Hall, Brecon, 📞 *01874 624437, www.breconbeacons.org*

One of many local food festivals in Wales designed to showcase the region's producers. It's not as razzamatazzy as the Abergavenny blow out, but you'll find a mouthwatering array of food. Organised by Brecon Beacons National Park Authority.

October.

Green Man Festival

Glenusk Park, Crickhowell, 📞 *01873 851643, www.thegreenman festival.co.uk*

Families are a big part of the fun at this ever-growing folksy-alternative festival in the verdant surroundings of Glenusk Park. Lots of music to suit eclectic tastes over the weekend, with good food stalls and a few alternative lifestyle workshops – possibly including knitting.

Mid August.

Hay Literary Festival

Various venues, Hay-on-Wye 📞 *0870 990 1299, www.hayfestival.com*

World-famous festival in book-shop-packed town. Its Hay Fever programme is for families and young people, with question and answer (and signing) sessions by the likes of *Alex Rider* author Alex Horowitz, and illustrator Quentin Blake.

Late May–early June.

Brecon

Brecon is a pretty little market town which children appreciate for its charm. You'll find family butchers, traditional greengrocers and lovely little cafes in the mainly Georgian buildings that line its narrow streets – as well as familiar chain stores and a good mix of restaurants. There's also a good indoor market hall open on Tuesdays and Fridays and the monthly farmers' market is the area's biggest. The town was established around a castle and priory built by William the Conqueror's half brother, Bernard de Newmarch, in 1093. The castle is now a hotel, although you can visit the grounds if you wish, and the priory was renamed Brecon Cathedral in 1923. It has a great heritage centre in the tithe barn next to the cathedral, and a fabulous cafe – **Pilgrim Tea Room and Hampers** – in the cathedral grounds. Entrance to the cathedral and heritage centre is free. The River Honddu flows from the north through the town and joins the River Usk near the old bridge. There are walks towards the castle along the river bank or you can walk the other way

towards the Brecon and Monmouth canal. The canal basin is a tourist draw in itself, and there are boat rides down the canal available in season.

Brecon Beacons National Park Mountain Centre ALL AGES

Libanus, Brecon, Powys, LD3 8ER, 📞 *01874 623366,* ***www.brecon beacons.org****. A few miles south of Brecon on the A470.*

This visitor centre is a great place to start your exploration of the Brecon Beacons. It has a large 3-D model of the mountains and surrounding towns, so you can get your bearings before going off exploring. It was only here that it finally dawned on us that the Black Mountains along the east Wales borders were completely different from Black Mountain, which is west of the Beacons. The Beacons themselves form a massive horseshoe-shaped, flat-topped range in between. At the centre you can also pick up tourist leaflets and buy guidebooks on walking, cycling, wildlife and local history. The café has a Taste of Wales menu and is a welcome sight after returning from one of the many walks through Mynydd Illtyd Common which start at the car park – although ours was not terribly successful. We never did find the standing stone we were aiming for, reminding us of the importance of carrying a good map on even the easiest walks. There's plenty of flat ground for children to play near the centre, and wonderful picnic spots with spectacular views of

Pen Y Fan – the highest mountain in south Wales.

Open daily except Christmas Day, July–Aug 9am–6pm, May–June 5.30pm, March, April, Sept, Oct 5pm, Nov–Feb 4.30. Café until 5pm March–Oct, 4.30 rest of year. **Admission** free, but with pay car park, £1 up to 2 hours, £2 all day. **Amenities** shop, café.

Brecknock Museum and Art Gallery ALL AGES VALUE

Captain's Walk, Brecon, LD3 7DW
☏ 01874 624121, **www.powys. gov.uk**

Our children were fascinated by the Victorian assize court room and traditional Welsh kitchen. The collection of unusually ornate Welsh lovespoons were not so appreciated but it's hard for adults not to marvel at the workmanship involved. There was also the AD800 canoe found at Llangorse Lake to admire, and although the children would probably have liked a few more buttons to press, we loved the fact that it was a good old-fashioned museum housed in the rather grand building of the former Shire Hall. There's also a good collection of contemporary Welsh art, sometimes for sale.

Open Tue–Sat 10am–5pm (all year, plus Mon 10am–5pm, Sun 12–5pm (April–Sept), Closed Sat 1–2pm, Dec 25/26, Jan 1, Good Friday. **Admission** adults £1, concessions £0.50 children free. **Amenities** gift shop.

South Wales Borderers Museum ★★★ ALL AGES

The Barracks, Brecon, LD3 7EB,
☏ 01874 613310, **www.rrw.org.uk**

This is a real boys' toys museum, with what is claimed to be the finest collection of weapons in Wales. The medal room alone has 3,000 medals. But the star attraction is probably the Zulu War Room, which outlines the heroic yet tragic 1879 Anglo-Zulu War in which the Royal Regiment of Wales (now reorganised into The Royal Welsh) played its part. Brecon has been a military town since its Roman occupation, and the barracks are the British Army's Welsh headquarters, while the Brecon Beacons are used for military training.

Open April–Sept, Mon–Fri, 10am–5pm, Sat, Bank Hols, 10am–4pm; occasional Sunday opening for special events; Oct–March, Mon–Fri, 9am–5pm (closed mid-Dec–mid Jan). **Admission** adults £3, children free. **Amenities** shop, with big stock of military books.

The National Showcaves Centre for Wales ★★★
ALL AGES FIND

Abercrave, Swansea, SA9 1GJ,
☏ 01639 730801/730284, **www. showcaves.co.uk**. On the A4067 near Sennybridge.

Definitely the best place to go in the Brecon National Park for a day out which will appeal to all ages. The underground caves are fabulous, but there's also a museum and fossil collection to see. Younger children love the huge dinosaur models which inhabit the site, and there's a Shire horse centre for older children, along with special breeds farm animals and some intriguing standing stones. But it's the caves that stand out. A series of them winds through the heart of the hillside, revealing underwater rivers, pools, waterfalls and, of course, stalagmites and stalactites. The caves were discovered by farming brothers Jeff and Tommy Morgan in 1912, and the giant Cathedral Cave was found by cavers in 1953. There's also the Bone Cave, where 42 human skeletons dating back to the Bronze Age were excavated, which we found a bit spooky – although its story was well told. The children liked the Dan-yr-Ogof caves best, following the winding path past illuminated stalagmites and stalactites, but the Cathedral cave was pretty impressive: two big waterfalls cascaded down through lights to the sound of classical music into a lake. You can even get married on a garlanded platform overlooking the waterfalls.

You could easily spend a day here. There are picnic areas, a millennium stone circle, Mr

Dinosaurs at the National Showcaves

Morgan's farm and a playbarn, too. Or you could stay next door at the self-catering cottages or the beautifully laid-out caravan and camping site (see p 117).

Open *daily, Easter/April 1–Oct 31; 10am–3pm (last entry varies with season). Also, February half-term and Santa Claus grotto in December.* ***Admission*** *adults £10.50, children £6.50. Free car park.*

Craig-y-nos Country Park
ALL AGES

Brecon Road, Pen-y-Cae, Swansea Valley, SA9 1G, ☎ *01639 730395,* ***www.brecon-beacons.com/www. breconbeacons.org/ forestry.gov. uk****. A few minutes south along the A4067 from the National Showcaves Centre.*

A perfect place for a picnic and gentle stroll, unless you fancy a hike. The 40-acre country park used to be the estate of the nearby Craig-y-nos castle – which belonged to opera soprano Madame Adelina Patti, who regularly sang for Queen Victoria – so some of the park still has a landscaped feel to it. There are lakes to walk around, woodland to explore, rivers and picnic benches in the meadows.

Open *daily, from 10am, except Dec 25.* ***Admission*** *free, but with pay car park (2 hours £1.50, all day £2.50.* ***Amenities*** *visitor centre, fishing permits, toilets.*

Henrhyd Waterfall ★★
ALL AGES **MOMENT** **VALUE**

Coelbren, near Glyn Neath, ☎ *01874 624437,* ***www.breconbeacons.org;*** ***www.brecon-beacons.com****. Follow the small signs at Coelbren on the A4221.*

With its 27m drop, this is the highest waterfall in South Wales and well worth making the effort to walk to – though possibly not with toddlers, babies or buggies. The path down from the National Trust car park is fairly steep, and then there's a bridge over the river Nant Llech and steep steps up the other side of the gorge to a narrow path that can be quite slippery. When we were there the waterfall was more of a delicate spray than a torrent, so following the path behind the waterfall was relatively easy, though it's not something which should be attempted without sturdy footwear or after heavy rain, and it would be dangerous for the very young. That said, our pair had never before experienced the magic of standing behind a waterfall, and pronounced it "cool" – and that was even after the exhaustingly-steep climb back to the car park.

Open daily. **Admission** free. **Amenities** National Trust pay car park.

> **INSIDER TIP »**
>
> The waterfalls in the Brecon Beacons are surprisingly difficult to find first time around, unless you have a good Ordinance Survey Map. You can buy these – or just study the maps on display – at the Mountain Centre run by the Brecon Beacons National Park, where you can also buy useful booklets produced by the National Park – and get a nice cup of tea from the café.

Henrhyd Falls, highest in South Wales

The Waterfalls Walk
`OLDER CHILDREN`

Pontneddfechan, near Glyn Neath, ℓ *01874 624437,* **www.forestry. gov.uk;** *www.brecon-beacons.com;* **www.breconbeacons.org**

There are several waterfalls walks along the rivers Mellte, Hepste, Pyriddin and Nedd Fechan, but during or after bad weather they can be quite dangerous, so families with young children should keep to routes recommended by the Brecon Beacons National Park such as in its Wildlife Walks booklet (£3.99). Try the gentle walk along the River Neath (Nedd Fechan) from Pontneddfechan, near Glyn Neath off the A465 and at the end of the B4242. Park near the Geopark Information Centre in the village and it is clearly marked from there to Sgwd Gwladus. It's a relatively easy walk of a couple of miles, much of it along a former tramway. Allow about 40 minutes each way. There are other waterfalls further up the river where it forks to the right, but this walk is not recommended for young children or weak walkers.

Open daily. **Admission** free, but with pay car park.

Porth yr Ogof ★ ★ ★
OLDER CHILDREN

Cwm Porth, near Glyn Neath, ☎ 01874 624437, **www.brecon-beacons.com/www.brecon beacons.org**

When we arrived at Cwm Porth car park we were all keen to walk to a waterfall. But if the £4 car park fee wasn't enough to put us off – fine for a day out, but not a swift stroll in the mist – the stony-faced National Park warden was. The car park is the start of a path down to Porth yr Ogof, one of the biggest cave openings in the UK, and also the start of the Four Falls Trail, a strenuous four-hour walk. Since it was only about four hours until dusk we decided against it, and received a nod from the warden in acknowledgement of our wisdom. We left without attempting any walk, although it would have been useful had the warden suggested the nearby Sychryd All Ability Trail to the Sychryd Cascades, which would have been within our capability. To be fair, though, it wasn't until later that we realised the warden had been absolutely right in discouraging us from

setting off so late in the day. Although the path to the caves is perfectly safe, the caves themselves are a notorious danger spot for people who have ignored warning signs about the cold, deep water. Also, one of the four falls – Sgwd yr Eira – was closed to the public because of overhanging rocks. So the moral of this story is to make sure you have footwear with good grip – even on the hottest summer's day – and that you get there early enough to make the most of the parking fee.

Open daily. **Admission** free, but with pay car park. **Amenities** National Park shop, café, toilets.

Sychryd All Ability Trail
ALL AGES

Dinas Rock car park, Pontneddfechan, ☎ 01874 624437/0845 604 0845, **www.breconbeacons.org/www. brecon-beacons.com**

At only 366m long this is ideal for a family with youngish children to enjoy the Brecon Beacons' waterfall country. The hard, level path through a narrow wooded gorge is also suitable for buggies. But constant supervision of children is essential.

Open daily. **Admission** free, but with pay car park.

Brecon Mountain Railway
ALL AGES

Pant Station, Merthyr Tydfil, CF48 2UP, ☎ 01685 384854, **www.brecon mountainrailway.co.uk**. Follow signs from the A470 and A465, three miles north of Merthyr Tydfil.

The ruins of Morlais Castle are above the disused Morlais

Quarries which this railway once served. Now vintage steam engines take holidaymakers along the narrow gauge track to the village of Pontsticill, with views of Pen-y-Fan in the Brecon Beacons, and continues by the side of the Taf Fechan Reservoir to Dol-y-Gaer. There's lots for youngsters as well as the ride. You can jump off at Pontsticill Station on the return journey where there's a lakeside snack bar, play area and picnic spot. There's another picnic area back at Pant, where you can also have a look around the workshop. Call ahead to make sure you're not visiting on one of the railway's random closed days.

Open Most days, Apr–Oct, with occasional opening in March, November and December (call for details). First train from Pant 11am, last train 4pm (occasionally 5.15pm). **Admission** details not available. **Amenities** free parking, restaurant, shop.

Garwnant Visitor Centre
ALL AGES

Off the A470, five miles north of Merthry Tydfil, 📞 0845 604 0845, **www.forestry.gov.uk**

This all-purpose place helps you to explore the Beacons. We enjoyed a picnic near one of the small car parks dotted around Llwyn-on Reservoir, and walked down to the shore where the children climbed trees. The Forest Frenzy low rope assault course for 7–15 year olds is great fun. There's also a play area for under 7s, a 10-minute trail beside a stream to a waterfall, and a moderate 3.2km trail through the forest. Two cycle trails (eight and 18km) have been designed to appeal to families, and a section of the Taff Trail runs through the area.

Open daily; 9.30am–6.30pm, April 1–Oct 31; 9.30am–4pm, Nov 1–Mar 31; Closed Dec 24, 25, 26. **Admission** adults £3.50, concessions £3, family £10. **Amenities** café, shop, toilets, car park.

Taff Valley Reservoirs ALL AGES
VALUE

Off the A470, north of Merthyr Tydfil, 📞 0845 604 0845, **www.forestry. gov.uk**

Three huge reservoirs all but fill the Taff Valley, offering great spots to walk and picnic. **Llwyn-on** is the largest and the first you get to driving north from Merthyr Tydfil. It's also the most popular of the three for fishing because both spinning and worming is allowed and it is regularly restocked with rainbow trout. Day tickets cost £13.50 from Garwnant Forest Centre. You can also walk around the whole of the reservoir (or do part of it with youngsters) and cycle around the lane that runs most of the way around the perimeter. **Cantref** Reservoir is next, going north up the A470, where you can fish for wild brown trout and regularly restocked rainbow trout. The day ticket costs £14, also from Garwnant Forest Centre. **Beacons** Reservoir is the highest, and in the shadow of Pen-y-Fan – south Wales's highest mountain. This is the smallest reservoir of the three, and run as a wilderness fishery because it is not restocked. But you can still catch wild brown trout and any rainbow trout that have survived from when stocking was carried out. Day tickets cost £8.50 from Garwnant Forest Centre, for fly fishing only. All three reservoirs offer cheaper, evening tickets, and all are only open for fishing during the fishing season, usually from mid-March to mid-October, although fishing for rainbow trout may be allowed at Cantref and Llwynn-on until January. No boats are allowed on any of the reservoirs.

Open daily. *Admission* free. *Amenities* parking, Café, shop, toilets, play areas, Taff Trail at Garwanant Forest Centre.

Llandovery

This old drovers' town has a twist typical of many Welsh rural communities: a new age contingent. So, as well as the the ruined motte and bailey castle from the 12th-century (with its Merlinesque statue of local hero Llewelyn ap Gruffydd Fychan), Victorian tea rooms, lovely cobbled market square and antique shops, you'll also find some interesting wholefood and craft shops. Llandovery is a good base for walking in the Tywi Valley, the Black Mountain, or exploring the Brecon Beacons generally. The **Brecon Beacons National Park Llandovery Heritage Centre** reveals the area's Roman history, and tells the story of highwayman Twm Sion Cati, a Welsh Robin Hood, and the Physicians of Mydffai.

This family of herbalists passed its secrets from father to son from the 12th to 18th centuries. These secrets, it has been claimed, were told to the first physician, Rhiwallon, by his fairy mother who lived in Llyn y Fan Fach – Lake of The Little Peak – in the Black Mountain. The same lake is associated with Arthurian Lady of the Lake legends. The **Heart of Wales Railway Line** runs through Llandovery (the station is on the A40, just after the western end of Broad Street). It's a particularly picturesque branch line running between Swansea and Shrewsbury.

Usk Reservoir ★ ALL AGES

Off the A40, at Trescastle, then along the minor road to Llanddeusant, ☎ *01495 769281/0845 604 0845,* **www.dwrcymry.com/www.forestry. gov.uk**

Only a few miles east of Llandovery is this very beautiful – but remote – reservoir. In fact, we thought we were never going to find it, but don't be put off by having to drive through a farmyard, up and down winding roads and over a humpback bridge followed by a sharp left turn – it's worth the effort. There is a far easier route if you take the second left turn at Trescastle rather than the one signposted for the reservoir, but what would be the fun in that? Usk Reservoir is a very peaceful place, popular with fishermen (who, it turns out, don't like little boys to skim stones...) and there are several marked footpaths into the Glasfynydd Forest

The historic streets of Llandovery

and a 10km family cycling route, which is a little more demanding than the one at Garwnant. It's also a tranquil spot for a picnic: you can just pull off the perimeter road and spread a blanket on the grassy banks or one of the little beaches. When we were there it was scorching hot and we did succumb to a paddle, but you must never swim in reservoirs because of the automatic equipment underwater, which can be operated without warning. Reservoirs are also much deeper and colder than they look. Fly fishing is permitted from March to October with day tickets from a dispenser (£1 coins required) at a hut on the western side of the dam wall. You'll also see Red Kites and the Marsh Fritillary butterfly here.

Open daily. **Admission** free.
Amenities car parking, walks.

Carreg Cennen Castle ★
ALL AGES **MOMENT**

Off the A483 near Trapp, four miles from Llandeilo, 📞 *01558 822291*
www.cadw.wales.gov.uk

In a country full of castles, Carreg Cennen Castle stands out as one of the most spectacularly located. It dominates the landscape, sitting on top of a limestone crag with a 90m sheer drop down the side of a cliff on one side. From the castle ruins you have an eagle-eye view over the Black Mountain in the west. The walk up to the castle begins at Castell Farm. Here you can get tickets from the craft shop and see the free-range farmyard animals, rare breeds and agricultural artefacts before attempting the steep trek to the top. For a more gradual climb there's a path through woods – but it's a 6.5km walk.

You need to take the path below the farm buildings and across a field towards Hengrofft Farm. Full details are in the Wildlife Walks booklet published by the National Park Authority (£3.99), which is aimed at families.

Open daily; 9.30am–6.30pm, April 1–Oct 31; 9.30am–4pm, Nov 1–Mar 31; Closed Dec 25. *Admission* adults £3.50, concessions £3, family £10. *Amenities* café, shop, toilets, car park.

Black Mountain (Llyn-y-Fan Fach) ★ OLDER CHILDREN MOMENT

From Talsarn, near Sennybridge, follow signs to Llyn-y-Fan Fach and park off the road at the start of land belonging to Dwr Cymru (Welsh Water), ☏ 01874 624437.

A big, bleak, mysterious mountain, which excites the minds of youngsters brought up on the likes of *Harry Potter*. This area has long been associated with legends and Llyn-y-Fan Fach has bagged one of the best. This is where King Arthur's Lady of the Lake appeared, and you don't get much more spine-tingling than that. Older children may enjoy the walk up Black Mountain to this natural lake, or tarn, which was created during the Ice Age (and modified more recently into a reservoir). The path takes you past the water treatment station and up a track to the dam. It's a 4.8km round trip, and takes about two hours. The lake is a lovely spot for a picnic, and there is a path further up the mountain – but this is not recommended for children. Don't forget to take wet weather clothes with your picnic, in case the weather changes.

Open daily. *Admission* free.

Pen y Fan Mountain
OLDER CHILDREN

Off the A470, north of Beacons Reservoir, ☏ 01874 624437, *www.breconbeacons.org/www.brecon-beacons.com/www.forestry.gov.uk*

There will always be families who want to climb to the top of mountains. We're not one of them yet, but the hike to the summit must be extraordinarily satisfying for older children. It can take several hours, depending on your route, so you should start relatively early and in good weather. The easiest route is from the Storey Arms car park on the A470, a 1600m north of the Beacons Reservoir, from which it should take 60–90 minutes to the top. Buy a Brecon Beacons National Park booklet and large scale Ordinance Survey map, and you can also check for other routes on websites such as *www.outdoorsmagic.com*.

Open daily. *Admission* free.

Talybont-on-Usk

This tiny little village is a bit of a magnet for people wanting to enjoy the beautiful surrounding countryside. The Monmouthshire and Brecon Canal and the Taff Trail pass through the village, providing easy family walking. You could try the five-kilometre Henry Vaughn Walk, a circular route, or for families with older children there's also access from the village to paths into the Black Mountains and the Brecon Beacons. The River Usk and Talybont reservoir are only a few miles away (you can canoe in the river during the closed fishing season with permits from the Welsh Canoeing Association). Many visitors are also attracted by the village's well-regarded pubs. The Star Inn is famous for its cask ales and has a large beer garden and B&B accommodation, while the White Hart has 4-star bunkhouse accommodation and offers good-value meals. The Usk Inn is an award-winning pub and hotel, which has a children's menu and family Sunday lunch.

Talybont Reservoir ALL AGES

Off the A40, at Trescastle, then head for Llanddeusant, 📞 *01495 769281/ 0845 604 0845,* **www.dwrcymru. com/www.forestry.gov.uk**

We stayed at the Danywenallt youth hostel only yards from Talybont reservoir, and you would be hard-pressed to find a better starting place to enjoy the area. Driving over the dam to the pretty old farmhouse turned-hostel was exciting in itself, but then there was the Taff Trail at the top of the drive which can be walked or cycled. There's a car park here and picnic area at Torpantau. Walk or ride eight kilometres up the Taff Trail (this section follows the disused Brecon and Merthyr Railway line) and you'll find a quiet moorland road above Blaen-yr-glyn, where you

can walk down to several waterfalls in the forest. There's also a car park here and picnic area. Back at the reservoir, fly fishing is permitted from mid-March to mid-October (day tickets available from the reservoir filter works).

Open *daily.* **Admission** *free.* **Amenities** *Taff Trail cycle route, fishing.*

Henry Vaughan Walk ALL AGES

Start at Talybont-on-Usk canal bridge, **www.breconbeacons.org**

Henry Vaughan was a 17th-century poet and doctor who grew up in Talybont Valley with his twin brother Thomas, a priest and alchemist. Much of Henry's poetry was inspired by the countryside, and is said to have influenced later poets such as Wordsworth. This walk is officially described as easy-access and takes you along the canal then into Talybont Valley past Vaughan Garden, where the brothers grew herbs and plants for medicines. There are picnic benches here, where you can lunch before continuing along the Brinore Tramroad. The trams were pulled uphill by horses to coal mines near Tredegar, then gravity was used to bring them back down to the canal. The path crosses over the River Caerfanell, then you begin the journey back to Talybont along the river bank and across fields back to the canal. The five kilometre walk should take an hour and a half if you don't stop for a picnic. Leaflets are available from tourist offices, but if you follow the blue Vaughan Walk swan markers you should be fine.

Open daily. **Admission** free. **Amenities** picnic spot at Vaughan Garden.

Crickhowell

This is a lovely little town, on the River Usk and just off the A40. Its best-known attraction is the 16th-century river bridge, which has 13 arches on one side but only appears to have 12 on the other. There are also the ruins of a 13th-century castle where you can picnic, and there are several walks up into the Black Mountains, nearby. But increasingly Crickhowell is known as a gourmet destination: there are several good independent food shops, and far more good restaurants and cafés than a town this size normally offers. The High Street alone has Askew's Family Bakery and Café, which sells superior ice creams, M T Cashell Family Butchers with a range of 20 sausages and a delicatessen that stocks 60 cheeses, and FE Richards & Sons family butchers, which also sells local fruit and veg. Also worth visiting is **Number 18**, a café, bar and brasserie on the High Street, which sells homemade soups and salads featuring oak-roasted salmon from the Black Mountains Smokery, which is also based in Crickhowell.

Tretower Court and Castle
ALL AGES

Tretower, Crickhowell, NP8 2RF, ☎ 01874 730279, **www.cadw.wales.**
gov.uk. Off A479 eight kilometres northwest of Crickhowell.

The transition of Wales from tribal battleground to peaceful, agricultural country is graphically illustrated in the remains of 13th-century Tretower Castle and its neighbour Tretower Court, a 15th-century manor house. The castle was built on the site of a 12th-century earthwork – built to control a route over the Black Mountains – but by the 1450s the area was peaceful enough for the castle to be abandoned in favour of a much more comfortable stone manor house. It was the ancestors of poet Henry Vaughan who built the house and lived in some style: there's a galleried courtyard and exceptional carved wooden shutters and panels inside the house. As castles go, Tretower isn't really one of Wales's best – but the castle and court together give an excellent illustration of Wales's medieval history. Take a picnic and perhaps choose a day when there's an historic re-enactment on.

Open Tue–Sun, 10am–5pm (Apr–Sept) Tue–Sun, 9am–4pm (Mar and Oct). **Closed** Nov–Feb and every Mon except Bank Hols between Mar and Oct. **Admission** adults £2.90, children £2.50, family £8.30. Under 5s free. **Amenities** free parking, gift shop, garden.

The Black Mountains ★★★
OLDER CHILDREN **MOMENT**

This range provides a natural barrier between Wales and England and, despite the name, they are a beautiful amalgamation of high

MT Cashell Family Butchers, Crickhowell

ridges and attractive valleys – for instance the Wye Valley, Usk Valley and Llanthony Valley. The highest peak is Waun Fach, at 810m although its neighbour Pen y Gadair Fawr at 800m is said to be the more interesting climb. One of the most distinctive, though, is Pen-y-Fal – Sugar Loaf Mountain – the conical summit that overlooks Abergavenny and is popular with walkers. The shortest route is from Sugar Loaf Car Park and View Point, just off the A40, west out of Abergavenny. There is also a peak known as The Black Mountain (not to be confused with The Black Mountain west of the Brecon Beacons) over which you can walk if you follow Offa's Dyke long-distance footpath. To be honest, though, we simply enjoy driving through the tiny, wiggly roads then parking high up for a stroll and breath of fresh air.

Open daily. **Admission** free but car park is pay and display.

Abergavenny

Traditionally viewed as the gateway to the Brecon Beacons, Abergavenny is possibly the finest market town in Wales. The Tuesday market is one of the country's most important, with more than 200 stalls inside and outside the market hall. Then there's the quieter, indoor-only Friday event and the 100-stall Saturday market. The farmers' market takes place on the fourth Thursday each month and there's also a flea market every Wednesday, an antique/collectors' market on the third Sunday and a craft market on the second Saturday. But it's the combination of markets and food that really sets Abergavenny apart from other market towns. The growing popularity of the Abergavenny Food Festival in September is the proof that this is becoming a bit of a foodie town, although if you want to avoid the crowds you'd be better off sticking to the weekly food-fests. There are other reasons for exploring Abergavenny, of course. There's the castle, one of the best examples of a motte and bailey castle in Britain; the museum, housed in a hunting lodge; and the keep built onto the remains of a Norman Castle – plus walks beside the River Usk.

Llanthony Priory ★ ALL AGES

Llanthony, Abergavenny, NP7 7NN, ☎ 01874 890487 (hotel), www. llanthonyprioryhotel.co.uk/www. cadw. Turn left off the A465 towards Llanvihangle Crucorney, then left after Skirrid Mountain Inn, and carry on for eight kilometres.

It may be ruined now, but Llanthony Priory is still a place of pilgrimage to many walkers thanks to the Offa's Dyke Path, which runs along a ridge between Llanthony and Olchon valleys. Many other people are also attracted by the peace of this romantic ruin, with its grassy sur-rounds, set in the secluded Ewyas valley – although the fabulous restaurant and bar housed in what is thought to have been part of the priory's cellar is a huge draw, too. It's a magical place – it wouldn't be a surprise to see hobbits on a summer's evening smoking clay pipes and supping ale from pewter tankards. The bar is part of the Llanthony Priory Hotel, which has four bedrooms arranged Rapunzle-like in the 12th-century tower, on floors off the stone spiral staircase. Unfortunately, the hotel doesn't accommodate children under 10.

There's plenty of space for run-ning around, and a horse riding centre next door, Llanthony Riding and Trekking.

Open *daily.* **Admission** *free, but pay car park.*

Goytre Wharf, Monmouthshire and Brecon Canal ★ ALL AGES

Goytre Wharf, Llanover, Monmouthshire, NP7 9EW, ☎ 01873 881069, www.goytrewharf.com. Heading north from Pontypool on A4042, turn left to Mamhilad and drive five kilometres.

This canal is one of the most pic-turesque in Britain, and follows the course of the River Usk for much of its 52km. Walking or cycling along the towpath is an excellent option for families because it's relatively flat and a haven for wildlife such as herons, kingfishers and buzzards. It also passes through or close to some fabulous market towns and vil-lages, starting with Brecon and continuing through Talybont, Llangynidr, Crickhowell and Abergavenny, then on to the once-industrial towns of Pontypool and Cwmbran before ending at Newport. You can use your own boat or canoe on the canal (British Waterways licences required – ☎ 01873 830328) or you can hire canoes at several places, including Goytre Wharf, near Llanover on the A4042. This eight-acre site includes a British Waterways Heritage Centre, craft and souvenir shop, café, bar, play area, a woodland walk and an aqueduct. There are also children's activities, exhibitions and events.

Open daily. *Admission* free.
Amenities heritage centre, exhibitions and events.

Talgarth

A busy little market town but once an important strategic site thanks to its position: Talgarth means end of the hills. Now it is also a good base for outdoor activities such as walking in the Black Mountains nearby. Among its many gentle attractions are the Pwll-y-Wrach waterfalls in Brecknock Wildlife Trust's **Pwll-y-Wrach Nature Reserve** just outside town. These ancient woods have bluebells in late spring and the unusual toothwort plant growing at the base of trees in summer. You may even see badgers and otters here. The **Woodland Trust's Park Wood**, on a ridge overlooking town, is also great for gentle walks and fantastic views. As for the town's strategic past, there is the medieval **Tower House** – a fortified house similar to a pele tower – one of only two such buildings in Wales. Talgarth Tower House is now the tourist office, where you can also find out about the ruins of Castell Dinas – a fairly well-preserved Norman keep south of the town. This is also one of the few towns where you can still see a regular cattle market. They take place on some Tuesdays and Fridays. Contact the tourist office for details (☎ *01874 712226*).

Llangorse Lake ALL AGES

East of Brecon, off the A40, (signposted), ☎ *01874 624437, www.* breconbeacons.org/www.brecon-beacons.com

There's an awful lot going on at Llangorse for the active family – and for those who just want to have a stroll, a picnic and a paddle, too. Llangorse is the largest natural lake in South Wales, and is a Site of Special Scientific Interest and a Special Area of Conservation It's home to at least 20 different bird species in winter – such as the great crested grebe, teal and tufted ducks – and in spring you can see birds such as ospreys migrating north. There's plenty of walking around the lake, too – it's 1.5km long and eight kilometres in diameter – and licences are available for fishing. But for those wanting more action, there's Llangorse Multi Activity Centre (see p 110).

Open daily. *Admission* free.
Amenities pay and display car park, National Park Village Information Agency, café, toilets, bird hide.

Hay on Wye

For a small town Hay has a huge reputation – not least for its eccentricity: it is twinned with Timbuktu and once declared independence from Britain. Hay is world famous for the hundreds of second-hand book shops, which attract tourists like bees to honey, but it was the **Hay Festival** – launched in 1987 – which put the town on the international culture map. During the 10 days of the literary festival, starting in the last week of May, it's best to stay away unless you've got tickets to the show. You certainly won't find anywhere to stay and the cafes will be full. The rest of the time Hay on Wye is a lazy, leisurely delight, and when the children are tired of poking around bookshops, antique and bric-a-brac shops or organic food stores (less than an hour for our two) you can wander down to the River Wye for a gentle stroll. **The Bailey Walk** follows the river bank on the town side for two and a half kilometres from Wyeford Road to the Warren – a local beauty spot where you can paddle in the river and have a picnic. You could also explore the town's Norman castle, though it's just a ruin and – predictably – a second-hand book shop. **The Offa's Dyke Path** and **Wye Valley Walk** both run through Hay, though the Wye Valley Walk is more suitable for families with young children. You can pick up a Walk Pack from the Hay Tourist Information Bureau, near the car park on Oxford Road. There are several lovely cafes and good pubs here, and the salmon fishing is well regarded. You'll need a rod licence and permit, which you can get from a fishing tackle shop and some hotels. If you've got a canoe you can launch it at Wyeford Road, but make sure you paddle clear of anglers – and swans.

For Active Families

Llangorse Multi Activity Centre OLDER CHILDREN

Gilfach Farm, Llangorse, ☎ *01874 658272, www.activityuk.com*

There is everything here for the active family or older children who want to get away from their parents for a few hours – or even

Hay on Wye is famed for its second-hand bookshops

Hay Festival

It's not every small town that can successfully host an internationally-acclaimed festival – yet Hay-on-Wye carries it off with ever-increasing ease. This lively little place – once half in Wales, half in England but now totally inside the Welsh border – attracts some of the world's best-known writers, politicians, musicians and other entertainers, as well as about 150,000 festival-goers. Of particular interest to families is Hay Fever, where children's authors read their work, talk about their favourite book characters and even give creative writing classes. There are activities for pre-schoolers, 5–7 years, 8–11 years, 12 plus and all the family. These include a variety of subjects ranging from baby yoga and puppet shows to journalism workshops aimed at 12–16 year olds and screen writing and film-making for over 10s. There's a similarly-impressive programme for adults, too, and lots of deck chairs to loll around in plus tasty, organic meals to buy from the food marquees. All in all a thoroughly civilised festival – if you can cope with the crowds.

days. Pony trekking (from age seven); climbing and similar activities (from age five) at the all-weather multi activity centre; Sky Trek (from age 12), which involves sailing through the air on ropes and harnesses for up to 200m, and Dingle Scramble where you scramble up dingles – gorges with waterfalls, pools and lots of mud. There are multi-activity fundays and three to five-day breaks. Bookings only. Accommodation can be arranged.

Open varies. **Admission** pony trekking from £13.50; Sky Trek from £23; activity sessions from £15.50; Dingle Scramble from £15.50.

Cantref Adventure Farm & Riding Centre

Cantref, LD3 8LR ✆ 01874 665223, www.cantref.com. Off A40 3.2km east of Brecon.

A farm and more. Firstly, there are the animals – goats, pigs, sheep and the like – with half-hourly treats such as lamb feeding, pig racing, pet handling (with rabbits and guinea pigs) and tractor and trailer rides around the enclosures. There are pony rides (£1, the day's only extra cost) as well as marked walking trails through arable fields and a wildflower meadow with beautiful views of the Brecon Beacons and special shows including sheep shearing and sheep dog trials.

The natural attractions are backed up by a huge indoor play area, the Mega Sledge (sledging on a plastic surface, apparently Europe's longest), paddle boats and the like.

A separate entity is the Riding Centre, which offers riding lessons around the farm and up into the hills, from four years up. There's a 20-minute taster (children and adults £6.50), and various options up to a day ride (11 and over, £43), or a two-hour hack for experienced riders (11 and over, £24).

The farm also has bunkhouses and a campsite (see p 115).

Open Adventure Farm, 10.30am–5.30am, daily March–Oct half-term, weekends and school holidays rest of year. Admission main season, adults £6.50, children 3-16/senior citizens £4.95, under 3s free, family ticket (2+3) £22.50; rest of year adults £3, children £3.95. Open all December with Christmas Grotto. Amenities shop, café, free parking.

Taff Trail ALL AGES

Starts at Brecon Canal Basin car park, wwwtafftrail.org.uk.

The Taff Trail covers 88km between Brecon and Cardiff and is designed for walkers and cyclists, with some sections suitable for horses. Much of the route is traffic-free, including the section that starts from Brecon Canal Basin. Walkers can follow the Monmouthshire and Brecon Canal tow path for three well-surfaced miles (ideal for fit families) to the first lock at Brynich. Here you'll find picnic tables, ducks to feed and other river wildlife to spot. You might get lucky and see a kingfisher. The Taff Trail continues for walkers along the canal towpath to Talybont-on-Usk, so you can join it for a leisurely stroll anywhere you like. Cyclists take a more off-road route nearby, then walkers and cyclists join the same path at Talybont Reservoir. It starts getting more difficult after that.

Beacons Way OLDER CHILDREN

From Abergavenny to Llangadog, www.breconbeaconspark society.org.

This is a 160km walk across the Black Mountains, Central Beacons and Pen-y-Fan – the highest mountain in south Wales. The average family can try bits of it, but it's as challenging as it sounds. It follows part of the route that forms the Cambrian Way – an even more hair-raising trip across every mountain between Cardiff and Conwy – on the north Wales coast. If you want to give it a go, the easiest section is between Carreg Cennen and Llangadog – a walk of just under 16km with an ascent of only 330m compared with the 600-1065m ascents in other sections. This last stage takes you through Cilmaenllwyd, Carreglwyd, Y Gaer Fawr and Bethlehem before reaching Llangadog.

Usk Valley Walk ALL AGES

From Brecon to Caerleon, near Newport, www.uskvalleywalk.org.uk

The Brecon Beacons part of this 77km walk mostly follows the Monmouthshire and Brecon Canal towpath, with a few diversions through woods and over fields. As such, it's quite lovely and a place where you can stroll rather than hike. After Abergavenny it follows the banks of the River Usk to Caerleon.

Brecon Beacon Legends

There are many legends about the mountains that now make up the Brecon Beacons National Park – some involving King Arthur and his knights. Wales is only one of several Celtic countries claiming the warrior king as its own, but Wales has some of the best stories. For instance, it is said that Arthur and his knights are sleeping in a cave at Craig y Ddinas, a crag near Glyn-Neath.

According to legend, a Welshman strolling through London with a particularly fine hazel walking stick was stopped by a man who asked to be taken to the tree from which the stick was cut. The Welshman took him to Wales where the man, who turned out to be a wizard, pulled up the tree.Underneath was a slab of stone which opened to reveal a cave, with a bell hanging in the entrance. Beyond were hundreds of sleeping knights and one particularly splendid warrior surrounded by silver and gold. The wizard told the Welshman he could take as much treasure as he could carry, but if he knocked the bell the knights would wake up and ask: "Is it day?", in which case he should reply: "No, sleep on." The Welshman had so much gold and silver he had to squeeze past the bell and, predictably, it rang. Since he had been warned by the wizard he knew what to say when one of the knights woke, and he escaped from the cave to live a very prosperous life.

Many years later, when he had spent nearly all his money, he returned to the cave to get more treasure. Again, he knocked into the bell as he squeezed past, but this time he could not remember exactly what to say when one of the knights awoke. Others too awoke to see him trying to steal their treasure, so they attacked him and kicked him out of the cave – battered, bruised and without a penny. The Welshman died a pauper and was never able to find the cave again. But the knights and their warrior king sleep on in readiness for the day when the Black Eagle and Golden Eagle go to war. Then they will save Britain from its enemies and Arthur will be king once more.

Offa's Dyke Path ★
OLDER CHILDREN

Offa's Dyke Centre, Knighton, Powys, LDN 1EN ☎ 0547 528753, www. offasdyke.demon.co.uk, www. nationaltrail.co.uk

It usually takes about two weeks to complete the full 285km from Chepstow in south Wales to Prestatyn on the north coast, but you can still enjoy it with children by taking little sections. The route became a National Trail in 1971, but only 112km of the path follows the course of the 8th-century earthwork. You can catch the Offa's Dyke Flyer – linked to the Beacons Bus – from Hay on Wye to the Llanthony Valley, where there's a particularly spectacular section of the Offa's Dyke Path which you can walk along to take you back to Hay.

Black Mountain Activities

Three Cocks, Brecon, LD3 0SD, 01497 847897, www.black mountain.co.uk. On A4078 several miles south west of Hay-on-Wye.

Heavy on the team-building and development training side of things, including for schools and colleges, there are also family and children's (from age 8) activity days throughout the summer holidays featuring canoeing, climbing, abseiling, orienteering, raft-building and gorge walking. From October to March there's whitewater rafting on the River Wye (from age 16). The centre also does mountain biking, kayaking, gorge adventures, archery and a number of other activities, some of which teenagers can take part in.

The centre's own 17th-century stone Black Mountain Lodge also offers B&B (with family rooms) plus evening meals. There is also a bunkhouse sleeping 16, and a camp site, with campers sharing bunkhouse facilities.

*Family activity days £55/36, half days £30/20. B&B family rooms, double with two children under 15 in bunk beds, tea-making facilities, £85. Camping £4pp. pm). Restaurant main courses from £9.25. **Credit** MC, V, AE.*

FAMILY-FRIENDLY ACCOMMODATION

There are lots of quaint country hotels in this region, along with a growing number of smaller, trendier places – and there are plenty of picturesque camp sites with none of the frenzy of coastal areas.

EXPENSIVE

Castle of Brecon Hotel ★

The Castle Square, Brecon, LD3 9DB, 01874 624611, www.brecon castle.co.uk

Not a castle in itself, but occupying the site of the original castle on a bluff in the centre of town, with wonderful views over trees and rooftops towards the mountains. Since opening as a coaching inn in the 18th century it has become a landmark in itself. Privately-owned and family-run, it has an old-school charm. In the midst of loving restoration – the Beacons View restaurant's Regency paint job and oak floors returning it to how it looked in 1809 – the feeling is historic and comfy but not stuffy. Children can share their parents' room for a small charge, and there are family rooms. Food under head chef Patrick Carney (who's worked with Marco Pierre White and Gary Rhodes) is charismatically British, featuring Powys lamb and mutton, game faggots and Welsh burgers as well as stylish fish and chips and pastas (which can be served in child portions).

*30 rooms. Double room from £100; children sharing £10, under 3s free. Family rooms from £110. Babysitting available. Dogs £10 a night. **Amenities** restaurant, bistro, bar, lounge, garden, car park. **In room** TV, tea maker.*

4 Smallbrook Terrace

Hay-on-Wye, 📞 *01242 513497,*
www.haywyer.com

A classy but very reasonably-priced townhouse with a cottagey feel only a few hundred metres from the centre of town and just up from the River Wye and its woodland paths and cycle routes. The house is on three floors and sleeps six in three bedrooms with king-size double beds. There are lovely wooden floors throughout and a slate open fire in the living room. A cobbled back yard (with chairs) leads on to a terrace garden with views over the hills. No TV or phone, but that's its charm. You can bring the dog, go for muddy walks, and return to a hot drink in the fully-equipped kitchen.

From £350 a week, £150 for a weekend of £195 for a 3-night break, including heating, linen, towels and logs for the fire.

Baskerville Hall Hotel

Clyro Court, Hay-on-Wye, HR3 5LE,
📞 *01497 820033, www.baskerville*
hall.co.uk. Just outside of town, on
the A438 to Brecon.

Built in 1839 by Thomas Baskerville, this huge, slightly creepy hall was immortalised by his chum Sir Arthur Conan Doyle (a regular visitor) in the Sherlock Holmes novel The Hound of the Baskervilles. At various times a school and health farm, the hall has been revamped into a smart hotel, but not one which ignores the needs of young, active visitors to the area.

There is also dormitory accommodation £16), and a camp site (£5) everyone gets to use the hotel pool and sauna, and if you're there at the weekend you get into the Hall's public disco. The Hall is set in 130 acres of fields and woodland, so great for walks even before you bother with the National Park slightly further afield. Children enjoy running around the huge halls and massive central staircase. Campers can bring their own hound (£2.50 a night).

Double rooms from £70; children under 12 sharing (in larger family rooms) are charged half-rate.
***Amenities** restaurant, bar, gardens, swimming pool, sauna, car park.*
***In room** TV, tea maker.*

Cantref Bunkhouse and Camping

Cantref, LD3 8LR, 📞 *01874 665223,*
www.cantref.com. Off A40 two
miles east of Brecon.

This is a lovely place to stay on a farm, with delightful views across to the Brecon Beacons and home to the Cantref Adventure Farm attraction and its associated riding centre (p 111). There are two bunk-houses, one an old stone farm building sleeping 24 in six bedrooms (for between two and six), the other an old Nissan hut, sleeping 10 in three rooms (two to four people). The buildings both have underfloor heating, common rooms and kitchens (in the larger building this makes for a smartly relaxing spot in the eaves). Both can be booked by the bed or room Mon–Thurs, with entire buildings needing to be booked at weekends, for a minimum of two nights – which means they're great places for family get-togethers, for less than £12 pp per night. The Adventure Park's café is open until late afternoon for anything from a cup of tea to a bowl of the hearty Welsh soup, cawl – but staff offer catering with advance notice.

The camp site is simple (toilets, hand basins and a water tap) but the tranquil setting is worth it.

Bunkhouses £12.50pp, Mon–Thurs. Weekends, large £290, small £120 per night, min 2 nights. Camping £3pp. No credit or debit cards.

Pencelli Castle Caravan & Camping Park ★

Pencelli, Brecon, LD3 7LX ☎ 01874 665451, www.pencelli-castle.com. Take A40 from Brecon towards Abergavenny; after 1.5km turn left on to B4558, then follow signs.

This small, pretty, well-tended site six and a half kilometres from Brecon and alongside the Brecon and Monmouth Canal is perfect for camper vans and caravans, while a tent-only field is right by the canal, where you can picnic as longboats glide past. There's a separate play area and a big grassy area for cricket and football, the posh shower block is centrally-heated, and there are two family rooms with double showers, changing areas and hair driers, plus a well-equipped laundry room with washers, driers, iron and ironing board. Mountain bikes can be hired on-site, to explore the many local paths and lanes, as well as the Taff Trail which passes through Pencelli village.

Camper vans and caravans £16–19 inc 2 adults; camping £8–9.50pp. Children (5–15) £4.50–5.50; under 5s free. Prices depend on season. **Facilities** *shop, disabled access.*

Brecon Youth Hostel ★

Groessffordd, LD3 7SW, ☎ 0870 770 5718, www.yha.org.uk

Making use of a lovely Victorian farm house in its own grounds with fantastic views over the countryside, there are family rooms which are clean and comfortable, if a little spartan, though there are plans for refurbishment. The self-catering kitchen is cramped, but well-equipped and sociable. If you don't want to cook, the restaurant provides tasty meals using local produce where possible, and the bar sells organic wine and beer. The best thing about this hostel though is the setting. On a summer's night you can sit on the veranda or on the lightning-felled tree in the adjoining field admiring the view with a glass of wine while your children run around to their hearts' content.

Ensuite family rooms available. Nightly rate from £14, under 18s from £10. Restaurant, TV room, games room, laundry, BBQ, parking.

Danywenallt Youth Hostel

Talybont-on-Usk, LD3 7YS, 0870 770 6136, www.yha.org.uk

There's a very lively atmosphere at this secluded old converted farm house – perhaps because most of the guests are buzzing with the excitement of having spent the day in the fabulously picturesque countryside, which starts right on the doorstep. There are also a couple of fields for children to run around in or play football without any worry of annoying grown ups. There's no self catering, but the restaurant provides very decent meals – and the huge cooked breakfast is included in the price. The hostel is right next to Talybont reservoir and within spitting distance of several waymarked walks.

Ensuite family rooms available. Nightly rate from £17.50, under 18s from £14. Restaurant, lounge, laundry, BBQ, parking.

Brecon Beacons National Park Caravan and Camping Site ★

Abercrave, Swansea, SA9 1GJ, 01639 730284, www.showcaves.co.uk. On the A4067, near Sennybridge.

A fabulous site, with a natural landscape feel that you would expect in the heart of the Brecon Beacons. There are grassy areas for tents, and hardstandings for caravans and campervans, with clumps of tree, lumps of rock, and grassy knolls for decoration. The site was redesigned a couple of years ago and it really is idyllic – a perfect base for walking and very convenient for the National Showcaves (you can book the site at their café). It's best to book in advance during school holidays.

Tents: adult £5, child £2, electrical hook-up £2 per night; caravans and camper vans £15 per night for two people, additional adult £5, child £3. Includes hook-up showers and awnings. Dogs welcome.

Danywenallt Youth Hostel is in the midst of beautiful countryside

117

FAMILY-FRIENDLY DINING

You might expect a place like this to be very traditional, but there's lots of organic stuff going on, and they like children.

Bridge Cafe ★

7 Bridge Street, Brecon, LD3 8AH, ☎ 01874 622 024, www.bridge cafe.co.uk. Right in the centre of Brecon, by the River Usk.

This lovely cafe and licensed bistro offers simple, muted décor, oak floors and a couple of sofas by the log fire. There are lots of seasonal, local ingredients, in summer leaning towards snacks and salads, but with casseroles and pies on cooler days. Children can enjoy simpler ham, egg and hummus options while the Aga-roasted peppers and the like please parents. They are famed for cakes, including chocolate made with Green & Black's bars, and there is also Fairtrade coffee and organic wine. There are three rooms upstairs for B&B – one has a folding bed along with the double for £55. Continental breakfast included, organic fry-up £3 extra.

Open *March–Oct, Wed–Fri, 10am–5pm; Saturdays, 10am–6pm; Sundays on Bank Holidays and school holidays, 10am–6pm.* **Main courses** *From around £5.*

Castle Street Restaurant

20 Castle Street, Brecon, LD3 9BU, ☎ 01874624392, www.castlestreet restaurant.co.uk. In the centre of Brecon, near the River Usk.

Organic, sustainable, and local produce combined with an inspired but sensible menu make this a Brecon delight in an 1840s Grade II listed town house. Sewin (sea trout) from Carmathen coracle fishermen and noodles with tofu sit alongside the children's favourite of organic pizza with home-made chips £6.50). There are Fairtrade wines and beers from the local Brecknockshire microbrewery. There are also several elegantly simple B&B rooms – a triple £60) can be booked with the single as a family suite (£75).

Open *Feb–Dec, Thurs–Sat, from 6.30pm, last orders 9.30pm. Extended hours during summer holidays.* **Main courses** *£6.95–11.75.*

Skirrid Mountain Inn ★★

Llanyihangel Crucorney, Abergavenny, NP7 8DH, ☎ 01873 890258, www.skirridmountaininn.co.uk. Just off the A465, 8 km north of Abergavenny.

This is the oldest pub in Wales, offering good food, outstanding real ales, and a lovely beer garden where you can enjoy wonderful views. The Skirrid has been an inn since 1110, and it was used as a court by the infamous Bloody Judge Jefferies. During the 1685 Monmouth Rebellion he hanged 180 of the rebels from a beam inside the pub – and people say the judge and his victims now haunt the building and its surroundings.

Open *Daily.* **Main courses** *£7.95–8.95.* **Credit** *MC, V.*

6 West Wales

WEST WALES

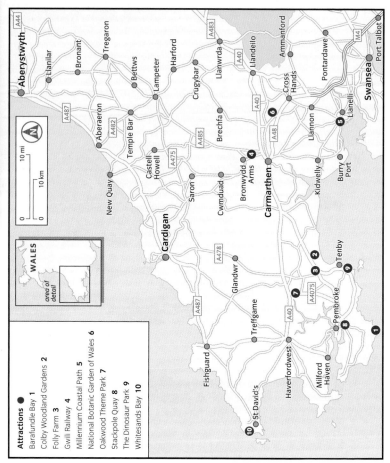

Attractions ●
Barafundle Bay **1**
Colby Woodland Gardens **2**
Folly Farm **3**
Gwili Railway **4**
Millennium Coastal Path **5**
National Botanic Garden of Wales **6**
Oakwood Theme Park **7**
Stackpole Quay **8**
The Dinosaur Park **9**
Whitesands Bay **10**

The wild west is a land of beaches that stretch off into the hazy distance, hemmed in by craggy cliffs, where you really do face the fact that (at least in the south) there's nothing between you and North America. Children love this great outdoors... the hidden coves, the desolation (sometimes), and the surprising warmth if you can find yourself a little nook. They forget about everything else as they bound down the winding paths toward the sea carrying bucket and spade, dashing into the foamy waves that mark this part of Wales, and then insisting on walking all the way back up for an ice cream from the café in the car park. Wildest of all is the Pembrokeshire coast, a magical place, until recently kept a well-guarded secret by people in the know. Increasingly it's a trendy new hotspot for visitors discovering the joys of the British seaside from bases in camper vans, luxury tents (in hilltop camp sites with sea views) and elegant holiday cottages.

This isn't just a spot for natural wonders, though – there are plenty of attractions, from castles to the only theme park in Wales – Oaklands. There's even a city out west – St David's, Britain's smallest – in reality it's a tiny town, granted city status because of its important – and tranquilly beautiful – cathedral. It's not right on the sea but is just a couple of kilometres from fantastic beaches.

After St David's the coast wiggles north-east past Fishguard, where ferry boats arrive from Ireland, then the delightful seaside resort of Newport. The rugged coastline between Newport and Poppit Sands – at the mouth of the River Teifi – is best seen from the Pembrokeshire Coastal Path, which starts at St Dogmaels, further down the estuary. Here, the countryside has already changed to a greener, lusher tapestry, heralding the start of mid Wales, over the other side of the River Teifi, in Cardiganshire – or Ceredigion.

ESSENTIALS

Visitor Information

Tourist Information Centres

Fishguard, Town Hall Fishguard, SA65 9AR, ☎ 01348 873 484, E: fishguard.tic@ pembrokeshire.gov.uk

Fishguard (Harbour), Ocean Lab, The Parrog, Goodwick, SA64 0DE, ☎ 01348 872 528, E: fishguardharbour.tic@pembs. gov.uk

Haverfordwest, 19 Old Bridge, SA61 2EZ, ☎ 01437 763110, E: haverfordwest.tic@pembrokeshire. gov.uk

Kilgetty, Carmarthen Road, SA68 0YA, ☎ 01834 814 161, E: info@tourismpembrokeshire.co.uk

Milford Haven, 94 Charles Street, SA73 2HL, ☎ 01646 690866, E: milford.tic@ pembrokeshire.gov.uk. Seasonal opening.

Newport, 2 Bank Cottages, Long Street, SA42 0TN, ☎ 01239 820912, E: NewportTIC@ pembrokeshirecoast.org.uk

Pembroke, Commons Road, SA71 4EA, ☎ 01646 622388, E: pembroke.tic@pembrokeshire. gov.uk

Pembroke Dock, Ferry Terminal, Pembroke Dock, SA72 6JZ, ☎ 01646 622753, E: pembrokedock.tic@ pembrokeshire.gov.uk

Saundersfoot, Harbour Car Park, SA69 9HE, SA72 6JZ ☎ 01834 813672,, E: saundersfoot. tic@pembrokeshire.gov.uk. Seasonal opening.

St David's, National Park Visitor Centre, 1 High Street, SA62 6SAW, ☎ 01437 720392, E: enquiries@stdavids. pembrokeshirecoast.org.uk

Tenby, Unit 2, Gateway Complex, SA70 7LT, ☎ 01834 842402, E: tenby.tic@ pembrokeshire.gov.uk

Areas in Brief

Before you reach the golden beaches of Pembrokeshire, there are other treasures to uncover on the journey west. The underrated county of Carmarthenshire has beautiful gardens and a coastline of tranquil estuaries, huge sandy beaches, and the regenerated former industrial wasteland around Llanelli, which has been transformed into the Millennium Coastal Park. But for most holidaymakers, west Wales really starts around Tenby, a bustling seaside town on the far side of Carmarthen Bay with a little neighbour, Saundersfoot, which is equally busy. From here you move into the far west where the sticky-out bits full of beaches and coves are as beautiful as you'll find anywhere in the world. Pembroke and Haverfordwest are busy market towns but you need to head further west for the true experience, a string of little seaside resorts with big expanses of beach alternating with tiny coves only accessible by a walk down the cliffs. Newgale is one of the biggest beaches, an easy drive from St David's, where the coast turns craggy with fiercesome cliffs and the occasional beach. But the seaside holiday gets back on track at massive Newport Sands before Pembrokeshire hands over the beach baton to Cardiganshire (Ceredigion) and mid Wales, after Poppit Sands.

Getting Around

By car If you're holidaying in Tenby and plan to spend your week in town you can get away without a car (parking here can be more difficult than Piccadilly in the rush hour), but anywhere else and a car is essential. Most of the more spectacular beaches are way off the beaten track and a long way from any bus route.

By train An 8-day Freedom of South Wales Flexi Rover ticket (*www.walesflexipass.co.uk*) gives use of trains on four days and buses for eight days as far north as Aberystwyth, and across the country for £45 (children 5–15 £22.50, under 5s free), with discounts at attractions and youth hostels. Trains get you to Tenby, Pembroke, Milford Haven, Haverfordwest and Fishguard, with buses serving the rest of the coast.

By bus Pembrokeshire has a Coastal Bus Service with a number of routes linking seaside spots with inland towns, such as the Puffin Shuttle (Haverfordwest-St David's) and the summer-only Celtic Coaster around the St David's peninsula. The Coastal Cruiser carries bicycles, surfboards and wheelchairs and runs between Pembroke and several popular beaches. There is a network of other services up the coast to Cardiganshire and east into Carmarthenshire. A West Wales Rover ticket (£6.30 adults, £3.15 accompanied children), sold on buses, gives you all-day travel in Pembrokeshire, Cardiganshire and Carmarthenshire. Services are run by an array of companies, so local council websites are the best source of information *www. pembrokeshire.gov.uk*, *www. carmarthenshire.gov.u*). For times and routes: *www.traveline-cymru. org.uk*.

By foot The Pembrokeshire Coastal Path meanders 300km from Amroth in the south to St Dogmaels in the north. Given its length, and the fact that 10670m of ascent and descent is said to be equivalent to climbing Everest, it's not a week's holiday. But each section is divine and wherever you are you'll find somewhere that works as a breathtaking stroll with younger children or as a serious hike with teenagers. Details on individual stretches (from around 6km) on *www.nt.pcnpa.org.uk* or just head for the coast and find somewhere to walk.

WHAT TO SEE & DO

Top 10 Family Experiences

❶ **Skipping into the sea** in the late afternoon at the virtually deserted, beautiful Barafundle Bay.

❷ **Eating fish and chips** on the harbour wall at Saundersfoot, before an early evening walk on the beach.

❸ **Exploring the rocks** at Marloes Sands on a shimmering hot day.

❹ **Watching the sun set** from the camp site at St David's Head while sausages cooked on the barbecue.

❺ **Running around the castle** at Manorbier after a morning on the beach.

❻ **Finding the burial chamber** in the Preseli Hills.

❼ **Viewing Tenby from the sea** on the boat ride to and from Caldey Island.

❽ **Playing on the ships** in the playground at Folly Farm Adventure Park and Zoo.

❾ **Messing about in the sand at Solva** while mum and dad (that's us) had a quiet drink outside the harbour pub.

❿ **Driving down the hill** at Newgale and seeing the coast stretch out for miles.

Family-friendly Festivals

Really Wild Food & Countryside Festival

St David's, ☏ 01348 840242, www. reallywildfestival.co.uk

A jolly do celebrating local nosh and its surroundings. Family-friendly Stalls sell all manner of stuff, from sausages to ice cream, there are cookery demos, crafts, coastal walks and you might even catch a rare sighting of TV naturalist David Bellamy, a patron.

Last weekend in August.

Pembrokeshire Fish Week

Countywide, ☏ 01437 776168, www. fishweek.co.uk

More fun than it sounds – events for children include snorkel safaris, rockpool rambles, crab catching, and seaside arts and crafts. The events take place in towns across the county and for the grown-ups there are historical fishing exhibitions, art workshops, photography competitions and classes on how to cook fish and shellfish.

Last week in June.

Laugharne Weekend

Various venues, Laugharne, www.the laugharneweekend.com

Literary festival celebrating Welsh voices and cult names in village where Dylan Thomas lived. The 2008 line-up had poet Roger McGough (author of many children's works) and Llanelli-born actor-writer Keith Allen (the sheriff in BBC's *Robin Hood*) alongside US rocker Patti Smith and Welsh novelists. Weekend £50, events from £5.

Late March.

Tenby Arts Festival

Tenby, various venues, www.tenby fest.co.uk

Huge range of music – from jazz to Welsh male choirs – plus drama, dance, photo and art exhibitions. Great for children is the Grand Parade of street entertainers, dancers and musicians opening the festival, and the sand sculpting competition.

Last weekend in September.

Pembroke Festival

Pembroke, various venues, ☎ *01646 680090, www.pembroke21c.org*

Lots of music, dancing and comedy, and children will love the colourful parades, treasure hunt, storytelling and barbecue. Includes the International Welsh Celtic Fiddle Competition.

Late August/early September.

Haverfordwest River Festival

Haverfordwest, various venues, ☎ *01437 763771, www.pembroke shirewaterway.org.uk*

A week of entertainment including medieval re-enactments, music and art, but also the ancient Beating the Bounds Ceremony, on the quay.

Early July.

Pembrokeshire Agricultural Show

County Showground, Withybush, Haverfordwest, ☎ *01437 764331, www.pembrokeshirecountyshow. co.uk*

The second largest agricultural show in Wales, and noted for its huge range of local produce, which should please the foodies among you. There are all the usual entertainments and competitions: girls will love the traditional show jumping and dog agility competition, while boys will be delighted by the vintage tractors and steam engines. And who can resist the best-in-show pygmy goats?

Mid to late August.

Narberth Food Festival

County Showground, Withybush, Haverfordwest, ☎ *01437 764331, www.pembrokeshirecountyshow. co.uk*

Narberth is regarded as food capital of Pembrokeshire and this festival has links with the good gourmets of Ludlow, in Shropshire. But although they take their local produce seriously, there's room for children's workshops, street entertainment and music – as well as cookery demonstrations.

September.

National Mud Festival

National Wetlands Centre Wales, Llwynhendy, Llanelli, Carmarthenshire, SA14 9SH ☎ 01554 741087, www.wwt.org.uk

You can't help but have fun here – although you might need a change of clothes. You can take a Mud Safari down the estuary at low tide and join in Wellie Wanging Competitions and the Mud-of-War version of the old favourite tug-of-war. You can make mud sculptures, mud huts and edible mud pies, and – especially for children – you can create your own Muddy Sea Creature, hear a muddy story or watch a video about mud and its role at the wetlands centre.

September.

LLanelli

The real draw here is not Llanelli itself. The first impression you get is of the traffic system that circulates around the Asda superstore (as splendidly chronicled in *Maybe I Should've Stayed In Bed* –Northdown Publishing, by Deke Leonard of famed rockers Man, a Milliganesque tale of young musicians growing up here). No, what you want is the coast. The Millennium Coastal Park (☎ 01554 777744, www. millenniumcoastalpark.com) is a 19km stretch along the Burry estuary, looking over to the Gower Peninsula. Once an industrial wasteland, it has been transformed into a nature reserve and outdoor activities area. Millennium Quays has a water sports centre; there's a promenade, visitor centre and coastal path/cycleway that links it to the National Wetland Centre at Penclacwydd, and Pembrey Country Park, and there's also a series of six well-stocked lakes which make up the Welsh National Angling Centre. The National Wetland Centre Wales, (☎ 01554 741087, www. wwt.org.uk) meanwhile, is a patchwork of lakes and lagoons near the estuary which is home to ducks, swans, geese – even flamingoes. The indoor Millennium Discovery Centre has been designed with children in mind – the highlight crawling though the tunnels of Water Vole City. Children also love exploring the water on a canoe safari, playing in the Swan's Nest Maze, watching out for giant dragonflies, and riding around the bike trail. Pembrey Country Park, (☎ 01554 833913, www. carmarthenshire.gov.uk) just outside Burry Port, has loads to do as well. There are cycle routes, woodland walks, an 11km sandy beach, equestrian centre, cafes, orienteering, pitch and putt, giant adventure playground, miniature railway, crazy golf – even a dry ski slope and toboggan run. And if you want to stay for more than the day, there's a top-of-the- range Caravan Club site. (☎ *01554 834369, www.caravan club.co.uk*).

Carmarthen

Carmarthen is the county town with a good selection of High Street outlets but it's the market that makes it different from other places. The St Catherine Street market claims to be the oldest in Wales, dating back to Roman times – and it's definitely one of the biggest. The indoor market is open Monday–Saturday, 9am–5pm, with an outdoor market on Wednesday and Saturday, and Farmers Market on the first Friday each month. There's little else to see in Carmarthen, though **Carmarthenshire County Museum** (☎ *01267 228696, www. carmarthenshire.gov.uk*), one and a half kilometres east along the A40 at Abergwili is good – not least because it is said to be Merlin's final resting place. The county collection is housed in the Old Palace of the Bishops of St David's, and is surrounded by beautiful parkland and a lake.

National Botanic Garden of Wales ★ ALL AGES

Llanarthene, SA32 8HG, ☎ 01558 668768, www.gardenofwales.org.uk. Just off A48 on B4310, 13km south of Carmarthen.

We really liked this garden, mostly because of its open aspect and attractive courtyards. The

space age tropical house is also fairly stunning. True, some of the planting still has a few years to go before it reaches maturity, but garden lovers will still be impressed. As for the children, they didn't even notice – too busy enjoying the children's play area and children's farm (summer only), running round lakes, and chasing butterflies.

Open daily, March–Oct, 10am–6pm; late Oct–early March, 10am–4.30pm. Admission adults £8, concessions £6, children (5–16) £3, family £17. Amenities cafés, souvenir shop, restaurant, free parking.

Gwili Railway ALL AGES

Bronwydd, Carmarthen. SA33 6HT ☎ 01267 238213, www.gwili-railway. co.uk. Just off A484 five kilometres from centre of Carmarthen.

This is the only historic standard gauge train in West Wales, using part of the former Great Western Railway Carmarthen-Aberystwyth line. The scenery of wooded hills and the River Gwili combine with beautiful engines and even a Victorian coach to conjure up the past, so the railway has been used in many TV and film shoots including the BBC's *Carrie's War.* You pass an old iron mill, cross the river and stop mid-journey at Llwyfan Cerrig, with its quarry backdrop, where you can take a break at the river-side picnic site and enjoy the miniature railway. Round it all off with cakes in the Café in the Coach back at Bronwydd station.

Open erratic, but basically May–Sept, most Sundays, some Wednesdays and also Wed–Fri in

August, plus some other Bank and school holidays. *Thomas the Tank Engine* days at Easter and October half-term with fairground, barbecue and entertainment. Santa's Magic Steamings in December. **Tickets** (which give all day travel): adults £5.50, OAPs £4.50, children (2–15) £3. Family tickets £15. Thomas days adults £8, children £6, families £25. **Amenities** cafés, souvenir shop, toilets, picnic areas, disabled access, free parking (no parking on Thomas days, when there are free buses from Carmarthen Showground).

Laugharne

A peaceful town on the serene River Taf estuary, with handsome Georgian buildings and pretty little cottages, a ruined castle and, of course, the Dylan Thomas Boathouse. This is where Thomas spent the last four years of his life, and 100 yards away is the shed where he wrote *Under Milk Wood*. They're worth a visit (01994 427420, www.dylandthomasboathouse. com) even if you only walk along the river path to see the truly inspiring views across the estuary. And if your children do agree to a quick look around, you can reward them with home-made cakes from the tea room. The Laugharne Festival takes place every three years to raise funds for the town's Cors Playing Field, which has an excellent children's adventure playground and is a good spot for a picnic. As for Laugharne Castle, it's on a beautiful site overlooking the river, and is under Cadw stewardship. A family ticket is £8.30 and it's open between March and October (01443 336000; www.cadw. wales.gov.uk). The nearest beach is Pendine – 11km long and famous for the Land Speed Record attempts by Malcolm

Dylan Thomas's writing shed, where he created *Under Milk Wood*

Campbell and his car Bluebird in the 1920s. The Sands of Speed Museum here displays the record-breaking car Babs – dug up from its grave in the dunes where it was buried after the crash that killed driver J G Parry Thomas. It has now been fully restored.

Amroth

The beach at Amroth and the cluster of seaside shops, pubs and cottages near the beach have hardly changed since the 1960s – probably thanks to Amroth being bypassed in the rush to Tenby. Amroth doesn't have the wild clifftop beauty of further around the coastline, but it does have safe bathing and all that's necessary for a good family seaside holiday. It is also the finishing (or starting) point for the Pembrokeshire Coast Path, and the beach itself is known for the drowned forest tree stumps visible at very low tides.

Colby Woodland Gardens ★★
ALL AGES

Amroth, SA67 8PP, ☏ 01834 811885, www.nationaltrust.org.uk. Off coast road at Amroth Castle, or follow signs from A477.

This is one of those places children instinctively like, full of trees to attempt to climb and great scope for hide and seek. It's also one of the best places in Wales to see rhododendrons, magnolias, azaleas and camellias in spring, and there are bluebell woods in late spring. The eight-acre valley has a sculpture trail, and new

planting schemes and paths are being created all the time.

Open daily, mid-March–Oct, 10am– 5pm. Admission adults £4, children £2, family £10. Credit MC, V. Amenities café, shop, free parking, picnic areas, disabled access.

Saundersfoot

This pretty seaside harbour village just east of Tenby manages to combine quaint surroundings with kiss-me-quick fun. Revellers pack pub patios and gardens as the sun goes down, but it's a child's delight. Our children loved buying fish and chips from the quayside chippy and eating them while sitting on the harbour walls – fending off seagulls. By day there are plenty of seaside options. The main beach stretches east from the harbour, a sandy strip at high tide, massive at low tide, and with all the benefits of Saundersfoot's shops and restaurants close by. Glen Beach heads in the other direction (connected at low tide), and is less commercial, with rock pools and cliffs as a backdrop. At the other end of the main beach, Coppet Beach is a pretty spot. Children love the echoing walk though the disused coal line rail tunnel (although it has its own car park), and through another tunnel to pretty Wiseman's Bridge where the beach changes from large rocks to soft sand.

Tenby

A proper seaside town in the nicest possible way. Tenby juts

Tenby is the most popular seaside resort in West Wales

out into the sea with a colourful harbour in the middle and long beaches on either side – North Beach, near the harbour and South Beach, backed by sand dunes once you get away from town. The medieval town centre with its huge, 13th-century town walls and castle ruins rolls down to the water. Up above are dolled up hotels and guest houses, smart shops, and restaurants that veer from the stylish to burger bars. By the quay there are stalls selling their catch, and places for a cheerful cup of tea. Even our children – vehement non-shoppers – enjoyed wandering the streets, many of which are narrow and winding, and the combination of beach and boats is beguiling. If there's a drawback it's that you can drive round in circles looking for somewhere to park, and the high season crowds are daunting.

Even though there are plenty of places to stay, most families pick somewhere just outside, often at one of the many pretty camping and caravan sites. If the sun fails to shine there are several non-beach entertainment options, including Tenby Castle. There's not much of it left, but there is plenty of grass to play and picnic on within what's left of the castle walls. At the bottom of Castle Hill is Tenby Museum and Art Gallery (☎ 01834 842809), the oldest independent museum in Wales, founded in 1878 by local amateur naturalists and archeologists who wanted to display their collections. Now you can also see art by Augustus and Gwen John and other prominent Welsh artists, and get a feel for the area's social history. But the National Trust's Tudor Merchant House, on Quay Hill, is possibly the most interesting attraction.

The tall, narrow house was built in the 15th century and is furnished with authentic Tudor fittings (☎ 01834 842279, www. nationaltrust.org.uk).

Silent World ALL AGES

Slippery Back, Mayfield Drive, Narberth Road, Tenby, SA70 8HR, ☎ 01834 844498, www.silentworld. org.uk. From A478 follow signs for North Beach car park (the best place to park).

You do need something indoors to fall back on in Wales, and if you're not going to be on the beach much better to come to a beautiful aquarium than wander around a shopping centre. Quirky and friendly, it is in a 19th-century chapel a swift walk from the town centre. There are lots of local creatures, and plenty of exotic ones, plus snakes, lizards, guinea pigs and a parrot. And it must be the only aquarium with a cat. There is also a toy box, brass-rubbing, drawing and quizzes.

Open daily 10am–6pm July–Aug; 10am–5pm April, May, June, Sept. Tues, Thurs, Sat, Sun 10am–4pm Feb, March, Oct–Dec. Daily in Feb and Oct half-terms. Admission: adults £4.50, children, OAPs £3, families £14. Credit MC, V. Amenities café, shop, disabled access.

Caldey Island ★ AGES 8 AND UP

Off coast at Tenby, ☎ 01834 844453, www.caldey-island.co.uk

Boat trips to Caldey Island leave regularly from Tenby harbour between May and September. It's a 20-minute journey to this peaceful island with its famous monastery lived in by Cistercian monks. Caldey has long been a holy island and was settled by Celtic monks in the 6th century.

Once there, visitors are free to wander among the trees and flowers, or see the chapel, church, priory and lighthouse. Children rise to the adventure, enjoying the ride and the Famous Five feel of being on a tiny island. Of course, you're not that cut off – there are shops selling perfume, chocolate and shortbread made on the spot, tea gardens and Post Office selling specially-franked covers. Nice to get away from it all with a picnic on the big sandy beach at Priory Bay.

Open Easter–October, Mon–Fri and most Saturdays. Boats roughly every 20 mins, 10am–3pm, last boat back 5pm. Admission (incl boat) adult £10, under 15s £5. Amenities café, shops.

The Dinosaur Park ★
AGES 13 AND UNDER

Gumfreston, Tenby, SA70 8RB ☎ 01834 845272, www.the dinosaurpark.co.uk. On the B4318 at Gumfreston.

There's lots to do here if the weather clouds over, including an astra slide, adventure golf, an off-roaders cicuit, sand diggers and similar activities. There's a good indoor play area, soft play pen and outdoor play area, plus fossil hunting, puppet show, treasure hunts and even a guinea pig village. And then there are the dinosaurs. We're getting used to the bizarre enjoyment children get from spotting fibre glass dinosaurs in British woodland settings, although looking forward to moving on. But overall, this is a good day's entertainment with plenty to keep everyone occupied.

Open Daily 10am–5pm March–Sept; 10.30am–4pm Oct (closed Mon and Fri). Admission: adults £5.95, children, OAPs £4.95, under 2s free. Amenities café, shop, disabled access.

Lydstep

Access to the beach at Lydstep is incredibly difficult – despite the National Trust ownership of Lydstep headland. You can't get there through the grounds of the privately-owned holiday village of Lydstep Haven – we've tried. The only access appears to be a rough track leading to Lydstep Head from Lydstep Village – not that we could find it. If you do manage it, you can get to Church Doors Cove, with its cathedral-like natural arch, and a series of caves that should only be explored at low tide. Alternatively, you can walk along the coastal path from Manorbier.

Manorbier

If it's possible to have a fairytale beach then this is it. The sands are red and grainy, with flat stones covering the top of the beach and a stream running through it – but it's still magical thanks to beautiful Manorbier castle, which virtually overlooks the beach. We're not the only people who have fallen in love with this pretty little village. Playwright George Bernard Shaw spent several months here

and novelist Virginia Woolf was a regular summer visitor. There's a good car park near the beach, but not too near, and the village has a few tea shops and a small general store.

Manorbier Castle ★
YOUNG CHILDREN

Manorbier, near Tenby, SA70 7TB, ☎ 01834 871394, www.manorbier castle.co.uk

Our children enjoyed charging round the grassy garden inside the castle, climbing spiral staircases up to the top of towers, and dreaming of what it must have been like to live in a castle. Imagine how impressed they were when we told them you can rent part of the castle for holidays. But you only have to pay the entrance fee to enjoy the fabulous views out to sea from the towers, the great hall and chapel.

Open Easter–September, daily, 10.30am–5.30pm; October–Easter, weekends and October half term holidays, 10.30am–5.30pm. Admission adults £3.50, children £1.50, OAPs £2.50. Amenities café, shop.

Freshwater East

A good family beach, with plenty of parking, beach shops and cafes. The wide, sandy beach is east-facing (Freshwater West is over the other side of the headland) and therefore sheltered from the prevailing westerly winds. You can walk east along the cliff top to Swanlake, an isolated and much more beautiful beach with firm sand and interesting rock pools. This can also be accessed through Swanlake Farm, where a field is used as a car park in summer. The farm has accommodation and tea rooms, which also serve Sunday lunch.

Stackpole Quay

B4319 south of Pembroke, following signs through Stackpole village.

A small sand and pebble beach and a little quay where a few boats might also be tied up, looked after by the National Trust. But the picturesque spot is only a starting point. There's the Stackpole Estate to explore, the splendid Barafundle Bay, a 15-minute walk along the cliffs, and a wonderful café near the quay.

Stackpole Estate ★★ ALL AGES

Old Home Farm Yard, Stackpole, nr Pembroke, Pembrokeshire SA71 5DQ, 📞 *01646 661359, www.national trust.org.uk/stackpole*

This is a delightful National Trust property that's basically the grounds of the demolished mansion of Stackpole Court. The land is now part of Stackpole National Nature Reserve and includes beautiful Bosherston Lily Ponds, where you can fish, Stackpole Quay (the starting point for the cliff walk to Barafundle Bay), the sand dunes of Stackpole Warren, and the outstanding beaches at Barafundle Bay and Broadhaven South. Parking is free at Bosherton Lily Park, but £2 at Stackpole Quay and Broad Haven South.

Open all year. Admission free, donations welcome. Amenities car parks, café.

Barafundle Bay

Part of the Stackpole Estate, this is a destination in its own right, being one of the most gorgeous beaches you'll ever find. From the Stackpole car park you first give in and buy the children an ice cream from the NT café and stand by the slipway watching classes of youngsters from activity centres jumping off the quayside. Then it's a steep walk up some steps before emerging on the clifftops for breathtaking views out to sea. The walk is a winner (as long as you've put the football away) before the steps curl down to the tranquil beach which, with its rocks and greenery, could pass for somewhere in *Pirates of the Caribbean*.

INSIDER TIP ▶

It can get crowded at Barafundle Bay, so try arriving late afternoon and you can relax as the throng drifts away, enjoying the balmy sun at what is often the nicest time of day.

Broad Haven South

A wonderful, wide, sandy beach, backed by dunes and with interesting rock formations and cliffs at either end – not to be confused with the far more commercial Broad Haven in St Bride's Bay. There's a big National Trust car park at the top of the cliffs with a beach shop and toilets. You can walk west along the

Barafundle Bay is one of the most perfect in Pembrokeshire

coastal path to St Govan's Chapel, a tiny medieval church built half way down the cliff. There are 52 steps cut into the rock face to get down to the 13th-century church, built where the 6th-century hermit St Govan once lived. It is said King Arthur's knight Sir Gawain is buried under the stone altar, and that water from the well (now dry) could cure rheumatism, eye and skin diseases.

Freshwater West

A wild, uncrowded beach with miles of sand backed by dunes. Swimming is too dangerous because of powerful rip currents, but it's a serious surfing beach.

West Angle Bay

A small, sandy bay, good for swimming and with a car park only yards from the beach.

Pembroke

A very pretty county town, and a nice place to visit although you're unlikely to want to stay here too long with the children. There's one main street with plenty of shops, restaurants and inns, which are, as we say, charming. Main attraction is Pembroke Castle, where the Tudor dynasty began (daily, April–Sept 9.30am–6pm; March and Oct 10am–5pm; Nov–Feb, 10am–4pm, adults £3.50, child £2.50, under 5s free, family £10. ☎ 01646 684585; www. pembrokecastle.co.uk), centrally located on Main Street. The Norman fortress has been impressively restored and even children who've visited more castles than they've had hot dinners feel the grandeur of the place. The huge, round keep, 23m high with 5.5m thick walls, is topped by a dome. There are

A New Kind Of Holiday Village

Bluestone is a great example of how family holidays in Wales have come on in leaps and bounds – yet respect the past. Sweeping across two woodland vales in Pembrokeshire Coast National Park, the brand new holiday resort manages to be both cutting edge eco-friendly, luxurious and nicely quaint. More than 350 lodges, cottages and studios (two to six bedroom) are built from local, sustainable materials, have solar panels to heat water and triple glazing. Yet the village centre looks like an historic hamlet, with little shops including a butcher's (with locally-sourced meat) and a baker's. A pub rubs shoulders with a plush spa, plus restaurants and a sports club. There's a children's club and nanny service, along with cycle hire, forest craft lessons and much more. Beaches are a short drive. A highlight is the Blue Lagoon, indoor and outdoor water park designed to look like a massive upturned coracle with the UK's largest indoor wave rider, flumes, rivers, pools hot tubs and wooden walkways, all heated by the same biomass plant which serves the main resort buildings. Bluestone guests get free access but the Blue Lagoon is open to the general public. *www.bluestone wales.com, www.bluelagoonwales.com*

towers, battlements, dark passageways and oak-beamed halls to engage the whole family. The nearby Tourist Information Centre is a place where children can design a heraldry shield, unlock the secrets of Black Bart's Treasure Chest, or complete a work sheet. There are also interesting models of the town down the ages and an imaginative interactive exhibition on the Pembrokeshire Coast Path.

Several miles north is Pembroke Dock, a separate town with some smart Victorian buildings, all built on a grid around the naval dockyard that closed in 1926. It's an area that's worth a browse, and there are striking views over the boats and Daugleddau River from Hobbs Point. The Gun Tower Museum,

a never-used 19th-century defence post (AprilSept, 10am4pm, adult £2, child £1, family £5 *www.pembrokedock. co.uk*) has exhibitions on the dockyard and town. The Rosslare ferry leaves twice daily, to Ireland, but the four-hour journey means it's more than a day trip. Neyland, on the other side of the Cleddau Bridge from Pembroke, has a beach along with impressive marina and waterfront development called Brunel Quay. It's a major sailing and watersports centre, has a waterside café, prom and picnic area, along with views of the bridge and the busy river traffic.

The estuary upriver from Pembroke is a charming place, known as the Secret Waterway, with a number of little beach and waterfront spots. The adjoining villages of Llangwm and Black Tar are both good for boating and watersports. Lawrenny and, in particular Lawrenny Quay (with pub and the Quayside café), are gorgeous places to start woodland walks. Several miles away is Creswell Quay, with lovely riverside strolls and the family-friendly Cresselly Arms pub.

Carew

This is a peaceful riverside village six and a half kilometres from Pembroke with an ancient Celtic Cross, a romantic ruined castle and restored tidal mill, plus plenty of picnic spots and grassy areas for children to tear around. The 11th-century cross is 4m tall and one of the best in Wales, while the castle, originally Norman, is a picturesque Elizabethan confection, including a walled herb garden and lovely walks.

Castle and mill open daily April– November, 10am–5pm. Family tickets for both are £8, adults £3, children £2. People arriving by public transport or bicycle get in free. The castle is also open daily during the winter from 11am–3pm (01646 651782, www.carewcastle.com).

Narberth

Good independent shops and a relaxed atmosphere make Narberth an ideal place to get away from holiday crowds. There are several art galleries in town and good exhibitions by

Pembrokeshire artists at Oriel Queens Hall, in the High Street (℡ *01834 861212*). Children, however, will probably be more impressed with the town's proximity to several of Pembrokeshire's most popular tourist attractions.

Oakwood Theme Park ★
ALL AGES

Canaston Bridge, Narberth, SA67 8DE, ℡ 01834 861889, www. oakwoodthemepark.co.uk. Off the A40 at Canaston Bridge, 13km east of Haverfordwest.

The only theme park in Wales, maybe not up there with the likes of Alton Towers, but rated one of the UK's Top 10. For bigger children there are a couple of seriously good rollercoasters, the state-of-the-art Speed, which climbs vertically, plunges, corkscrews and loops, and Megafobia, a traditional clackety-clack wooden monster. Ours loved the

Smugglers Island, Oakwood Theme Park

Snake River Falls waterslide, the Bobsleigh sledge ride and the Treetops Coaster. Lots for younger children too – rides, roundabouts, Techniquest science room and the like. Set in pleasingly landscaped country grounds, there are buses from Tenby and Swansea in high season – see website for details. Only 200 yards from the park entrance is Oakwood's Family Entertainment Centre, with ten pin bowling and the Crystal Maze – open all year.

Open March 31–September 30, 10am–5pm (August, until 10pm). *Admission* standard (age 10 and up) £14.75, junior (3–9) £13.50, OAPs £10, under 3s free, families £53. There's a 15% online discount if you book at least 3 days in advance. *Credit* MC, V. *Amenities* cafés, shops, free parking.

INSIDER TIP ▶▶

Go to Oakwood on a Friday – park bosses say it's always quieter as Saturday is changeover day for weekly holidaymakers, and they're all putting their cozzies back in the suitcase. It certainly worked for us with pleasingly short queues in mid-August.

Folly Farm Adventure Park & Zoo ★★ ALL AGES FIND

Begelly, Kilgetty, Pembrokeshire, SA68 0XA 📞 *01834 812731, www. folly-farm.co.uk. At St.Clears roundabout on A40 take A477 to Tenby, then A478 road for Narberth.*

We were, to be honest, a bit sceptical of the wimpy name, but our children loved this place (better than Oakwood), and we did too. Pembrokeshire World of

Goats might have been a more apt name – although not very snappy. There were goats everywhere – in the big shed for petting and feeding, in pens alongside llamas as we went past on the tractor-drawn train, and in pens near more exotic creatures such as the Brazilian tapirs, bongos (forest antelope), racoons and spiny porcupines. Both zoo and farm were excellent, but there was more. A mammoth modern barn housed the biggest undercover vintage fairground in Europe alongside an up-to-the-roof climbing adventure with walkways and slides. Adults could watch from coffee bar or pub. And out towards the zoo was the best adventure play equipment we've seen, beautifully constructed wooden pirate ships, one split asunder and sinking into the ground. Folly Farm is a pretty place to walk with something new to look at

Folly Farm Adventure Park and Zoo

around every corner – and the children made their visit last as long as they could.

Open Saturday–Sunday, December– mid March (daily during February half-term), 10am–4pm, then daily – until 5.30 up to July; 6pm, August, 5pm, September, 4pm, November, December. *Admission* adults £6.95, children 3–15, OAPs £5.95, under 3s free. *Credit* MC, V. *Amenities* cafés, shops, parking, disabled access.

Haverfordwest

An interesting old market town and an important port until the railways arrived in the late 19th century, Haverfordwest has an impressive ruined castle, some fine Georgian buildings, and a museum. From our family's point of view though, it's best remembered for the giant super-market on the roundabout near the road to St David's, a place where you can stock up with burgers for the camp site barbie well after other shops have closed. If you're not out at the beach, like we always were, there are plenty of other places to shop here. The indoor Riverside Market (Mon–Sat), built on stilts and overlooking the River Cleddau, has everything from food to pets, and a little café with river views. Across the pretty footbridge is Riverside Quay, a car-free spot with big High Street names. The quaint streets here are overlooked by the ruins of Haverfordwest Castle. The former prison in the grounds features artefacts, including leg irons and part of a cell door and the adjoining

museum has a painting of the castle by Sir William Pitt. (£1, OAPs, £0.50, children free, *www.haverfordwest-town-museum. org.uk.*)

Marloes Peninsula

Fewer holidaymakers head for this far flung corner compared with the beaches around Tenby and St David's, which is great for those of us who want to keep this area to ourselves, though, Dale is well-known among the yachty crowd and on a sunny, summer weekend has a friendly, jolly atmosphere. The town beach is shingly and full of boats and water sports enthusiasts, so if you want sand head to West Dale Bay, one and a half kilome-tres west of the village on the other side of the peninsula. You have to walk down a footpath near privately-owned Dale Castle, then down steep steps, so it's not the most family-friendly. Also, swimming is dangerous when the tide's going out because of undertows. The next beach is Marloes Sands – our favourite beach in Wales (although Mwnt is a close second). The walk through fields from the National Trust car park may put people off, but it's all part of the attrac-tion to us. The children love spotting wild flowers and butter-flies and looking out for a first glimpse of the beach. If the tide is out the beach is simply breath-taking – a large expanse of firm sand with some soft stuff at the top and jagged, layered cliffs with matching outcrops of rock sticking at an angle out of the sand like shark teeth. One of our fondest memories is nestling in alcoves among the cliffs on a warm but cloudy day, with the beach all to ourselves, cooking sausages on a portable gas stove – miles better than any Mediterranean experience. There's also a good youth hostel here.

At the western end of the beach you can walk out to Gateholm Island at low tide, where Iron Age artefacts have been found. Further west, at Martin's Haven, you can get a boat from the harbour over to Skomer Island from spring until autumn, every day except Mondays. Contact Dale Sailing on 📞 01646 603123, www. pembrokeshireislands.co.uk. Once there you can visit the National Nature Reserve, home to all kinds of birds – including the fabulous Puffin – but you need to take your own food and drink.

St Bride's Bay

A great curve of coast, which extends 48km from Wooltack Point, south-west of Haverford-west, to St David's. Here you'll find pretty little seaside towns with hills rising up behind them, and beaches bookended by cliffs. There's picturesque Little Haven and busy Broad Haven, with its wide open beach, seafront shops, cafes and pubs. The beach at Druidston is sandy and unspoilt, but parking is limited to the sides of the coast road, so arrive

early. The only access is along two paths to the cliff tops then a steep climb down. There's a fab-ulous family hotel and restaurant here, the Druidston (p 147). Access to sandy Nolton Haven is easier. There's a car park, beach shops and cafes, then you come to the pride of St Bride's: Newgale, a beach that will be forever loved, certainly by our family. Here the A487 from Haverfordwest to St David's hits the coast, plunging down the hill into a heavenly vista with cliffs rising at either end. The flat, perfect sand stretches for five kilometres and the road squeezes between it and the Sands Café, a pub, a couple of shops and a busy campsite, which can resemble a pop festival in high season. There's a pay car park (free parking for the café). We've been here a number of times and it's never less than magical – sometimes in the morning the cliffs are shrouded in a light sea mist, sunlight filtering through the haze. By late afternoon the west-facing skies are awash with gold. And no matter how busy it gets (and it's limited by the park-ing) there's plenty of room for everyone to set up camp, play cricket or football, bodyboard or surf.

Solva

This one-street village with picturesque harbour and small boaty beach has transformed itself over past decades. Most of the buildings are painted in technicolour shades – a bit

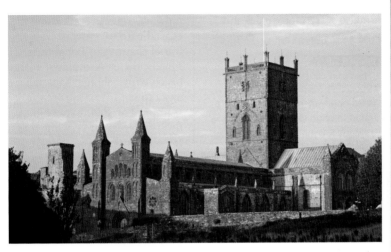

St David's Cathedral, St David's

garish but a huge improvement on the dun-coloured buildings of the past. It is a bit of a yachty tourist trap, with most shops selling things you don't really need. But you'll also find good pubs, cafes and restaurants, a 100-year-old woollen mill, and collectable art at Simon Swinfield's gallery (📞 *01437 721114*).

St David's

This is a bit of a disorientating place, as instinct tells you this should be a seaside spot – or at least a cliff-top eyrie. In fact it's a rather packed, small town. Its main (and almost only) street is awash with tourists in the summer, looking for something to do, or somewhere to park. There's a goodly selection of restaurants, cafes and bars, and shops selling surf gear, but little else to do except visit its raison d'etre: St David's Cathedral (*www.stdavidscathedral.org.uk*;

cadw.wales.gov.uk). It's beautiful and contains lots of gleaming ecclesiastical relics, but is not a must-see for youngsters when they can sense the sea is close. It's free to visit, although a £3 donation is suggested; tours are £4/£1.20. For us, a walk up and down the road outside was enough. St David's is, however, a place for boat trips, which mostly go from Whitesands Bay a couple of kilometres away. Voyages of Discovery (*www.ramseyisland.co.uk*, 📞 *01437 721911*) and Thousand Island Expeditions (*www.thousand islands.co.uk*, 📞 *01437 721721*) both specialise in voyages around the RSPB reserve of Ramsey Island with its seabird colonies and hundreds of seals. Only 40 people a day are allowed on to the rugged, cliff-ringed island, and they go with Thousand Island. Other trips scoot among islands packed with puffins and gannets, while you can also search for whales and porpoises.

Whitesands Bay

This is St David's most popular local beach although there are a few more hidden among the cliffs. To get here go west from the city on the A487 then left on the B4583. This is a very wide, very popular beach and very crowded in summer. Swimming is largely safe and there are sand dunes to play in, a large car park, beach shops and cafes. Backtracking east along the coast you'll find a rocky cove at St Justinian's, also known as Porthstinan, where there's a small car park and lifeboat station. St David's other main beach is further east at Caerfai, a lovely sandy beach which you get to by turning left off the A487 from Solva just past the city's main car park. The beaches north of Whitesands Bay are mostly small and hard to get to, often with slate-grey shingle turning to sand as the tide goes out. Abereiddy is one of the more accessible, and a good place to search for fossils. A slate quarry at the northern end of the beach has been flooded to form the Blue Lagoon. Next is Abercastle, a tiny beach, and a port until the arrival of the

railways. You can walk along the coastal path to a prehistoric burial chamber at Longhouse. Finally, there's Abermawr, a large beach with a shingle bank falling away to sand. You can see the stumps of an 8,000-year-old drowned forest at very low tide. It's not easy to get to though: a single track signposted off the main A487 takes you to the beach, but parking is on the verge – so a bit tight.

Fishguard

A complicated place for such a small town: the centre of Fishguard is on a cliff top, with the main road carrying on down to pretty Lower Town, a tumbling tangle of streets dropping towards the sea and Old Port. Meanwhile Goodwick, once a village and now an extension of Fishguard, is back towards Strumble Head. Here you'll find a sandy beach, promenade and the ferry terminal to Rosslare, in Ireland. Here fast ferries take just two hours for the crossing, so day trips are possible (☏ 08705 421126, www.stenaline.co.uk). Lower Town, where the 1970s film of Dylan Thomas's *Under Milk Wood* was made, is a pretty place to pop into with its picturesque setting at the mouth of the River Gwaun and its wooded valley. Little boats bob and you can walk up the hill to the old fort for fab views. Goodwick has all the shops and usual amenities of a seaside village, including the Fishguard Bay Hotel, a stylish coastal property that was once a

Great Western Railway hotel. Goodwick beach – sand and shingle – is a charming spot, with its green, tree-lined backdrop. There's plenty of parking and you can visit Ocean Lab (daily April–Oct, 9.30–5pm/6pm summer holidays, Nov–March 10am–4pm, free, ☎ 01348 874737) a child-friendly look at marine life led by Ollie the Octopus, with soft play area (under 5s), cyber café and tourist office. Fishguard is famed for the last invasion of Britain, when French troops landed nearby in 1797. Cobbler's wife Jemima Nicholas was the 'Welsh Heroine' who nabbed many invaders single-handed. The French negotiated their surrender at the Royal Oak Inn and laid down their arms on the beach. The bizarre incident is commemorated in a Bayeaux Tapestry-style creation on show in the Town Hall.

Lota Park is a good place for children to play. Nearby is Strumble Head, a high, windy spot, the nearest point to Ireland, where you get great views of passing ferries as well as the lighthouse, which sits across a tiny footbridge (not open to the public) on the tiny rocky isle of Ynys Meicel.

Dyfed Shires & Leisure Farm ALL AGES

Carnhuan, Eglwyswrw, SA41 3SY ☎ *01239 891288, www.leisurefarm. co.uk. A487/B4329 junction, 1.2km south of Eglwyswrw, on Fishguard-Cardigan road.*

Here you can see mighty Shire horses, daily dolled up in brassy finery and after the children tire of gawping you can entertain them with all sorts of indoor and outdoor play activities from slides to quad bikes and the dreaded crazy golf.

Open Easter–Oct 31, days vary but mostly Mon–Sat, 10.30am–5pm. Admission: adults £5, children 2–15/OAPs £4, under 2s free. Credit MC, V. Amenities café, shop, free parking, indoor and outdoor picnic areas, disabled access.

Dinas Head

This is one of the most beautiful stretches of the Pembrokeshire Coastal Path and older children might be interested in the chance to explore some of the tiny secret coves around what is known locally as Dinas Island. You can park by the beach at Pwllgwaelod, which is just a few miles north of Fishguard (take the A487 and turn left to Bryn Henllan). The beach has greyish sand with wonderful rock pools for children to explore. There's a footpath suitable for buggies that crosses the head for just over a kilometre through Cwm Dewi to link Pwllgwaelod with another small beach, Cwm-yr-Eglwys. This is much smaller, but east-facing – so sheltered if the wind's blowing from the west. The cliffs are low and wooded, with easy to get at rock pools, and reddish sand. It's about four kilometres around the coastal path between the two beaches. There are also the remains of a storm-battered church, and in the spring the woods are carpeted with bluebells.

Newport

Families return to Newport year after year, not just for the beautiful coastal scenery but also the town's growing reputation as a food-lover's holiday destination. You can get organic bread daily at Hughes Bakers, locally grown or produced goods from Wholefood of Newport, and excellent but simple meals and good coffee at the Canteen in Market Street. Newport also has a strong sense of being Celtic, there's a small Neolithic burial chamber near the bridge across the River Nevern. But it's the countryside that really draws families back – and in particular Newport Sands. It's the best beach in north Pembrokeshire, and the sands stretch for miles across the river. At low tide you can walk over from Parrog, the town's small, shingly beach, but it's safest to drive around to the huge car park at Newport Sands then let the children loose to run wild for as far as they can see.

Poppit Sands

The last beach in Pembrokeshire before you cross into Cardiganshire (Ceredigion), and one of the few accessible beaches after Newport Sands, Poppit Sands is a similarly massive, flat expanse, thanks to its position at the mouth of the River Teifi – perfect for cricket and rounders. The beach is backed by sand dunes, with striking views across to Cardiganshire's cliffs. To find it turn off the A487 just south of

Cardigan on to the B4546 and meander through narrow village roads – including historic St Dogmaels, where the Pembrokeshire Coast Path officially starts – until you arrive at the seashore where you'll find people cramming cars on the verge to avoid the £4 parking fee. If you're staying a few hours it's reasonable, though, and the children loved the openness, which, depending on how you view it, can be rather breezy – or great for kite-flying. You can often see porpoises, seals and dolphins here, too. There are toilets and a scout hut-style café with home-made cakes. The beach is on the Poppit Rocket bus service which links Cardigan and Newport.

Preseli Hills

Although not in the same league as Snowdonia or the Brecon Beacons, the Preseli Hills are worth a look, if only because children will love The Lord of the Rings-style feel. There's the 'bleeding yew' at St Brynach Church, in Nevern, which oozes reddish sap, and will continue to do so – according to legend – until a Welsh prince takes command at Nevern Castle. Unfortunately the castle is just an overgrown mound now. The churchyard also has a beautifully-carved 4m high Celtic cross.

Just south of Nevern is the largest exposed Neolithic burial mound in Wales – an amazing sight. Pentre Ifan is like a scene out of Narnia, where you might expect to see Aslan roar at any

Pentre Ifan in the Preseli Hills is the largest exposed Neolithic burial mound in Wales

minute. It is believed to date back to 3,500BC. The bluestones of Stonehenge were carved out of these hills at Carn Menyn, thought to be a covered burial chamber. Nearby is the Golden Road, a Neolithic sunken lane, which was once a major trade route. Now it's a lovely walk and will take you to the 13 standing stones known as Beddarthur – or Arthur's Grave.

Castell Henllys Iron Age Fort ★ ALL AGES

Meline, near Crymych, SA41 3UT, 📞 *01239 891319, www.castell henllys.com. Just off A487 between Newport and Cardigan.*

If your children love standing stones and burial chambers they'll probably like this reconstruction of a real Iron Age fort, too. Authentic thatched roundhouses have been built on the exact site of the originals – providing a real-scale reconstruction of a hillside fort 2,000 years ago. There's a smithy, grain store,

animal quarters and a chieftain's house, as well as a modern exhibition centre telling the story of the people who used to live here. The children can also inspect the site of an archaeological dig and explore a sculpture trail.

Open April–Oct, daily, 10am–5pm; Nov–March, Mon–Fri, 11am–3pm. *Closed late Dec–early Jan.* *Admission adults £3, children £2, family £8; winter admission £2.* *Amenities shop.*

Newcastle Emlyn

This lively market town features interesting old buildings, not least the ruined 13th-century castle where the last dragon in Wales is said to have been killed. Much of the castle was destroyed during the Civil War in 1648, but it's still good for scrambling around, and there are picnic tables in the grounds and a path beside the River Teifi. The river runs through the town on its way to Cardigan Bay, and further downriver is Cenarth Gorge and its famous waterfalls, where traditional coracles are still used. Here you can visit The National Coracle Centre (01239 710980, www.coracle-centre.co.uk) and a clutch of craft shops and cafes. A few miles away, at Abercych, children might like to see organic cheese being made at Glyneithinog Farm. Caws Cenarth Cheese (01239 710432, www.cawscenarth.co.uk) open Mon–Sat, 9am–5pm, and free. Even Prince Charles has been there. Also near Castle Emlyn is the National Wool Museum (01559 370929, www. museumwales.ac.uk), in the village of Dre-fach Felindre, off the A484. Housed in restored mill buildings it has a wonderful collection of Welsh blankets, shawls and costume. Families can follow a special Woolly Tale trail and children can have a go at carding, spinning and sewing. It's a lovely museum, with coffee shop and picnic area – and it's free too.

Teifi Valley Railway ★ ALL AGES

Henllan, Newcastle Emlyn, SA44 5TD, 01559 371077, www.teifivalley railway.com. On B4334 Llangranof-Carmarthen road, just south of A475 junction.

The railway offers a charming journey beside the Teifi River for 3.2km between Henllan and Newcastle Emlyn, along what, in the 19th century, was going to be a Carmarthen-Cardigan line but never reached the latter. Steam and diesel locos serve several intermediary stations on the narrow gauge line. Your ticket lets you ride all day, so you can hop off and explore woodland walks to see the waterfalls, have a picnic, play free crazy golf or quoits and get ice creams from the tearooms.

Open April–Oct, mostly daily but usually closed Fri except in summer holidays. Call to check. Christmas service some days in Dec. Tickets (pay once, ride all day): adults £5.50, OAPs £5, children £3.50, disabled children £3. Under 3s free. Family tickets £16, dogs £0.50. Amenities café, gift shop, railway charity shop, toilets, picnic tables, free crazy golf and quoits, disabled access, free parking.

For Active Families

West Wales is full of centres where you can climb, sail, run and jump. And while many might on the surface seem more suitable for Outward Bound types, there are lots of family options to explore from a day to two weeks.

Sealyham Activity Centre
AGES 8 AND UP

Wolfscastle, Haverfordwest, SA62 5NF, 01348 840763, www. sealyham.com. On A40, halfway between Haverfordwest and Fishguard.

This no-frills centre in grounds of Sealyham Hall offers specialist courses in surfing, kayaking, climbing (and that team building stuff), but also has a family option. You (minimum of eight people, age 8 and up) stay in hostel-style accommodation and can fit a session of each of the three activities daily, or others such as mountain biking, dinghy sailing and coasteering (scrambling along the coast). It's knockabout stuff which brings everyone together. The centre offers daily non-residential variable activity packages for 8-16 year olds in spring/summer holidays (£30).

Open variable, year-round. Prices one day full board £36, plus £20 per activity, per day. Amenities tuck shop, recreation room, extensive gardens, woodland, river and lakeside walks.

Heritage Canoes ★
AGES 3 AND UP

Teifi Marshes Nature Reserve, Cilgerran, Pembrokeshire, SA43 2TB, ☎ 01239 613961, www.cardiganbay active.co.uk. Turn off A478 at Pen-y-Bryn, south of Cardigan, and follow brown Wildlife Centre signs.

Proper Canadian canoes, like out of a '50s American movie, take you along the River Teifi through the Cilgerran Gorge and nature reserve, a spot unnavigable by powered craft. Guides help you spot otter tracks (sometimes even otters) as well as herons, cormorants, dragonflies and salmon, then get you ready for the gentle rapids at the end of the two-hour journey.

Heritage Canoes also links with Adventure Beyond, to form Cardigan Bay Active, which offers an array of activities on and off water. There is kayaking in the gorge, sea kayaking, climbing and coasteering (clambering and splashing along the coastline), all around £30, from age 10.

Open year-round Tickets: adults and unaccompanied children £25, children under 14 £15, families £75 Credit MC, V. Amenities parking.

Pembrokeshire Activity Centre
★ AGES 8 AND UP

Cleddau River Centre, Cleddau Reach, Pembroke Dock, SA72 6UJ, ☎ 01646 622013, www.princes-trust.org.co.uk. Pembroke Dock, just off A477.

A purpose-built £2.5m centre created in conjunction with the Prince's Trust with £500,000 of equipment and up to 30 instructors is more geared to schools and groups of youngsters, but age is no limit (as long as you're at least eight), and families can book along with anyone else for courses (mostly one and two days) in sailing, canoeing, kayaking, climbing and more. There's smart accommodation in a pair of large 'houses' with plenty of bedrooms, used for groups year-round, with public bookings at weekends and during holiday periods.

Open year-round. Prices 1 day kayaking, £70. Amenities café, climbing wall, showers, changing rooms, disabled access, common rooms, football play areas.

Llys Y Fran cycle route ★★★
AGES 7 AND UP VALUE

Llys Y Fran Country Park, Haverfordwest, Pembrokeshire, ☎ 01437 532273/532694, www.cycle pembrokeshire.com. On B4329, 16km north west of Haverfordwest.

A delightful 11km off-road family bike trail around the Llys Y Fran reservoir is great for youngsters as

Pembrokeshire Coast National Park

The Pembrokeshire Coast National Park is as hard to get your head around as it is your feet. It's effectively a coastal strip which encompasses the Pembrokeshire Coastal Path, a 300km walk that takes in an inspiring landscape of cliffs, beaches, wooded estuaries, dramatic hills and peaceful wildlife havens. The Park, and Path, starts in the east at Amroth, just before you get to Tenby, and (after an inland diversion around an MoD site) gets almost as far as Pembroke Dock. The Path continues, crosses the Cleddau Bridge over Milford Haven (the estuary) and heads west again. Just the other side of Milford Haven (the town) it rejoins the Park where it skirts the headland, with views over to wild Skomer Island then heads up along stunning cliff tops, past St David's and Fishguard all the way to St Dogmaels just before you get to Cardigan. Between Fishguard and Cardigan the Park swells out to encompass the lovely Preseli Hills, while there's an unconnected riverside section just in from Pembroke.

The Path is a mammoth undertaking, and even committing yourself to part of it requires time and effort. But the great thing from a family perspective is that it really is a path that follows the coast, so you only have to park the car and you can take a stroll through scenery that's up there with anywhere in the world. Rugged stretches that slow down serious hikers are like adventure playgrounds to young children. Sometimes you're on cliff tops (like skirting Barafundle Bay in the south), sometimes you're on the beachside (such as Newgale Sands as you get towards St David's).

Elsewhere are views of gorgeous inlets leading to peaceful beaches, dark smugglers caves, and spectacular natural formations such as the Green Bridge of Wales (near Bosherston, just west of Barafundle), a natural rock arch shaped by the sea. There are lonely islands, like monastic Caldey Island or uninhabited Skokholm and Skomer, which are home to colonies of a wide variety of birds, rare flowers and wildlife. And chances are you'll even see seals.

As you walk you see the ancient footprint of humans – Norman castles, Celtic crosses, medieval churches, abandoned quarries and lively quays.

the path is wide enough for two abreast, chatting. Offering a mostly solid, even surface, there are a couple of spots for a muddy dash. Sometimes you're by the water's edge, sometimes you dart into the woods and along little valleys with tree-lined streams. There are some ups and downs, but the well-maintained path means most youngsters should be able to handle it. Bikes can be hired at the café at the park entrance, or ride your own for £1. The park, with imposing dam and grassy banks, is great for picnics.

Open year-round. Prices entry free, bike hire variable, ride-your-own £1. There are also boats for hire.
Amenities shop, visitor centre, angling (with equipment for disabled).

VenjureJet ★ ★ ALL AGES

Llanon, Trefin, SA62 5AE, ☎ 08000 854786, www.venturejet.com

These boat trips, mostly from Whitesands Bay near St David's are more than just a pleasure cruise. The fast jet-propelled dinghy-like boats whiz you out to see seals, cliff-nesting birds and porpoises, sometimes even whales, as well as nipping you into caves. No age limit, but not really for younger children. Jet Therapy (14 and over) gets you wet with lots of handbrake turns.

Open Variable, year-round. Prices 90-minute trip, adults £20, children under 14 £12. Jet Therapy (1 hour) £18

FAMILY-FRIENDLY ACCOMMODATION

Pembrokeshire is getting to be seriously chic, so there are some smart hotels and an awful lot of upmarket holiday cottages and apartments. An awful lot of camp sites too – many of which are discreet and charming. Before you book you just need to beware of the huge caravan parks that litter some areas.

EXPENSIVE

Atlantic Hotel

The Esplanade, Tenby, SA70 7DU, ☎ 01834 842881, www.atlantic-hotel.uk.com

This grand old hotel looks out over the sea from Tenby's cliff-top seafront, with views of sweeping South Beach, Caldey Island, Castle Hill and the island fort of St Catherine. There are stylish but unfussy rooms, an indoor pool (plus whirlpool and steam room), the old world charm of Carrington's restaurant (with good children's menu) and a comfy lounge. Parents can relax in the sea-facing gardens while youngsters play safely on the beach.

42 rooms. From £102 double. Babies under two £9.50, age 2–4 £12.50, 5–10 £20, 11–15 £25.50. Amenities: 2 restaurants, bar, car park. In room: radio, TV, tea maker.

Fishguard Bay Hotel ★

Quay Road, Goodwick, SA64 0BT, ☎ 01348873571, www.bayhotelfishguard.co.uk

Big imposing place set in woodland with fab sea views and access to coastal walks. Big, comfy rooms

60 rooms. From £80 double. Extra beds £25, cots £10, for duration. Amenities restaurant, bar, car park. In room: TV, tea maker.

MODERATE

Druidstone ★ ★

Broad Haven, Pembrokeshire, SA62 3NE, ☎ 01437 781221, www.druidstone.co.uk. Take B4341 from Haverfordwest to Broad Haven, turn right to Nolton. Take second Nolton turn, then follow signs to Druidston Haven.

This family retreat is set amid huge, wild gardens on the grassy cliffs above the beach of Druidston Haven, just outside Broad Haven on St Bride's Bay. The stone house, dating from 1850, is part hotel, part chummy holiday home welcoming not only children but pets. Some of the hotel rooms have en-suites, some don't, and there are cottages converted from stables and outbuildings sleeping up to 10. Hotel rates are B&B (breakfasts include St Bride's Bay mackerel and organic black pudding). The restaurant is highly rated and heavy on organics and local seafood, a place that attracts far more than residents. There's children's high tea at 6 (£4), a varying menu of favourites but with a healthy edge, taken at a massive table in the former farmhouse kitchen (which doubles as a private dining room). This would be a great place for an extended family get-together, with the option of a set meal (12+) or buffet (25+).

There's also a sitting room, TV room and cellar bar. The place has been run since the early '70s by former hippy types Rod and Jane Bell and irregular musical events still happen, including appearances by Rod's ex-flatmate Andy Davis, who had hits with the Korgis and whose '70s band Stackridge, recently reformed, play engaging music that our Georgia sings along to in the car.

You can walk down to the beach with its caves and rocks, stroll along the Pembrokeshire Coast Path, or hop on the Puffin Shuttle bus to St David's or Marloes Sands.

11 rooms, 7 cottages. Double from £68 per night; cottages, self-catering, from £315 per week. If sharing, age 3 and under free, then £5–8 depending on age. **Amenities** *restaurant, bar, car park.* **In room** *TV, tea maker.*

Caerfai Farm ★

St David's, Pembrokeshire, SA62 6QD, ☎ 01437 720548, www.caws caerfai.co.uk. Turn left at junction as A487 enters St David's from Haverfordwest.

Organic farm (their milk makes Gianni's ice cream and they make cheese on site) with accommodation that would be organic if it could be (the farm is hoping to install a wind generator to power the whole place). Four cottages (two converted from stables and granary with exposed beams), with a wealth of stone and wood, sleep between two and six, with the option of an extra cot in each. Then there's the simple camp site with sea views (Caerfai Bay, 200m away), with shower block. Cottages and campers share a farm shop and St David's is up the road.

Cottages £230–450 per week (2 bed) up to £295–850 (6 bed). Short breaks available out of season. Camp site, £6.50 pp per night, children £3. Cottages open all year, camp site Whitsun-late Sept. **Amenities** *farm shop.* **In cottages** *full kitchen, TV, open fire or stove.*

INEXPENSIVE

Moreton Farm

Moreton, near Saundersfoot, SA69 9EA, ☎ 01834 812016, www.moreton farm.co.uk. On the A478 heading south, several kilometres before Tenby.

Pleasing camping and caravan site in a secluded setting is a kilometre's walk (down a tree-lined footpath) from the beach delights of Saundersfoot. Apart from the simple, grassy spaces for bring-your-own accommodation, there's also a selection of two-bedroom (sleeping six) Pine Lodges, and three cottages and the original farmhouse, sleeping 4/6. The place is far enough from the village crowds to feel like a real getaway, and the children liked the walk (even if the uphill return can be a slog). Lots of room for fun, with play area and climbing frame.

*Lodges and cottages £170–235 for 3-night weekend or Mon-Thurs, £220–505 for a week. Prices include sofa beds and bed linen. Tent/camper/caravan + 2 people, £12–15 per night, extra child or adult £2. **Amenities** Launderette, shop, play area, modern toilet and shower blocks. **In lodges/cottages:** fitted kitchen, TV.*

Manorbier Youth Hostel

Manorbier, SA70 7TT, 0870 770 5954, www.yha.org.uk. Take B4585 towards Manorbier, turn left by Skrinkle housing estate and follow YHA signs.

A strangely modern-looking youth hostel, but a fairly comfortable one set in its own grounds and only a few hundred yards from the coastal path. The views are exceptional and accommodation includes family rooms with en suite bathrooms. There's good access over the cliffs to Skrinkle Haven and Lydstep Haven as well as Manorbier.

Adults from £14, under 18s from £10 a night.

Marloes Youth Hostel ★

Runwayskiln, Marloes, SA62 3BH, 0870 770 5958, www.yha.org.uk. Follow B4327 from Haverfordwest for 11 miles and turn right to Marloes. At village church turn left to car park. YHA Marloes Sands is down a private track on left approx 200 metres

Several farmhouse buildings have been transformed into comfortable accommodation, but the farmhouse is probably best for families and has three- and four-bed rooms. The setting is fantastic, the sea just a few minutes walk away – and the beaches absolutely glorious. Boat trips to Skomer Island from nearby Martin's Haven.

Adults from £13.95, under 18s from £7.50 a night.

Stackpole Inn

Jasons Corner, Stackpole, SA71 5DF, 01646 672324, www.stackpole inn.co.uk

This family-run pub is a 15-minute stroll from Barafundle Bay with B&B accommodation in separate building in the grounds. There are four double rooms, two with sofa beds. Meals use local fish, seafood and meat (lobster, crab, mackerel, lamb), and there's a decent children's menu for around £5

*4 rooms. Double room £70, plus £10 per child under 13, £15 13 and over (max 4 people). **Amenities** car park.*

Creswell Quay Cottages ★

Creswell Quay, 0870 770 5750, www.cottagesforgroups.com

Centre point is the riverside Mill, a stylish conversion into accommodation for nine (plus a couple of children's z-beds), but with the adjoining three cottages (the Stores, Miller's House and Miller's Cottage) there's accommodation for up to 29 (plus more z-beds), suitable for the biggest family get-together. On the estuary upriver from Pembroke, six and a half kilometres from Oakwood theme park, the nearest beach is 13km, with Tenby and Saundersfoot an easy drive. There's a riverside garden, and a pub nearby. The Cleddau with its wooded banks is ideal for small boats and kayaks, and there are stepping stones across. One of many options from a specialist in large accommodation.

5 bedrooms (The Mill); 15 in total. The Mill from around £500pw; in total from £1,500 (fuel extra Oct–May). **Amenities** *all have full kitchens, barbecues; some have laundry. DVDs, open fires.*

St David's Camping and Caravanning Club Site ★
MOMENT **VALUE**

Dwr Cwmwdig, Berea, St David's, SA62 6DW, 📞 *01348 831376, www. campingandcaravanningclub. co.uk. Take Fishguard road from city, turn left at first sign to Whitesands Bay, ignore second and go several kilometres.*

The evening we sat outside our tent gazing at the sea and sunset with a bottle of wine, barbecue sizzling, as the children played will long stay with us. The site sits on a hilltop an easy drive from St David's (and on a fairly direct route to Haverfordwest) with views over fields, which then drop away to the shore.

Small and friendly (although there's no play area), and the site takes tents, caravans and camper vans. Beach is a mile away.

Low season £4.40 (£2.15), mid season £5.15 (£2.15), high season £6.95 £2.25) per night per adult (child), plus £2.90 pitch fee. **Amenities** *shop/ office, showers, toilets.*

Freshwater East Caravan Club Site ★ VALUE FIND

Trewent Hill, Freshwater East, SA71 5LJ, 📞 *01646 672341 www.caravan club.co.uk. Just off the B4584, turn right into Trewent Hill, then follow club sign.*

Not only is this lovely site minutes from Freshwater East – a safe, sandy beach – it's also only a walk across the cliff from Barafundle Bay, and a short drive from Broad Haven South, Stackpole and Manorbier. The site is tree-lined with both grass and hardstanding pitches. Tents are welcome, and there is a play area.

Low season £4.20 (£1.30), mid season £5.35, peak season £5.50 (£2.15) per night per adult (child), plus pitch fee of £4.70 (low) and £7.10 (peak). There are also saver and value seasons – see website for dates. **Amenities** *shop, showers, toilets, laundry.*

FAMILY-FRIENDLY DINING

From chip shops to stylish restaurants to pubs which welcome children, there's an array of styles and foods that you wouldn't have bargained on a few years back.

Cwtch* ★★★ FIND

22 High Street, St David's, SA62 6SD, ☎ 01437 720491, www.cwtch restaurant.co.uk

Ah, this is the stuff – a place with a children's menu that tempts older children rather than assuming than everyone under 16 wants chicken nuggets. For £6 they can have a selection of things which are, give or take a dollop of chive and garlic butter, adult dishes – lamb brochettes with couscous, various pastas (none of them spag bol) and a 4oz Welsh black rib eye with potatoes (OK, that one has a £1.50 surcharge, but still good for the money). And this is a stylish place, artily informal, the brainchild of a former ad exec (you can tell by the asterisk in the title) with slate and wood floors, blackboard menus and such. The menu is awash with local products – St Bride's Bay sea bass and potted crab, Carmarthen ham, and lots of Welsh cheeses. It's not strictly expensive, with three courses for £26 and wine from £13, but you're not going to get away without buying the children the rich chocolate tart.

*Open April–Oct, Tues–Sun, orders 5.30–10pm. Nov–March, Wed–Sat, orders 6–9.30pm. **Main courses** £15–18.50. **Credit** MC, V.*

MODERATE

The Captain's Table

The Harbour, Saundersfoot, SA69 9HE, ☎ 01834 812435, www.the captainstable.co.uk

Overlooking the sea, this jolly pub-style bar and restaurant features big screen sports indoors, barbecues and live music outdoors. The menu is surprisingly adventurous with fish (plaice, cod, etc) and meat (lamb, duck) in rich sauces, a grill menu (16oz rump steak around £14), and favourites such as curries and pasta. Children can get the usual sausage/burger £2.95), or can move up to a 6oz rump steak (£6.95) or smaller portions of adult dishes such as spag bol or battered cod. There are also lunchtime specials, sandwiches and wraps – eat in or out. There's also a good choice of real ales, and house wine around £8 a bottle.

*Open Daily. **Main courses** £5–15. **Credit** MC, V.*

Pam Pam

2 Tudor Square, Tenby, SA70 7AD, ☎ 01834 842946

At this happy family restaurant adults can enjoy a variety of dishes with a local influence, whether chicken stuffed with leeks and Welsh brie or lamb loin with black pudding, along with Welsh steak and fish, and more obvious dishes such as pasta. The children's menu features lamb chops, pasta, sausages and the like and there are high chairs, booster seats and enough colouring and balloons to keep even the liveliest child happy.

*Open daily, 10am–10pm. **Main courses** £4.50–around £10. **Credit** MC, V.*

Something's Cooking ★ VALUE

The Square, Letterston, SA62 5SB,
📞 *(01348) 840621, www.something cooking.co.uk. Several kilometres outside Haverfordwest on A40 to Fishguard.*

This cheerful chippie-and-more has even had its praises sung by seafood guru Rick Stein when its fish dishes won an award. It's all done with homely panache – children adore the servers in their ties and boaters bringing out vast plates of crispy cod (a respectable £4.99, with chips and tartare sauce). There's plaice, skate, homemade fish and crab cakes, and sometimes halibut and sea bass (you can ask for your fish to be poached), and starters such as whitebait and potted shrimps. There's a selection of reasonably-priced wines too. The £3.85 children's menu includes cod, scampi, chicken burger and sausages, with chips, peas or beans, ice cream with flake and a drink. There are lunchtime specials, and a lunchtime/evening takeaway option with child's cod, chips and drink £1.99.

Open Tues–Sat, 10am–10pm, Mondays July–Aug. Main courses £4.50–10. Credit MC, V.

Fecci & Sons Ice Cream Parlou

Upper Frog Street, Tenby, SA70 7JB,
📞 *01834 842503*

Known locally as Top Geo's, after late founder Geo Fecci, this historic spot serves creamy Italian ices, including lots of old-fashioned sundaes and floats, as well as breakfasts, light lunches, coffee and afternoon tea.

Just around the corner in Lower Frog Street is Fecci's Restaurant (📞 *01834 842484*), a converted coaching inn which is now an excellent fish and chip spot with locally sourced food.

Open Daily, 8am–late afternoon. Credit MC, V.

Sands Cafe ★★

Newgale, St Bride's Bay, SA62 6AS
📞 *01437 729222, www.newsurf.co. uk. Where the A487 from Haverford-west to St David's dips down to the sea.*

It's THE place at big Newgale beach, smart and modern yet with the friendliness of a local café and a clientele that ranges from surfer dudes to parents with babies. Sands has a deck and even a lawn overlooking watermeadows. Food takes in favourites such as fish and chips alongside baguettes (crab, etc), and homemade hummus with pitta bread. Ice cream is Gianni's, made with organic milk from Caerfai Farm (a renowned producer just outside St David's).

Open daily, 9.30am–5pm in winter, earlier and later in summer and holidays. Main courses £5–10. Credit MC, V.

7 Mid Wales

MID WALES

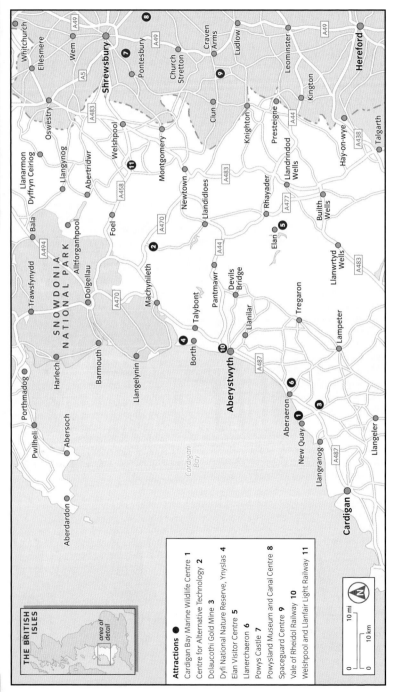

Attractions ●

Cardigan Bay Marine Wildlife Centre **1**
Centre for Alternative Technology **2**
Dolaucothi Gold Mine **3**
Dyfi National Nature Reserve, Ynyslas **4**
Elan Visitor Centre **5**
Llanerchaeron **6**
Powys Castle **7**
Powysland Museum and Canal Centre **8**
Spaceguard Centre **9**
Vale of Rheidol Railway **10**
Welshpool and Llanfair Light Railway **11**

THE BRITISH ISLES

area of detail

0   10 mi
0   10 km

The heartland of Wales is a mystical, magical place of mountains and hills, greenery and gold (or at least old gold mines), not to mention one of the country's finest coastal stretches. There are bustling market towns and quiet villages, often away from the tourist fray, as well as an endless collection of reservoirs, rivers, forests and other places where the young can run free.

The area stretches from the Brecon Beacons National Park in the south to Snowdonia National Park in the north, and to the very edge of the Pembrokeshire Coast National Park in the west. The seaside here starts at Cardigan (just across the estuary from the end of the Pembroke Coast Path) and continues up to the Dyfi estuary, after which you're really in North Wales. There's the gentle wonder of sweeping Cardigan Bay with its holiday towns, such as New Quay with its timeless seaside fun, and the more sedate university town of Aberystwyth. Along this coast are some of the finest beaches in Britain, on what is the UK's first Marine Heritage Coast, a Special Area of Conservation famous for its resident population of dolphins and porpoise.

But you only need to go a handful of miles inland and you find the green and pleasant scenery rising up to the forest-clad Cambrian Mountains that form the backbone of Wales. Further south and you are in the Brecon Beacons, 835 square kilometres of national park – half of it over 300m.

Here you will find the highest mountains in Wales outside Snowdonia, some of the most beautiful waterfalls in the country, the National Show Caves with their impressive stalactites – and miles of countryside made for walking, horse riding, cycling and any other number of outdoor sports. And don't forget the border towns: Welshpool with its markets and Knighton with its long distance footpaths – both Offa's Dyke and The Glendwr Way.

Mid Wales has everything: beaches, mountains, market towns and rolling green countryside. The one thing it doesn't have is the crowds.

ESSENTIALS

Visitor Information

Tourist Information Centres

Visit Carmarthenshire Tourist Board www.visitcarmarthenshire.co.uk

Aberaeron, The Quay, Aberaeron, SA46 0BT, ☎ 01545 570602, E: aberaerontic@ceredigion.gov.uk

Aberystwyth, Terrace Road, Aberystwyth, SY23 2AG, ☎ 01970 612125, E: aberystwythtic@ceredigion.gov.uk

Bala, Penllyn, Pensarn Road, Bala, LL23 7SR, ☎ 01678 521021, E: bala.tic@gwynedd.gov.uk

Borth, High Street, Borth, SY24 5HU, ☎ 01970 871174, E: BorthTIC@ceredigion.gov.uk

Builth Wells, The Groe Car Park, Builth Wells, LD2 3BL, 01082 553 307, E: brectic@ powys.gov.uk

Cardigan, Theatr Mwldan, Bath House Road, SA43 1JY, 01239 613 230, E: cardigan@ ceridigion.gov.uk

Knighton, Offas Dyke Centre, West Street, Knighton, LD7 1EN, 01874 622 485, E: brectic@ powys.gov.uk

Lake Vyrnwy, Unit 2, Vyrnwy Craft Workshops, Lake Vyrnwy, SY10 0LY, 01691 870 346, E: laktic@powys.gov.uk

Llandrindod Wells, Auto Palace, Temple Street, Llandrindod Wells, LD1 5HU, 01597 822 600, E: llandtic@ powys.gov.uk

Llanidloes, Mount Street, Llandiloes, SY18 6EY, 01686 412 285, E: cspllanidloes@powys. gov.uk

Machynlleth, Royal House, Penrallt Street, Machynlleth, SY20 8AG, 01654 702 401, E: mactic@powys.gov.uk

New Quay, Church Street, New Quay, SA45 9NZ, 01545 560 865, E: newquaytic@ceredigion. gov.uk

Newtown, The Park, Back Lane, Newtown, SY16 2NH, 01686 625 580, E: newtic@ powys.gov.uk

Presteigne, The Judge's Lodging, Broad Street, LD8 2AD, 01544 260 650, E: presteignetic@powys.gov.uk

Rhayader, The Leisure Centre, North Street, LD6 5BU, 01597 810591, E: rhayder.tic@powys. gov.uk

Welshpool, Vicarage Garden, Church Street, Welshpool, SY21 7DD, 01938 552043, E: welctic@powys.gov.uk

Areas in Brief

Heading north, you cross the river bridge at Cardigan and there's an immediate change in the scenery. The headlands seem to loom less large and the inland vistas are gentler. That said, there are still exciting, hidden beaches, Mwnt particularly – although it's not hidden from the crowds. There are no major seaside towns here. New Quay is the nearest thing, and there are lots of little villages with neat beaches. As the coast heads north the beaches largely disappear, replaced by dark rock and black sand expanses. Aberystwyth is the main town in the north of the region, and tries for a holiday feel despite its disappointing beach. The area ends with the rather quirky resort of Borth, with its long stretch of open sand that becomes wilder as it heads north, ending in one of the coast's beauty spots – Ynyslas – the point where the beach, awash with shells and sheltered by massive dunes, sweeps round into the Dyfi estuary. It's a tucked away spot where you park on the sand and the children can run and play. Inland from Aberystwyth are the Cambrian Mountains, an area that runs virtually from the Brecon Beacons up to Snowdonia. It's a quiet, sparsely-populated region of mountains, forests, lakes and reservoirs, which is fast becoming an adventure playground for anybody who loves the outdoors – whether walking, cycling, horse riding, canoeing, orienteering or just picnicking.

Getting Around

By car There's no fast way to get through Mid Wales – most of the roads are winding, and dual carriageways are few and far between. That said, public transport is an even slower option.

By bus TrawsCambria, ℅ 0871 200 2233, www.pticymru.com/ Traws.htm, is a network of services between major Mid Wales towns and from Aberystwyth to Cardiff in the south and Bangor in the north. These are run by several companies including Arriva Cymru, ℅ 0870 608 2608, www.arriva.co.uk, First Cymru, ℅ 01792 582233, www.firstgroup. com, Express Motors, ℅ 01286 881 108, www.expressmotors.com, GHA Coaches, ℅ 0871 200 2233, www.ghacoaches.co.uk, Richards Brothers, ℅ 01239 613756, www. richardsbros.co.uk and Stagecoach, ℅ 0871 200 2233, www.stagecoach. com.

Don't forget, there are very few services on Sundays.

By train Mid Wales is not well served by trains, though there are services to Welshpool and down to Aberystwyth and

Cardigan

Barmouth on the west coast, and a line that heads down through Llandrindod. Several other lines pop up a short way from Cardiff. For more details: National Rail Enquiries (℅ 08457 484950, www.nationalrail.co.uk) or Arriva Trains (℅ 0845 6061 660, www.arrivatrainswales.co.uk). A North and Mid Wales Flexi Pass (adults £45, children £22.50, concessions £29.70), allows four days train and eight days bus travel in an eight day period. (℅ 0845 6061 660, www.walesflexi pass.co.uk).

One-day Rover Tickets are also available in certain areas. Information: ℅ 08457 484950, www.nationalrail.co.uk. For more specific information about times and routes: www.traveline-cymru. org.uk.

By foot There are several long-distance paths that traverse Mid Wales, including Offa's Dyke,

The Wye Valley Walk, Cambrian Way, Ceredigion Coast Path, Glyndwr's Way, Dyfi Valley Way, Elan Valley Way and Severn Way. This is the best way to see the beauty of Mid Wales, and even if you can't tackle a major hike you can always find a short section for a family walk.

WHAT TO SEE & DO

Top 10 Family Experiences

❶ Splashing in the surf at Mwnt and building sand boats on the beach.

❷ Watching red kites as they circle the feeding station at Bwlch Nant yr Arian – Forestry Commission woodland at Ponterwyd.

❸ Running in sand dunes at the Dyfi National Nature Reserve at Ynyslas.

❹ Playing French cricket on the beach at Aberporth.

❺ Watching the dolphins from the cliffs at Craig Yr Adar near New Quay.

❻ Playing with puppets at Aberystwyth's Ceredigion Museum, housed in a beautiful old music hall.

❼ Playing hide and seek among the clipped yew trees and woodland walks at Powis Castle, near Welshpool.

❽ Eating Holgate's Honey Ice cream at Aberaeron's Seafood Festival.

❾ Enjoying the views from the Vale of Rheidol Railway through the wooded valley.

❿ Walking the boardwalk around Tregaron Bog.

Family-friendly Festivals

Play in the Bay – Cardigan Outdoor Festival

Cardigan Bay resorts, 📞 *01239 615554, www.visitcardigan.com*

There's almost a week of action for adults and children at a number of coastal resorts where you can turn up and experience surfing, climbing sailing and more at a bargain price, with extra discounts for booking the full programme.

Spring Bank Holiday weekend.

Cardigan River & Food Festival

Quay Street/Somerfield car park, Cardigan, 📞 *01239 615554, www. visitcardigan.com*

This free event has become one of Wales's leading food fests – with the riverside setting meaning that lots of boaty things are thrown in. Watch out for organic burgers and sausages, chocolate and ice cream, and for the grown-ups there's fish, Welsh whisky, Welsh wines and more. Entertainment includes boat trips, coracle demos, duck races, clowns, folk music, fairground rides and cookery demos.

Second weekend in August.

Aberaeron Seafood Festival

The Quay, Aberaeron, ☏ 01545 570445, www.hiveonthequay.co.uk

A whole school of stalls runs from the inner harbour to the harbour mouth cooking up fish and shellfish – try the barbied mackerel. Brass bands, jazz, shanty singers and the crowds pouring out of the bar at the Harbourmaster Hotel make it loud and party-like, even before the end-of-evening live music on the pier head, and the crabbing competition, while honey ice cream from Hive on the Quay make it a children's favourite.

Early July.

Lampeter Food Festival

University of Wales, Lampeter Campus, ☏ 01570 423981, www. cardiganshirecoastandcountry.com

There's free entrance, free entertainment and free parking at this celebration of Welsh food, held on the campus of the University of Wales, in Lampeter. The area is strongly linked with the organic farming movement and the festival has grown from local interest in all things organic. But as well as food there are children's activities, folk dancing and live entertainment.

Late July

Royal Welsh Show

Showground, Llanelwedd, Builth Wells, ☏ 01982 553683, www.rwas. co.uk

This four-day show attracts 200,000 people to a festival of farming and much more, including a Shetland pony Grand National, a Ukrainian Cossacks horse display, motorcycle stunt team, carriage driving and trained ducks.

Late July.

World Bog Snorkelling Championships

Llanwrtyd Wells, ☏ 01591 610666, www.llanwrtyd-wells.powys.org.uk

One of those 'make your own fun' events that has been going on for more than 20 years. Competitors have to complete two lengths of a 55m trench cut through the dense Waen Rhydd Peat bog, wearing snorkels and flippers, but without using conventional swimming strokes. (In early July there's a cycle race using bikes with lead-filled tyres to complete the underwater course).

August Bank Holiday.

Victorian Festival

Temple Street, Llandrindod Wells, LD1 5DL, ☏ 01597 823441, www. vicfest.co.uk

There's a full programme of family events during this annual celebration of Llandrindod Wells's Victorian heyday. These include a village fete and Welsh ladies tea party. There is also street entertainment and the town's shops take on a Victorian look, with the townsfolk dressing up as Victorians, too.

Last full week of August before the Bank Holiday.

Workhouse Festival

*Llanfyllin, 📞 07890 458561, www.
workhousefestival.co.uk*

This three-day music and theatre
festival has a definite alternative
feel to it, with a healing area and
green crafts. Families are well
looked after with their own,
quiet, camping area and free
entry to under 12s accompanied
by a paying adult. Children's
entertainment includes storytelling, circus skills and
workshops – and there's plenty
to keep the grown ups happy,
too. No dogs or fires allowed.

Early July.

Gregynog Festival

*Gregynog, Newtown, SY16 3PW,
📞 01686 625007, www.gwyl
gregynogfestival.org*

If your children are seriously
interested in classical music con-
sider taking them to this leading
festival in the former home of
Gwendoline and Margaret
Davies – the sisters who
bequeathed the largest collection
of Impressionist paintings and
drawings outside Paris to the
National Museum & Gallery in
Cardiff. Luminaries such as
Ralph Vaughan Williams, Gustav
Holst and Adrian Boult all played
at the festival, which was started
by the sisters in 1932. Family
tickets and reduced entry for children are available at some events,
and admission to the grounds is
free during the festival.

Mid June.

THE COAST

The Mid Wales coastline
includes some of the most spectacular beaches in the country.
The Mwnt to New Quay stretch
contains some fabulous little villages with sandy beaches, high
cliffs and rock pools. Two of the
best beaches – Mwnt and
Penbryn – are owned by the
National Trust (NT), and much
of the headland here is NT
owned, with access to coastal
paths along bracken-covered
land. The coast is less picturesque
further north, although there are
colourful small towns and villages along the way, but the sand
dunes of Dyfi National Nature
Reserve, at the mouth of the
Dovey estuary are a Californian
dream. Much of this region is
now known as Ceredigion, but
the old county name of Cardiganshire lives on in many
places – including this book.

Cardigan

A Georgian market town stuck
serenely in a 1970s time warp
with plenty of independent
shops but, like most towns, not
hugely interesting to children.
However, if you decide to join
the large volume of traffic
squeezing down its narrow
streets you'll find special events
virtually every weekend in the
summer months. These include
the carnival, several regattas, and
a couple of festivals. If you are
visiting on a quieter day there's a
nice spot at the end of Bridge
Street (after passing the Black

Lion Hotel, the oldest coaching inn in Wales) where you can sit on the stylish new stone steps of Prince Charles Quay overlooking the River Tiefi, maybe eating chips from the seven-day-a-week Quick Chip across the road. Cross the bridge and you find the trendy Fforest Outdoor shop and café where you can have a cappuccino and locally-made cakes while buying a canoe, or maybe booking a canoe excursion (see For Active Families). Next door is Cardigan Heritage Centre with its quaint history of the area and selection of local biscuits and the like on sale. Also worth visiting is the handsome, two-storey Cardigan Guildhall, one of Wales's most historic buildings – and the venue for Cardigan market on Thursdays and Saturdays.

Cardigan Island Coastal Farm Park ALL AGES

Gwbert, Cardigan, SA43 1PR
01239 612196, www.cardigan island.com. North from Cardigan along the B4548 to Gwbert.

This farm, with its rare breeds animals, sits on a headland only a few hundred yards from Cardigan Island nature reserve and has one of the best views along this coast. You can often see Atlantic grey seals and their pups on the rocks below the headland, and bottlenose dolphins swimming in the sea. The views are heavenly and children love meeting Dilwyn the donkey, pigs, sheep, goats, rare breed cattle, jersey cows, Shetland ponies, Welsh mountain ponies,

rabbits and guinea pigs. You may also see rare choughs and skylarks flying overhead. Other attractions include tractor and trailer rides, an adventure playground and sand pit.

Open daily, mid-March–end October, 10am–6pm. Admission: £3.50 (14 and over), £2.50 (2–13), OAPs £3.20, under 2s free. Amenities parking, café, picnic areas, shop, adventure playground, sand pit.

Gwbert Beach

Gwbert beach on the north side of the Teifi estuary (B4548), is the nearest beach to Cardigan town, has lovely sand and is south-west facing. However, the tide can change the shape of this beach drastically and swimming here could be dangerous. It is not so much a family beach as a place for sailing, sea fishing and extreme sports, but the Gwbert Hotel, right on the beach, does good pub meals.

Mwnt

Several kilometres north of Cardigan off the B4548, this is a classic Welsh beach, not least because of the tiny, meandering, hedge-lined lanes that lead to the cliff-top car park. On our last visit we made it in OK, but as we were leaving someone was trying to haul a caravan down the hill, creating complete gridlock and involving lots of standing round with hands on hips and re-directing cars into farmers' fields. The view from the grassy, windswept National Trust

Mwnt beach has everything – sand, cliffs and rock pools

car park (pay but free for NT members) is awesome: a sandy beach with crashing waves, sheltered by rock faces on three sides. Steps descend past a snack kiosk (with home-made Welsh cakes) to the friendly, sometimes crowded, sands. The children adore the place – running into the water, playing beach cricket, and dashing back up the steps for an ice cream. Families with buggies will find those steps quite challenging, though. The tiny 15th-century whitewashed church on the cliff top is still in regular use and may be open for visitors.

Aberporth

Another small village, this one is more accessible than some of the others along this stretch of coast. A small headland creates two sandy beaches that become one huge one as the tide goes out. There is very little else here, though there are plenty of walks along the cliffs for families with

older children. The Ship Inn (📞 *01239 810822*), which overlooks the sea, has a children's menu as well as good pub food for adults, and the Beach Café (📞 *01239 810294*) is the place to go for ice creams.

Felinwynt Rainforest Centre ALL AGES

Felinwynt, Cardigan, SA43 1RT
📞 *01239 810250, www.butterfly centre.co.uk. Six and a half kilometres from Aberporth on the B4333 to Mwnt, off the A487 at Blaenannerch.*

This is basically a large humid greenhouse, but a great place to escape the weather if things turn wet. You can enjoy the warmth of a tropical rainforest while the children tiptoe round trying to spot exotic butterflies and birds. There's also a shop where they can agonise over how to spend their holiday pocket money while mum and dad have a quick cup of tea in the café.

Open daily Easter–Oct, 10.30am–5pm; Oct, 11am–4pm. Closed Nov–March. Admission Adults

(14–59) £4, Child (3–14) £2, over 60s £3.75, under 2s free, family £11. **Amenities** *free car park, shop, cafe.*

Tresaith

More a hamlet than a village, with just one shop, a café and a pub, Tresaith is nevertheless a great family seaside destination. The pretty, sandy beach joins with neighbouring National Trust-owned Penbryn beach as the tide retreats. Its most remarkable feature though is the waterfall which cascades over the cliffs from the River Saith. The Ship Inn serves children's meals until 7pm daily, or you can buy freshly-cooked pizza to take away. It also has four en suite hotel rooms (☎ *01239 811 816, www.shiptresaith.co.uk*).

Penbryn Beach

This is a difficult place to get to but the kilometre-long, unspoilt, golden sands are well worth it (turn off the A487 at Sarnau and follow signs to Penbryn). There's a drop off point near the beach, but parking is 370m away, so it may not be a good option if you've got very young children and a lot of paraphernalia. There's a woodland walk from the car park to the beach, and rock pools for children to play in when they're tired of making sandcastles. There are no amenities on the beach, but a small NT shop and café is open during the summer at the pay and display car park (free to NT members).

Llangrannog

This tiny village runs down a narrow valley to a truly beautiful beach, one of the most striking along this stretch of coast. Llangrannog (also spelt Llangranog) features magnificent rock formations, wonderful rock pools, and the odd cave in the cliffs for bold explorers. The beach can become crowded in high season, but thankfully its size doubles when the tide goes out, revealing access to neighbouring Cilborth Beach. You can also get to Cilborth by the path over the National Trust-owned headland – Ynys Lochtyn – and there are steps down the cliff to the beach. The most stunning rock formation at Llangrannog is 15m-high Carreg Bica, which, legend has it, was the tooth of a giant called Bica, who lived in the county. He had to spit out the tooth to cure his toothache, and it has been there ever since. Parking on the seafront is very limited, but there's a large car park signposted along a left turn at the top of the hill just before the shops. Along the narrow seafront there's home-made ice cream at the Patio Café, a fish and chip shop, and the Baguette Bar. The Pentre Arms pub does B&B and has seats in front overlooking the beach (see p 186), while the Ship Inn has a stylish outdoors area and serves good food.

New Quay harbour is right next to the town's sandy beach

New Quay

A quaint town that tumbles down the hillside into a little harbour, a lovely curving beach and a traditional seaside resort: ices, lollies, lilos and pubs jostling for attention with green hills rising all around. Dylan Thomas lived in a cottage across the bay and his classic *Under Milk Wood* is believed to be partly based on the town and the people he met here. He drank in the Blue Bell, and there's a Dylan Thomas Trail around places thought to feature in the book; fine if the children are studying Thomas for their GCSEs, but youngsters are more likely to be impressed by the toffee fudge Upton Farm ice cream on sale, or the dubious delights of the Famous Pound Shop. The beach, nestling inside the stone slipway and pier, isn't huge and can get busy – but is soft, sandy and safe. From the pier you can often see the Cardigan Bay dolphins playing. A path

from the centre of town takes you away from the bustle and up onto the cliffs for spectacular views, especially from the National Trust spot Craig Yr Adar (Bird Rock). You'll see many types of gull, along with kestrels and often seals and bottlenose dolphins and can get a closer look at wildlife from various boat trips. Afterwards there are plenty of fish and chip options, both eat-in and take-away including the Mariner, Captain's Rendezvous, all within a few yards of each other.

Cardigan Bay Marine Wildlife Centre ★ ALL AGES

Glanmor Terrace, New Quay, SA45 9PS, 📞 *01545 560 032, www. cbmwc.org. In the centre of New Quay, overlooking the harbour.*

This charitable trust monitors and studies bottlenose dolphins, grey seals, porpoises and other sea creatures and is based in a lovely listed building, free to enter. There's a whole floor of information, interactive displays and fun things for children to see and do, along with an area where they can sit and draw their discoveries. The centre runs trips on its Dolphin Survey boat, which give a real insight into the Bay's inhabitants.

Open daily April–September, 10am–5pm. *Admission: free. Boat trips: adults £16, children under 12 £10 (2 hours, longer trips available).*

Aberaeron

The main street runs through Aberaeron like any other little town, but off to one side is the delightful harbour area – like something in Brittany but with colourfully-painted Georgian buildings. There are nice pubs and a good fish and chip shop in Alban Square, plus a couple of upmarket restaurants at the harbour. Try Hive on the Quay (www.hiveonthequay.co.uk), a stone shop-restaurant that's home to Holgate's Honey Ice cream, and serves fresh fish from the boats that also supply the neighbouring fish shop. The Harbourmaster Hotel (www.harbour-master.com) also has a first-class restaurant and welcomes 'well-behaved children', whatever they are. The beach, however, is disappointing – seaweed-covered stones with a little black sand here and there. No surprise, then, that the town attracts a yachty crowd and, increasingly, people who like good food. The Harbourmaster organises Aberaeron Seafood Festival along the quay in July, which is great fun.

Llanerchaeron ★ ALL AGES

Ciliau Aeron, near Aberaeron, SA48 8DG, ☎ *01545 570200, www. nationaltrust.org.uk*

Children love playing in the gardens of this wonderful country estate, which has survived largely unaltered since the 18th century. There are colourful walled kitchen gardens, a dairy, laundry, brewery and salting house and woodland walks around the grounds. The Villa was designed by John Nash in the 1790s and is virtually untouched. The Home Farm is now a working organic farm with cattle, sheep and pigs. Children can watch lambing and hay making, depending on the season, and explore the traditional outbuildings.

Open Wed–Sun, 11.30am–4pm, mid March–mid July; Tue–Sun, 11.30am–4pm, mid July–early Sept; Wed–Sun, 11.30am–4pm, early Sept–late Oct. *Closed* Mon, except Bank Hol Mons; Tue, early Sept–mid July; late Oct–late March. *Admission* adult £6.40, children £3.20, family £16; Home farm and garden only: adults £4.80, children £2.40. *Amenities* free car park, café, farm shop, gift shop, picnic areas.

Aberystwyth

This respected university town has an oddly bohemian yet bookish feel to it – the inevitable result of being a student town and hub of Green politics – but it's not a place that made our children's eyes light up on arrival. The nondescript centre has the usual clutch of charity shops and High Street stores, and you get the feeling that this

Aberystwyth's Ceredigion Museum is a must for families

is a place to visit rather than spend a holiday.

The little horseshoe-shaped North Beach is dark and shingly, hemmed in by tall Edwardian B&B-type places. A gentle seafront stroll takes you past an ornate John Nash-designed college building, and up to the ruins of the castle built by Edward I during his conquest of Wales – open at all times and free. The children enjoyed exploring them and playing on the huge climbing frame in the little park below, which has a grassy area and picnic tables. As you round the small, rocky headland the view opens out with a long, blustery prom and the more attractive South Beach, which ends at the little harbour. At the other side of the harbour Tanybwlch has a quiet shingle beach, with Pen Dinas hill fort (free) rising 120m above. The Cliff Railway, dating from 1896, creeps up 130m Constitution Hill at the far end of North Beach to a café and picnic area. But possibly the best free family entertainment is Ceredigion Museum (Terrace Road, www.ceredigion.gov.uk) housed in the Edwardian Coliseum music hall. The wonderfully atmospheric museum has an engaging collection of reconstructed rooms, farming implements and the like, with a colouring area for children.

Walking through town you'll find Ultra Comida (31 Pier Street, ☎ 01970 630686) a deli-restaurant that has a curious Spanish/Welsh/French remit (tapas, local cheeses) while MGs deli-takeaway (14 Great Darkgate Street, www.mgees. co.uk) is a coffee bar with fresh sandwiches and snacks along with bottles, jars and boxes of food and drink. Everything is sourced in Wales, mostly in

Cardiganshire. Also, try The Dolphin with its original-looking early 1960s décor (47 Great Darkgate Street – (01970 624081) for takeaway or sit-down fish and chips. Alternatively, the farmers market is the first and third Saturday of every month.

Vale of Rheidol Railway
ALL AGES

Park Avenue, Aberystwyth, SY23 1PG, (01970 625819, www.rheidol railway.co.uk. Near the centre of Aberystwyth, next to the mainline station.

This railway used to serve the lead mines in the Rheidol Valley and carry passengers through inaccessible and rugged territory. It was British Rail's last steam railway – only privatised in 1989 – and now runs from Aberystwyth to the legendary Devil's Bridge, where there are walks to Mynach Falls, Devil's Punchbowl and Jacob's Ladder. There are hopes to extend the

line further than the current stretch of nearly 20 kilometres, which takes about an hour each way.

Open daily April–October, first train 10.30am, last train 2pm or 3.45pm on some high season dates. Phone for details. Admission: adult £13.50 (return), children 3–15 (first 2 per adult) £3, then £6.50, OAPs £12, under 2s free. Dogs £2, no bicycles.

Borth

A curious little seaside town just north of Aberystwyth – Borth features one long road running alongside the beach – slightly claustrophobic where the town section starts because there are buildings on both sides of the road, shutting out the sea view. Leave the car in the free car park at the T-junction near the strange, modern supermarket and cross the road to find a three kilometre stretch of sandy beach. When the tide's in this is a narrow strip

Borth beach has firm sands perfect for all sorts of fun

of smooth stones up against the sea wall, but when it's out it's really out and, if a trifle wind-swept, has a certain wild charm (not to mention donkey rides). The town has a railway station near the shops, and the Friendship Inn has a beer garden and family room.

Drive through and out the other side for one of the real delights of this coast. The road ends amid giant, white sand dunes of the Dyfi National Nature Reserve at Ynyslas, at the mouth of the River Dyfi (Dovey), with Aberdyfi (Aberdovey) across the water. You can park on the hard sand, and the feel is California cool. People waterski in the estuary, and our children had a whale of a time throwing themselves down the dunes and running across the shell-strewn sandflats to the unspoilt Twyni Bach beach. There's a modern, wooden building, across a meandering boardwalk, which has smart, clean toilets and a little snack bar. A truly wonderful find, and a glorious place to picnic or walk – but swimming is too dangerous.

Borth Animalarium ALL AGES

Ynisfergi, Borth, SY24 5N,A 📞 *01970 871224, www.animalarium.co.uk*

Apart from the beach this is Borth's only family attraction – an off-beat collection of unwanted pets including a leopard, snakes, iguanas, monkeys and crocodiles. It also gives a home to animals that pet shops and zoos can no longer keep, and to animals rescued by the RSPCA and other organisations. This could be a real education for any child convinced there's room at home for something exotic, but there are also domestic animals which children can feed, plus an indoor ball pool for under 8s, outdoor play area and pet shop.

Open daily April–October, 10am–6pm; Nov–March, 11am–4pm. *Admission adult £7.50, child £5.50, concessions £6.50, family £24, under 3s free. Amenities free car park, café, shop, play areas.*

THE INLAND TOWNS

If you're looking for peace, quiet and traditional towns and villages in rolling green countryside then check out this area. One of the best days we ever had in Mid Wales was when we visited a small country show at Tregaron, near Lampeter. There were local children taking part in horse jumping and dressage competitions; local farmers showing off their prize sheep, and families parading their pet dogs. In the village hall there were giant marrows, carrots and beans competing for the best in show titles, flower arrangements vying for the 1st place rosette, and painted stones by more children. It was a wonderful day for everybody – whether they were competing in the show or just sampling home-made cakes from the tea stall, like us. A taste of the real Wales.

Lampeter

It looks like an unassuming country town but Lampeter boasts the oldest university college in Wales, Saint David's University College. After Oxford and Cambridge Universities, it's the oldest degree-awarding institution in England and Wales. The student population add an extra dimension to what has been a market town since medieval times, and which still has regular cattle markets and a horse fair, as well as the weekly market. Lampeter Museum, housed in the town library and open during library hours, has a small collection of local artefacts, including the town's original Royal Charter. At nearby Pontryhdyfendigaid is the remains of Strata Florida Abbey where the Welsh poet Dafydd ap Gwilym is buried.

Dolaucothi Gold Mine ★

AGES 5 AND UP

Pumsaint, Llandwrda, Carmarthenshire, SA19 8US, ☎ 01558 650177, www.nationaltrust.org.uk

Our children were incredibly excited at the idea of panning for gold here, and had so much fun swilling muddy water around in tin pans that we didn't get around to actually going down the gold mines – a tour which covers some of the Roman workings, and tunnels from the 19th and 20th centuries. Babies and children who need to be carried cannot be taken underground, but there is loads for children to enjoy above ground. There's an activity room, an exhibition on mining and plenty of scope to play Thomas the Tank games following the narrow gauge tracks of the equipment left behind when the gold mines were abandoned in the 1930s. There are also woodland walks, fishing and – completely hidden from sight – a touring caravan site.

Open daily, 10am–5pm, late March–late Oct. Christmas shop: open Wed–Sun, 11am–4pm, early Nov–late Dec. Admission adult £3.40, child £1.70, family £8.50. Underground tour: adult £3.80, child £1.90, family £9.50. Amenities free parking, café, gift shop, walks, picnic areas, fishing.

Rhayader

A small, historic market town on the banks of the River Wye, Rhayader is the oldest town in Mid Wales, dating back to the 5th century. The town was named after a waterfall on the Wye that was blown up in 1780 so a bridge could be built. The waterfall is still there, but not as exciting as it used to be. Rhayader provides an excellent base for exploring the nearby Elan Valley, much of which was flooded by the Victorians to build reservoirs that now provide water for Birmingham. Elan Visitor Centre (☎ 01597 810880, www.elanvalley.org) is signposted off the B4518 out of Rhayader and has an exhibition about the reservoirs and the natural history of the area, an information desk and audio-visual show, plus shop, café, picnic spots and a play area. There are also guided walks and children's activities, although it's best to book these. The Elan reservoirs and River Wye provide fantastic fishing opportunities, and the final stretch of the Wye Valley Walk goes through Rhayader to the river's source at Llangurig. Rhyader is also on the doorstep of the Cambrian Mountains, where visitors enjoy mountain biking, horse riding, bird watching, fishing, walking and other outdoor activities. Bicycles can be hired in town, and the Sustrans National Cycle Route 8 can be picked up on the outskirts of town.

Red Kite Feeding Station
ALL AGES

Grigin Farm, South Street, Rhayader, LD6 5BL, ☎ 01597 810243, www.gigrin.co.uk

We had never seen so many red kites in our lives as when we were travelling through Mid Wales, and the reason is the growing numbers of Red Kite Feeding Stations. As well as Grigin Farm there's another at Cors Caron, near Tregaron, one at Bwlch Nant yr Arian, near Ponterwyd and at Llanddeusant, in the Brecon Beacons. At Grigin Farm, beef is put out to attract the kites – although you're sure to see other birds try their luck too. An absolutely fantastic sight as the beautiful birds of prey swoop down to dine.

Open daily, 1pm (feeding at 3pm in summer, 2pm after clocks put back in winter). Admission adult £4, Child (4–15) £1.50, OAPs £3, under 4s free. Amenities free car park, hides for bird watching.

Machynlleth

The ancient capital of Wales. 'Mach' is a small market town in the lower Dyfi Valley, about 16 kilometres from the coast. The town was the site of Owain Glyndwr's Welsh Parliament in 1404 and is still a seat of Welsh culture and politics, although these days it's mainly Green. This makes for some interesting shops and cafes – for instance the vegetarian and Fairtrade Quarry Café, and wholefood Quarry Shop. The main street is Heol Maengwyn, where you'll find the town's most recognised landmark – the 19th-century clocktower, nearly 24m tall – and the busy Wednesday market. Most of the shops here are independent traders, including the High Street master butcher William Lloyd Williams, who sells meat from local farms, including his own. Three mountain bike routes – Mach 1, 2 and 3 – start from the car park in Heol Maengwyn. They are fairly long, serious routes but older children might be able to complete the early sections of them, particularly Mach 1 and 2. See *www.dyfimountainbiking.org.uk* for information, where you can also find out about the Cli-Machx route in the Dyfi Forest. This has the longest descent in Wales, so it's not for beginners, but there's plenty of informal free-riding in the forest, too. Old Parliament House (☎ 01654 702827) is open Monday to Saturday from Easter to September. The black and white half-timbered town house and adjoining building is home to the Owain Glyndwr Centre where you can find out all about this legendary Welsh hero. Entrance is free. Opposite is Plas Machynlleth the 17th-century mansion home of the Marquess of Londonderry. The building and grounds were bequeathed to the people and until recently housed the Celtica Museum. That has now closed and there are hopes to open an arts centre.

Museum of Modern Art
ALL AGES

Hoel Penrallt, Machynlleth, SY20 8AJ, ☎ 01654 703355, www.moma wales.org.uk

Workshops for children and adults are held in July in this innovative gallery, which has six exhibition spaces with work by some of the best artists in Wales. The museum is part of a complex of buildings that centre on the Tabernacle, a former Wesleyan chapel restored for use as an auditorium in the 1980s. The buildings are now the venue for the August Machynlleth Festival.

*Open Mon–Sat, 10am–4pm. **Closed** Dec 23–26 and Jan 1. **Admission** free; charge for concerts, theatre and festival events. **Amenities** art for sale.*

Centre for Alternative Technology ★ ★ ALL AGES
GREEN

Machynlleth, SY20 9AZ, ☎ 01654 705950, www.cat.org.uk. North out of Machynlleth on the A487 towards Dolgellau.

If ever a little acorn grew into a giant oak tree, this is it. CAT has mushroomed from an experiment by idealists in the early 1970s to one of the world's leading eco-centres. And it's growing all the time. What was once a disused slate quarry has been transformed into hours of fun for the family. Honestly. There are the sort of interactive displays that children seem to

Centre for Alternative Technology, Machynlleth

understand intuitively and, for the grown ups, demonstrations of organic gardening, sustainability in the home, and examples of environmentally responsible buildings. You can even stay in one of two self-catering Eco Cabins on the site, which each sleep 18 people. There's also an adventure playground, tinies' play area, and free children's activities during school holidays, plus a covered picnic area, wholefood and vegetarian Taste of Wales restaurant, and a gift and book shop.

Open daily, late March–late Oct, 10am–5.30pm; late July–early Sept 10am–6pm; late Oct–Easter, 10am–dusk. Closed Christmas and early January. Call for details. Admission March–Oct adult £8.40, children (5–15) £4.20, concessions £7.40; winter £6.40/£4.20/£5.40. Under 5s free. Amenities car park, restaurant, shops, play areas, picnic areas.

Tregaron

This market town is near to the mountainous source of the River Teifi and nestles at the Southern end of Cors Goch Caron, a huge red-tinged marshland that is a National Nature Reserve and famous for the variety of its bird-life. There's a boardwalk trail around the marshland – Tregaron Bog – information about which can be found at Tregaron Red Kite Centre and Museum (℡ 01874 29877, *www.ceredigion.gov.uk*), which is housed in a Victorian School. Children love the old classroom with its blackboard, teacher's desk, ink bottles and slates, and

you can find out about birdlife on the bog, including the Red Kites, which are fed at 2pm in winter. The museum is open Mon–Sat, April–Sept, 10.30am–4.30pm and most winter weekends from 12–4pm. There's a shop, café and small car park. Admission is free.

Cors Caron, the Tregaron Bog
ALL AGES VALUE

On the B4323 at Maeslyn, between Tregaron and Pontrydfendigaid

Free, and a great place for the children to let off steam, this is one of Britain's few remaining raised peat bogs, beside the river Teifi just outside Tregaron on the edge of the Cambrian Mountains. It's an area of eerie beauty, where sphagnum moss has, over thousands of years, created a small dome. An old railway line, now a path, runs alongside, while a circular boardwalk lets you stroll through the centre. There's also a lake, which is usually alive with wildfowl, and a parking area where you can picnic.

Rhiannon Welsh Gold Centre
ALL AGES

Main Square, Tregaron, SY25 6JL, ℡ 01974 298415, www.rhiannon.co.uk

Rhiannon Jones is one of the few jewellers who works with real Welsh gold, but as well as buying Celtic design jewellery here you can see the workshops and an exhibition telling the story of Welsh gold. There's also a craft centre and tea room.

Open normal shop hours. ***Admission*** *free.* ***Amenities*** *exhibition, workshops, tea room, craft centre.*

Llanfyllin

This is an ancient and pretty little town, in the foothills of the Berwyn Mountains. There are no big attractions, but Llanfyllin is home to the Workhouse Festival (*www.workhousefestival. co.uk*, 📞 *07890 458561*) in June/July. It has children's workshops and entertainment as well as a huge range of bands and acts – from Breton dance bands to psychedelic trance. The workhouse itself is one of the best preserved in Wales and is being restored. You can walk up Market Street and into the hills to see St Myllin's Well, an ancient holy site, or drive over to nearby Llanrhaeadr-ym-Mochnant to see the highest waterfall in Wales. Pistyll Rhaeadr has a 73m drop and can be reached down the charmingly named Waterfall Street.

Lake Vyrnwy ALL AGES

RSPB Lake Vyrnwy Nature Reserve, Bryn Awel, Llanwddyn, SY10 0LZ, 📞 *01691 870278, www.rspb.org.uk*

This was the first of the Welsh reservoirs created to supply water to English cities – in this case Liverpool – and there's a flooded village under the lake, as a display at the visitor centre explains. You can see the ruins when the water level is low enough, but most people come to this RSPB-run nature reserve to see the birds and explore the beautiful countryside. There are a few hides around the lake and car park where you can watch birds and special trails for children, including a nest-box trail. The whole family is likely to enjoy the sculpture park trail, started by local sculptor Andy Hancock in 1997, which now has more than 50 pieces of work from artists all over the world. There's also a playground, picnic benches and you can hire bikes from the Artisans Craft Shop (📞 *01691 870317*) near the visitor centre. Paths include the 21km circular route around the lake. Canoe, kayak and boat hire and instruction are available at Bethania Adventure (📞 *01691 870615*) near the dam, and fishing licences are also available.

Open daily, 10.30am–5.30pm, April–Dec; 10.30am–4.30pm, Jan–March. ***Admission*** *free.* ***Amenities*** *visitor centre, bird hides, playground, sculpture trail and marked walks.*

Builth Wells

Once a spa town thanks to its saline and sulphur mineral waters, Builth is mainly Victorian and Edwardian-built. Although its spas are now closed it is still a handsome place on the banks of the River Wye. There are plenty of shops to nose around, although children will be more interested in the Royal Welsh Agricultural Show – biggest in Britain – which takes place in July. (*www.rwas.co.uk*, 📞 *01982 553683*). Other events at the Royal Welsh Showground include The Mid Wales

Mouthful, a food festival, plus shows connected with gardening, horses and working dogs.

Llanwrtyd Wells

Surrounded by the Epynt and Cambrian Mountains, this former spa's claim to fame is as Britain's smallest town. But it's really best known for holding some of the maddest competitions in Wales. This is where The World Bog Snorkelling Championships and The Mountain Bike Bog Leaping Point-to-Point takes place every August Bank Holiday Monday, not forgetting The Man v Horse Marathon, in June. For details call ☎ 01591 610666 or go to www.llanwrtyd-wells.powys.org.uk. The town is also a good base for more mainstream outdoor activities.

Vale of Rheidol

The River Rheidol floods into the sea at Aberystwyth after a spectacular journey through this narrow, winding valley. It's instantly remote and wonderful – and possibly best seen from the Vale of Rheidol Railway (p 167) – which links Aberystwyth and Devils Bridge. There's also a 27km signposted Rheidol Cycle Trail from Aberystwyth harbour to Devil's Bridge along back roads and cycle routes. But it's also easily accessed by car and there are many beautiful sights to see as you drive over Plynlimon (Pumlumon in Welsh) the highest mountain in Mid Wales and part of the Cambrian Mountains. Cwm Rheidol Reservoir (☎ 01970 880667) is up a narrow, riverside road that forks off from the A44 at Capel Bangor. It's a pretty place to picnic, there's a nature trail, and it's floodlit during the evening. A free information centre gives details of the Rheidol Hydro-Electric Scheme and there's a free tour of the power station and adjoining fish farm. Nearby is the Magic of Life Butterfly House (www.magicoflife.org, ☎ 01970 880928, £4) a warm, indoor spot for a wet day.

Devil's Bridge (☎ 01970 890233) is one of those little places that seem to exist only for the tourist throng. Here, three roads come together to cross the white waters where the River Mynach plunges 91m into the River Rheidol, and three bridges sit almost on top of each other across the gorge. At the bottom is the 11th-century original, then the 18th-century stone version, then the modern road bridge. You have to put £1 in the coin-operated turnstiles to get down the steep, wet steps to the crashing noise of the river and the Punch Bowl, several rock basins created by the water's force. A longer walk (£2.50/children £1.25) takes you to Mynach Falls. It's a place loved by children, although it can be very busy, not least because of the day trippers using the Vale of Rheidol steam railway. The 600-acre Nant-y-Moch Reservoir (☎ 01970 880667) further up the valley off the A44 is also a lovely

Vale of Rheidol Railway runs through spectacular countryside

place to walk, cycle, picnic and fish. A few miles south, in the Ystwyth Valley, is Hafod (℡ *01974 282568, www.hafod.org*), a lovely 18th-century estate, hailed as one of the finest examples of a Picturesque landscape in Europe. It has wonderful woodland walks originally laid out in the late 18th century and now restored to guide you to fantastic views. Hafod is off the B4574. Entrance free.

Bwlch Nant yr Arian ★★
ALL AGES FIND VALUE

Ponterwyd, SY23 3AD, ℡ 01970 890694, www.forestry.gov.uk/ wales. Sixteen kilometres east of Aberystwyth on the A44.

This Forestry Commission woodland is simply stunning. There's an All Ability Lakeside Trail of less than a kilometre, which even young children will be able to enjoy walking around without getting too tired. There are other marked walks including

The Miner's Trail to the silver-lead mine (see p 176), and guided walks for a small fee. There are playgrounds – including a toddlers' area – and several picnic sites. Also mountain bike trails, but they are graded as difficult so unsuitable for most children. The highlight is daily Red Kite feeding at 3pm in summer and 2pm in winter. From the visitor centre terrace and a number of other spots you can watch the beautiful birds of prey swoop down, and there's even a video system with cameras around the lake, giving close-up views. The eco-friendly visitor centre has a restaurant – and a sedum roof which filters rainwater into toilets and a bike washer.

Open daily, 10am–5pm April–Oct, 10am–dusk in Nov–March. Admission free, but parking costs £1.50. Amenities visitor centre, restaurant, orienteering trails.

Llywernog Silver-Lead Mine Museum and Caverns ALL AGES

Llwernog, Ponterwyd, SY23 3AB
☎ *01970 890620, www.silvermine tours.co.uk. Fifteen minutes from Aberystwyth on the A44.*

A dark and cavernous delight dating back to the mid 19th century when silver mining was a boom industry locally (and before big, new Australian and American mines flooded the market). The mines were abandoned, until 1973 when the museum opened. Now you can tour the mines (wearing helmet lamps), there's a self-guided trail around the mine site above ground, and children can enjoy panning for silver-lead and iron pyrites.

Open Mon–Sat except Feb and spring half-terms, Easter and summer holidays, 7 days; June–Aug and school holidays, 10am–6pm, March– May 10am–5pm, Sept/Oct 11am– 5pm. Closed Nov–March. Admission adults £7.25, children (4–15) £4.25, family £20, OAP/student £6.50. Amenities free car park, gold panning, shop, cafe, picnic site.

Llandrindod Wells

Its historic spa may be closed but Llandrindod Wells's Victorian architecture makes it a remarkably handsome town, one that appeals to youngsters on a stroll. The Rock Park Spa's renovated pump rooms are now used by the Llandrindod Wells Complementary Health Centre (☎ *01597 822997*), and in the same Victorian complex you'll find the Heritage Centre and Tea Rooms with a display of photographs from the town's heyday, as well as a good menu. But the main reason for visiting is to catch the Victorian Festival in the last couple of weeks in August. Shops are transformed with Victorian window displays, cars are banned, and everybody dresses up to enjoy the street entertainment and events such as music hall. The nine-day celebration ends with a torchlight procession to the lake and firework display.

THE BORDER TOWNS

The border between Wales and England was a moveable feast, even up to the 1960s. Roughly speaking it has always been between the Welsh mountains to the west and the English rivers to the east. Many of the towns in this corridor were fortified, which is why there are the remains of so many motte and bailey castles as well as more substantial fortresses. As peace became the norm, these towns grew into market towns, characterised by half-timbered medieval buildings. Ironically, it is said that the towns on the Welsh side of the border have more of an English culture and outlook than those on the English side. Whatever, they never fail to delight, and you can always find some ancient site for youngsters to scramble and run free.

Welshpool

A magnificent example of a Welsh Marches town, this nestles in the upper reaches of the Severn Valley. Welshpool regards itself as one of the gateways to Wales, and has two castles to prove it. The oldest, a 12th century motte and bailey, is simply a tree-covered earthwork with – bizarrely – a bowling green, but it's a good place for children to let off steam. More impressive Powis Castle is less than a kilometre south, and one of the best properties and gardens in the National Trust's collection. However, if you do visit what's left of the motte and bailey you could call into the nearby Old Station Visitor Centre, (Severn Road, ☎ 01938 556622) housed in the former railway station, where there's tourist info, speciality shops and a restaurant. A new railway station has been built nearby. The town has many medieval 'black and white' timber framed buildings and the only cockpit in Wales – although there has been no cockfighting since it was outlawed in 1849. The Montgomery Canal passes through, and an old canal warehouse is now Powysland Museum and Canal Centre. You can walk along the towpath to Newtown – an easy 21km section of the Severn Way, which follows the Severn from its source in Plynlimon to Bristol (*www.severnway.com*). The Offa's Dyke path is to the east, and Glyndwr's Way finishes here. Welshpool has long been an important market town, with Saturday and Monday markets still held in the Town Hall, where there's also a farmers' market (first Friday of the month). The livestock market is Europe's biggest.

Powysland Museum and Canal Centre ALL AGES VALUE

Canal Wharf, Welshpool, SY21 7AQ, ☎ 01938 554656, www.powys.gov. uk; www.powys.mysite.wanadoo-members.co.uk

This museum in a 19th-century warehouse by the Montgomery Canal features a collection of colourful canal boats with information about canals and railways, along with fascinating history and archaeology displays from private collections of the Powysland Club, the oldest county historical society in Wales, which founded the museum in the 19th century. The old photos and maps seem to engage children. Outside you can take short cruises down the canal, and you can also hire boats. Call ☎ 01938 553271 for hire info.

*Open Mon, Tue, Thur, Fri, 11am–1pm and 2–5pm; May–Sept Sat and Sun, 10am–1pm and 2–5pm Oct–April, Sat 11am–2pm. Closed Wed, winter Sun, some public holidays. **Admission** adult £1, children free.*

Powis Castle ★★
ALL AGES FIND

Welshpool, SY21 8RF, ☎ 01938 551929, www.nationaltrust.org.uk. 1.5km south of town on High Street (A490), or drive down the A483 towards Newport.

There's something for everybody at this wonderful medieval castle with its world-famous Italianate gardens. It's on the site of a 12th-century fortress built by the Welsh princes along a rocky ridge, giving it views across rolling countryside. It was remodelled many times over the next several hundred years to provide a comfortable home for the Earls of Powis. Consequently it has one the best art collections in Wales – plus a museum housing the treasures of Clive of India, whose son married into the family. But it's the garden that the castle is most famous for, particularly its clipped yews, herbaceous borders, terraces and woodland walks, all of which are places for children to run and hide.

Open Mid–late March, castle: closed, garden: Mon, Thur, Fri, Sat, Sun, 11am–4.30pm; April–June, castle: Mon, Thur, Fri, Sat, Sun, 1–5pm, garden 11am–6pm; July and Aug, also open Wed; early–mid Sept, castle: Mon, Thur, Fri, Sat, Sun, 1–5pm, garden 11am–6pm; mid Sept–late Oct castle: Mon, Thur, Fri, Sat, Sun, 1–4pm, garden 11am–4.30pm. *Closed* Tues, most Weds, late Oct–mid March. *Admission* adult £9.45, children £4.70, Family £23.60; garden only: adults £6.75, children £3.40, Family £16.90. *Amenities* free parking, shop, plant sales, restaurant, garden tea room, self-catering holiday cottage.

Welshpool and Llanfair Light Railway ALL AGES

Raven Square, Welshpool, or The Station, Llanfair Caereinion, 📞 *01938 810440, www.wllr.org.uk*

The original steam trains, which used to pull carriage-loads of farmers and their produce to market, are still being used on this remarkable little railway,

Powis Castle

which was built with the help of public donations in the mid 19th century. Now it's a great way to see the 13km from Llanfair Caereinion to Welshpool. Vintage carriages have viewing balconies at both ends.

Open Late March–late Oct, daily in June, July and Aug by days vary in other months. First train leaves Llanfair at 9.45am, last train leaves Welshpool at 5pm. Closed Nov, Dec (except Santa Specials), Jan, Feb, most of March. Admission return adults £11.20, children first child per adult free, others £5.60, under 3s free, OAPs/National Trust members £10.20. Amenities shop, tea room and picnic site at Llanfair, parking at both stations.

Newtown

Newtown's major claim to fame is its Santa Run (Saint Nick carried through town on a fire engine, handing out sweets), but it also has a couple of quirky museums. The WH Smith Museum in the High Street (01686 626280, Mon–Sat, 9am–5.30pm, free) reveals this chain store's history using displays and memorabilia. It's above a real WH Smith shop which has original 1920s fixtures and fittings, and is a nostalgia trip for the whole family – children feel an immediate affinity to somewhere related to the purchase of DVDs and *Doctor Who* magazines. The Robert Owen Museum is inside the Town Council offices (Broad Street, 01686 626345, Mon–Fri, 9.30am–12pm and 2–3.30pm; Sat, 9.30–11.30am, free). This

may not be quite so interesting for children, but it includes the books and letters of one of the world's most important social reformers. Newtown-born Owen set up the Co-Operative movement to help impoverished workers during the industrial revolution. Dubbed Britain's first Socialist, Owen's museum has become a site of pilgrimage for politicians and trades unionists. Among those Owen tried to help were textile workers, and Newtown Textile Museum (Commercial Street, 01686 622024, May–Sept, 2–5pm, Mon, Tue, Thur–Sat, free) shows a typical 19th-century weaver's cottage with a living area on the ground floor and handloom on the first floor. The weaving industry was particularly important in Newtown, where flannel was produced and, during the 1850s, sold by the Pryce Jones family through the first mail order business in the world. And, yes, there is also a Pryce Jones Museum (01686 626911, Station Yard), which opens on request.

Montgomery

At this pretty little market town, with a ruined castle and medieval and Georgian buildings, there's a good local history collection at Old Bell Museum (01686 668313, Arthur Street, Easter–Sept, Wed–Fri and Sun, 1.30–5pm; Sat and Bank Hols 10.30am–5pm, adults £1, children £0.25), but probably the main reason for coming here is to walk one of the best-preserved sections of Offa's Dyke long distance footpath. You can join the path just outside town on the B4386, where the Ditch reaches an impressive 6m high – something like it would have looked when it was first built – which the children find great fun.

Knighton

You can't ask for a better border town than Knighton, with its pretty half-timbered houses and narrow, winding streets. It's only metres over the Welsh side of the border – leaving its railway station in England. The fact that this area was fought over so much is illustrated by the estimated 24 castles or ruins in a 32km radius of the town. Even more significantly, Offa's Dyke actually runs through the town. The path is one of the main reasons people come here – particularly to visit the Offa's Dyke Centre (West Street, ℡ 01547 528753, daily, April–Oct, 9am–5.30pm; Mon–Fri, Nov–March), which also houses the tourist office. An exhibition outlines the history of the dyke (the mystical, other-worldly element fascinates youngsters) and there is a park next door with play area and car park. The centre is half way along the full length of Offa's Dyke, which stretches from Chepstow to Prestatyn, but it is at the start of Glendwr's Way National Trail – named after the Welsh warrior Owen

Gledwr. The 220km walk meanders west through Mid Wales to Machynlleth then back east to finish at Welshpool.

Spaceguard Centre ★
OLDER CHILDREN **FIND**

Llanshay Lane, Knighton, LD7 1LW, ℡ 01547 520247. www.spaceguard uk.com. Off the A4113 to the east of town.

There are two main purposes behind the Spaceguard Centre. One is to monitor the threat to Earth of an asteroid or comet smashing into it, which is rather spooky in a Quatermass sort of way. So let's concentrate on the other one, which is to explain the wonders of the universe in a way that anybody can understand and enjoy them. You also get to see some huge telescopes, the largest Camera Obscura in Europe, a planetarium and a real-time satellite image downlink in the weather sensor suite. And there's the all-important gift shop. Great fun particularly for older children, although younger ones still appreciate the giant machinery.

Open Wed–Sun and Bank Hols, tours at 10.30am (May–Oct), 2pm and 4pm. Admission adults £5, children £2.50. Amenities car park.

Presteigne

Another sleepy border town, with England across the River Lugg. This medieval market town used to be on the main London coach road and was the county town of Radnorshire, which explains why such a small place has so many wonderful buildings.

The Judge's Lodging ALL AGES

Broad Street, Presteigne, LD8 2AD, 📞 *01544 260650, www.judges lodging.org.uk*

The most accessible of Presteigne's impressive buildings is the 1829 Shire Hall, where travelling judges would reside while they dealt out justice. All the furniture here is original – it had been stored in the attic when it fell out of fashion – and the interior had hardly been changed since it was first installed. Curiously, it's very child-friendly – youngsters are encouraged to sit in the judge's chair and look through his books to get a real feel for the period at this award-winning museum. There are activities during school holidays and a special children's guidebook. An audio guide adds to the atmosphere as you are introduced to the characters – the judges, the servants and the felons – who made this building tick.

Open daily, 10am–5pm, March–Oct; Wed–Sun, 10am–4pm, Nov-Dec. Closed late Dec-March Admission adults £5.25, children £3.95, family £15, concessions £4.75. Amenities shop.

For Active Families

Cardigan Bay Watersports ★
AGES 8 AND UP

Sandy Slip, Glanmore Terrace, New Quay, SA45 9PS, 📞 *01545 561257, www.cardiganbaywatersports.org. uk. Above the beach in the centre of town.*

Offers dinghy sailing, power boating, windsurfing and kayaking in the beautiful, sheltered surroundings of Cardigan Bay – everything from short beginner sessions to expert courses, from fun experience to serious training and children and those with disabilities are all catered for. There's limited parking around the harbour – best to use the pay car park at entrance to village.

Open April 1–October 31. Prices taster, adults £12.50, under 16s 10; sailing/windsurfing £17.50/£15, inc equipment. Kayaks, windsurfers and sailing boats also for hire. Amenities changing rooms, showers.

Llain Activity Centre
AGES 8 AND UP

Llanarth, SA47 0PZ, 📞 *01545 580127, www.llain.co.uk. Off A487, follow brown signs at Cei Bach left turn just before Llanarth.*

This family-run centre is a one and a half kilometres from the sea between New Quay and Aberaeron and specialises in residential courses of 2–5 days for schools and clubs, offering kayaking, climbing, abseiling, zip-wire, archery, assault course, orienteering and more. Youngsters adore the new sky tower with its high wire thrill rides. But there are also by-the-day options for adults and families. A day would generally involve four activities for a very reasonable price with a family package and there are new all-inclusive family holiday weeks in July and August. Accommodation is in chalets, or a lodge which sleeps

Beach Life

The coast of Cardiganshire (Ceredigion) is a paradise for those who want wild (and sometimes windy) beaches in dream settings. Huge cliffs, huge views, huge sunsets and huge stretches of sand for the children to play on. There are the famous ones – Mwnt, for instance. But there are others, less grand in some cases, and less accessible in others. There's pretty, uncrowded Cei Bach, and Cwmtydu (limited free parking near the beach and parking further back along the Llwyndafydd road) both close to New Quay. Even further off the beaten track is Seal Bay, only accessible by coastal path from Cwmtydu, and Traethgwyn, between New Quay and Cei Bach. Tresaith, is wonderful for watersports, and its wide, sandy expanse is a children's favourite, but lack of parking keeps away the tourists. There's the little town of Aberporth, which has two separate beaches with two pay car parks between them, and the National Trust beach of Penbryn, between Llangrannog and Tresaith (NT car park, £1.50, is 800m from the beach.

40 in small dorms, and there are three meals a day, and no hidden extras.

Open year-round for daily activities, April–Oct for residential breaks. Prices 1 day from £18, family (2 + 2) from £60. Family week for 4, £899, plus £109 per extra person under 16, £129, 16 and over.

Wye Valley Walk   OLDER CHILDREN

Wye Valley AONB Office, Hadnock Road, Monmouth, NP25 3NG, www. wyevalleywalk.org

It might take a couple of weeks to walk the 219km from Chepstow to the Plynlimon Mountains north of Rhayadar, where the River Wye starts. But that doesn't mean you can't have a stroll along the river at some of its more accessible sites in Mid Wales, such as Builth Wells, Rhayader and the Hafren Forest, where it links with the Severn Way. If you do want to complete the whole

walk you can get sections stamped in a River Wye Passport as you complete them, but each of the official seven sections is between 27 and 39km long, so only older children will really enjoy them. One tip is to start at Hafren Forest and head south. It's marginally easier because it's more or less downhill. The walk crosses in and out of Wales and England, and is marked by a leaping salmon logo. Free guided walks are often available in the summer. Details should be on the offical website above.

Ceredigion Coast Path ★★
ALL AGES FIND

www.ceredigion-coastal-footpath. com

This coastal path links established routes to run from Ynyslas, just north of Borth, down to Cardigan – joining the Pembrokeshire Coastal Path at

Poppit Sands as it takes in the sweep of Cardigan Bay. It's just over 96km, but short walks over headlands from one beach to another and back can be completed in a few hours. The website has maps and details of walking festivals and circular walks.

Elan Valley Trail ALL AGES FIND

From Cwmdauddwr to Craig Goch reservoir, near B4518, www.elan valley.org.uk

The easy, 13km path along the former Birmingham Corporation Railway line is open to walkers, cyclists and horse riders. It begins at Cwmdauddwr, west of Rhayader, and finishes at Craig Goch reservoir. You can join the path at several marked points along the B4518. There is also an unmarked Elan Valley Way that broadly follows the aqueduct which carries Birmingham's water supply. This is 206km and goes through the Wyre Forest

and Llandrindod Wells ending up at Frankley on the outskirts of Birmingham.

Glyndwrs Way OLDER CHILDREN

Starting point, the Clock Tower, Knighton, or Welshpool's canalside park, www.nationaltrail.co.uk

A dragon logo marks this 217km trail set up in 2000 to highlight the triumphs of Owain Glyndwr – crowned Prince of Wales. It starts at Knighton, goes west to Machynlleth then east to Welshpool, passing through moorland, woodland and forest and taking in views of Cadair Idris, Lake Vyrnwy and the Cambrian Mountains. Most of the 16 sections are less than 16km, but children may only want to walk a couple of kilometres so it's best to go to accessible places such as Knighton (where you can also walk Offa's Dyke), Hafren Forest, Machynlleth, Lake Vyrnwy and Welshpool – where

Looking over Craig Goch

you can also walk Offa's Dyke or the Montgomery Canal.

Offa's Dyke Path OLDER CHILDREN

Offa's Dyke Centre, Knighton, Powys, LDN 1EN, 0547 528753, www. offasdyke.demon.co.uk; www. nationaltrail.co.uk

You'll want to allow two weeks to complete the 285km from Chepstow in the south to Prestatyn on the north coast, which doesn't really make for the average family holiday. But you can do sections with children, and they'll be most enchanted walking the 8th-century earthwork (only 112kmof the path runs along it). Some of the best-preserved sections of the Dyke pass through Mid Wales, such as the 21km stretch from Kington (in England) to Knighton.

Severn Way OLDER CHILDREN

From Plynlimon to Bristol, England, www.severnway.com

The longest river walk in Britain follows the course of the Severn, starting at its source at Hafren Forest in Plynlimon. The first section meanders between the trees at Hafren (Welsh for Severn), and is good for family strolls, before continuing to Llanidloes, 26km away, do-able if you've got ruddy-cheeked teenagers. However, you may prefer to just visit the source of the Severn, which is a trek in itself from the car park and picnic area at Rhyd-y-benwch in the forest. There are plenty of other forest trails, too.

FAMILY-FRIENDLY ACCOMMODATION

There are lots of smart cottages to rent deep in the countryside, and lots of traditional inns and hotels in the towns. The coast has a wealth of cottages and apartments to rent, and discreet and charming camp sites too, though the coastal area is still blighted by caravan parks.

MODERATE

Trericket Mill

Erwood, Builth Wells, LD2 3TQ, 01982 560312, www.trericket. co.uk. On A470 Brecon-Builth Wells road, between Llyswen and Erwood.

This 'veggie guesthouse, bunkhouse and camping' occupies an idyllic spot not far from the Brecon Beacons National Park. Whether you want quaint B&B, simple shared bunkhouse or picturesque camping, it's here in the woods by the side of a stream. The guesthouse is a former watermill, which used to grind corn for the Llangoed Estate and the machinery and grain bins form an evocative backdrop in the dining room. The three twin/double rooms are perhaps more suited to grown-ups but the traditional stone bunkhouse in the midst of the apple orchard is ideal for families. Two rooms, cosy with wooden floors, have four beds. There are a few pitches for tents and camper vans around the orchard, campers sharing the bunkhouse's bathroom facilities. Food is on offer for all. Breakfasts feature home-made bean, basil and tomato sausages, Welsh cheese, home-made jam – and the mill's own chicken and duck eggs. Three-course dinners are £16 or there's a one-course option (£7). Food is local, mostly organic, and even the water comes from the Mill's own supply. The relaxed feel is a joy for youngsters, and the place is a great base for exploring the Park and the Wye Valley.

Guesthouse from £56 double room, bunkhouse £12pp, camping £6pp with child discounts depending on age. Open early February–early Jan. Facilities lounge with TV, wood-burning stove, free hot drinks and WiFi. Bunkhouse has outdoor kitchen, barbecue and dining area.

Elan Valley Hotel

Nr Rhayader, Powys, LD6 5HN, 01597 810 448, www.elanvalley hotel.co.uk. Turn west off A470 on to B4518 in Rhayader and follow signs.

This smart but friendly little family-run hotel amid charming scenery is just half a mile from the Victorian dams of the Elan Valley reservoir. There are pretty rooms, and safe places for the children to play outside and the restaurant is stylish with delights such as Welsh lamb and beef from around £10, available in child's portions at half price. Youngsters can also get the usual sausages and nuggets type food both here and in the Farmer's Bar, which serves lighter meals. The Elan Valley Visitor Centre is a pleasing stroll, while Rhayader,

with its quirky shops, is just over three kilometres away.

10 rooms. Double room from £70; children 11–14 sharing £12, 4–10 £7, under 4s free. Dogs £6 a night (4 rooms only). 2 cots and bedding, high chairs and baby listening devices available free. Reduced rates for children in own room depending on availability. Amenities gardens, car park. In room direct dial phone, Internet access, TV, tea maker, hairdryer.

Coed Parc Farm

Lampeter, SA48 8NU, 01570 422402, www.coedparcfarm.co.uk. Just outside Lampeter on the A485 to Tregaron.

This is a farming area and there's nowhere better to stay than on a farm. Coed Parc is a pretty place in a charming valley, which has been family-run since the 18th century, offering traditional décor and views over the farmyard and across fields into Lampeter. Animals to look at include miniature spotted ponies and there's a pool table, darts and other games. Meals are available on request and there are lots of woodland walks from the door.

5 rooms. From £50 double. Extra beds free. Amenities: Meals, lounge, parking. In room: TV, tea maker.

Aberporth Express ★★

Cardiagan Heritage Coast footpath between Aberporth and Tresaith. 01239 851 410, www.underthe thatch.co.uk

A converted Edwardian railway sleeper carriage offers views across Cardigan Bay and beaches in either direction from two oak-panelled double bedrooms, one with a single train bunk, suitable only for a child. There's a kitchen with cooker and microwave, lounge with 1920s stove, flat-screen TV and CD player, dining compartment and shower room. There's also a deck and garden where you can sit and gawp at the dolphins swimming past. Parking is 275m away along the footpath. You can fish for sea bass and mackerel from the rocks, and there's a beachfront café and pub a short stroll away. It's one of a number of eclectic properties, including gipsy caravans and thatched cottages, from an innovative restoration and conservation group.

From £369 per week.

Pentre Arms Hotel

Llangrannog, Llandysul, SA44 6SP, 01239 654345, www.pentrearms. co.uk. On the seafront at Llangrannog.

You can't get closer to the beach than the Pentre Arms, so if you fall in love with Llangrannog's charms this is a good place to stay. There are only eight rooms in this traditional inn, some available as family rooms with en suite bathrooms.

8 rooms. From £95 family room B&B. Amenities meals, lounge, parking.

INEXPENSIVE

Cardigan Bay Camp Site ★★

Cross Inn, near New Quay, SA44 6LW, 01545 560029, www.campingand caravanningclub.co.uk. Turn off the A487 to the A486, then follow signs to Cross Inn.

This is an excellent Camping and Caravanning Club family camp site with caravan and campervan pitches available. It's quite large but well laid out so there are plenty of hedges and trees to look at rather than just canvas and caravans. The children's facilities are great, with a field reserved for ball games as well as a separate play area. The toilet and shower block is modern, and there are laundry facilities and a shop. New Quay is less than a 10-minute drive and there's a quirky little grocery and general store in Cross Inn where you can buy locally-produced goods. Great for access to the more interesting sandy beaches such as Llangrannog, and for the coastal path nearby.

90 pitches, non-members welcome. Low season: pitch £2.90, adult £4.40, child £2.15 per night; peak season: pitch £4, adult £6.95, child £2.25 per night. Amenities toilets, showers, laundry, disabled access, dogs welcome.

Doldowld Caravan Club Site, Llandrindod Wells

Rhayader, LD1 699, 01597 810409, www.caravanclub.co.uk. Just off the A470.

This site is on the banks of the River Wye, so perfect for the Wye Valley Walk and the National Cycle Route 8 is also nearby as is fishing at local lakes and reservoirs, with the Elan Valley only a few kilometres away. It's very simple – no play area, toilets or showers.

50 pitches for caravans and campervans. Low season: pitch £3.90, adult

£3.20, child £1.10 per night; peak season: pitch £5.20, adult £4.25, child £1.80 per night.

Rhandirmwyn Camp Site, Llandovery

Near Rhandimwyn, SA20 ONT, ☏ 01550 760257, www.campingand caravanningclub.co.uk. Off the A483.

A wonderfully remote – and therefore quiet – camp site with caravan and campervan pitches also available, there's plenty of space here for children to play, with a field for ball games and a play area. The site, in the Tywi Valley, is within a few kilometres of the Brecon Beacons, and you could enjoy a day trip to the beaches near Cardigan with ease. The beauty of this site is the unspoilt countryside all around it, enhanced by a high standard of washing facilities. There are also lodge holiday homes to hire.

90 pitches, non-members welcome. Low season: pitch £2.90, adult £5.15, child £2.25 per night; peak season: pitch £2.90, adult £7.60, child £2.35 per night. Amenities toilets, showers, laundry.

Borth Youth Hostel ★

Morlais, Borth, Cardigan, SA24 5JS, ☏ 0870 770 5708, www.yha.org.uk. On the main road through Borth, heading towards Ynslys.

Only a hop, skip and jump from the sandy beach at Borth and a kilometre or two from the fantastic sand dunes of the Dyfi National Nature Reserve, this hostel is a great place for families to spend several nights. It has family-sized rooms plus a games

room, television room and internet access. It also has its own grounds and you can use the barbecue while you watch the sun setting over the sea.

Rooms sleep four, six and eight. Adults from £8.95, children from £6.95. Meals available. Amenities restaurant, BBQ, games room, TV and Internet, laundry room, parking.

FAMILY-FRIENDLY DINING

There's plenty of choice here, in smart pubs, family restaurants and and hotels, both traditional and newly-stylish.

EXPENSIVE

Gwesty Cymru ★★

19 Marine Terrace, Aberystwyth, SY23 2AZ, ☏ 01970 612252, www. gwestycymru.com

This swish restaurant (and small hotel) is right on the seafront with stunning Cardigan Bay views. It serves up favourites, Welsh and otherwise, with, as they say, a contemporary touch – like Cannon of Ystwyth Valley Lamb in a herb and Dijon mustard crust, with bubble and squeak, green beans and a bacon, shallot and Thyme sauce (£15.50). Children can get sized-down dishes or a simple selection of individual dishes. Accommodation includes several elegant family room options, such as top-floor suite with sofabed, from £110 double plus £20 per child.

Open Mon–Sat, noon–3pm, 6–10pm. *Main courses* £11.50–17.95. *Credit* MC, V, AE.

MODERATE

Old Watch House

South John Street, New Quay, SA45 9NP, ☏ 01545 560852.

Serving pleasing fish, chips and more, this is right on the quay-side. Adults can be (slightly) adventurous with John Dory, chips and mushy peas (£12.99) or whitebait salad (£8.50) while children get a decent £3.30 menu with nuggets, burgers and the like.

Open Daily. *Main courses* £5–15. *Credit* MC, V.

Hive on the Quay ★★

Cadwgan Place, Aberaeron, SA46 0BT, ☏ 01545 570445, www.hiveon thequay.co.uk

Set in a single-storey stone converted wharf on the waterfront in a pretty Georgian town, it's easy to miss this stylish but friendly café behind the honey ice-cream counter running along the front. Eat homemade delights, mostly organic and local, in the pleasant white-painted café conservatory or courtyard. Grown-ups might like a whole lobster salad, crab or grilled mackerel, while young-sters would enjoy the pastas, frittata, free range chicken and other dishes, available in children's portions. There are also sandwiches (from around £3), home-made cakes – and Holgate's Honey Ice Cream in all the usual flavours and others such as goose-berry, and melon and ginger.

Open Spring Bank Holiday–September, 10.30am–4pm (August, 5pm). *Main courses* £4–24. *Credit* MC, V.

INEXPENSIVE

Horse & Jockey Inn

Station Road, Knighton LD7 1DT, ☏ 01547 520062, www.thehorseand jockeyinn.co.uk

This big, friendly family-run pub was a 14th-century coach-ing inn. Now it's got lots of room, serves good beer (it's a free house) and has good food. Children love the crispy pizzas, from £3.50 (23cm), while adults can restore their energy with 225g rump steaks with all the trimmings (£8.50), sea bass, lamb shank, and vegetarian risotto and enchilada served alongside a simple children's menu. A two-course Sunday lunch is £8.95. You can eat in the restaurant, or sit out in the courtyard.

Open Pub daily 11am–11pm (10.30pm Sun and Bank Holidays). Food, Mon–Sat noon–2pm, 6–9pm; Sunday all day. *Main courses* £3.50–15. *Credit* MC, V.

8 North Wales

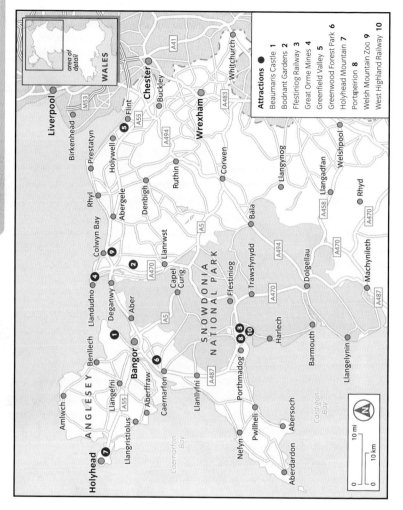

area of detail

WALES

Liverpool

Birkenhead

Prestatyn

Rhyl

Colwyn Bay

Llandudno

Deganwy

Benllech

Aber

Llangefni

Aberffraw

Caernarfon

Amlwch

Llangristiolus

Holyhead

A N G L E S E Y

A55

Bangor

Llanllyfni

Nefyn

Pwllheli

Abersoch

Aberdardon

Caernarfon Bay

Cardigan Bay

Holywell

Flint

Abergele

Denbigh

Ruthin

Llanrwst

Capel Curig

A5

A470

Corwen

Bala

Trawsfynydd

Ffestiniog

Harlech

Barmouth

Llangelynin

S N O W D O N I A   N A T I O N A L   P A R K

A487

Porthmadog

Chester

Buckley

Wrexham

A41

A483

A494

A5

A494

A470

A470

A458

Whitchurch

Llangynog

Llangadfan

Welshpool

Dolgellau

Machynlleth

Rhyd

A487

10 mi

10 km

0

0

N

Attractions

Beaumaris Castle 1
Bodnant Gardens 2
Ffestiniog Railway 3
Great Orme Mines 4
Greenfield Valley 5
Greenwood Forest Park 6
Holyhead Mountain 7
Portmeirion 8
Welsh Mountain Zoo 9
West Highland Railway 10

Our children were initially shocked by how long it took to get there. ("Nine hours," was all Georgia could say when asked how the journey was. "Nine hours" – although that was a gentle meander the length and breadth of the country.) However, they soon perked up and loved every minute as this is where the juxtaposition of sea and peaks is at its best. They were more partial to the wilder coastal destinations than the busy resorts, but enjoyed themselves wherever they went – and there really are lots of spots to discover. This is a land of contrasts. There's north Wales the coast, a place of frantic, packed holiday towns; there's north Wales that sticks out into the sea, with quiet, far-flung places like the Llyn Peninsula and Anglesey. There are the border towns with their English influences, and there's the might of Snowdonia, in some places green and verdant, in others windswept and rocky – a region unto itself but dominating the rest of the north with its dramatic presence.

That these worlds exist side by side, and often only a few kilometres apart seems sometimes quite incredible, but it does mean that when you (and probably the children) have tired of donkey rides and Wimpy Bars on the coast, you can escape to wide open spaces to run, climb, paddle, kick and roll. It has to be said that in high season, particularly Bank Holidays, you might not be able to make the transition as quickly as you would like, given the traffic pouring into (and cruising between) Rhyl and Llandudno. But once out into the hills and mountains you can lose yourself, walk, cycle or horse ride along the many marked paths, explore the forests and woods, canoe or windsail on the lakes, climb the rocks or try any number of other outdoor sports with adventure centres to suit most ages and all abilities.

You can get an insight into the region's turbulent history by visiting the numerous castles and learn about the spirit of these hard-working people in the heritage museums now set up in old slate and copper mines. And you can have fun at the many family-orientated attractions that are available all over north Wales, offering entertainment come rain or shine. But, above all, fall in love with the wild and majestic countryside.

ESSENTIALS

Visitor Information

Tourist Information Centres

North Wales Tourism Head Office, 77 Conwy Road, Colwyn Bay, LL29 7LN, ☎ 01492 531731, www.nwt.co.uk

Bangor, Town Hall, Ffordd Deiniol, Bangor, LL57 2RE, ☎ 01248 352786, E: bangor.tic@gwnedd.gov.uk

Caernarfon, Oriel Pendeitsh, Castle Street, Caernarfon, LL55 1ES, ☎ 01286 672232, E: caernarfon.tic@gwynedd.gov.uk

Colwyn Bay, Imperial Buildings, Station Square, Colwyn Bay, LL29 8LF, ☎ 01492 530478. www.colwyn-bay-tourism.co.uk; E: colwynbaytic@conwy.gov.uk

Conwy, Conwy Castle, Conwy, LL32 8LD, ☎ 01766 830360, E: conwytic@conwy.gov.uk

Holyhead, Stena Line, Terminal 1, Holyhead, LL65 1DQ, ☎ 01407 762622, E: holyhead@nwtic.com

Llandudno, Library Building, Mostyn Street, Llandudno, LL30 2RP, ☎ 01492 876413, E: llandudnotic@conwy.gov.uk

Llanfairpwllgwyngyll, Station Site, Llanfairpwllgwyngyll, Isle of Anglesey, LL61 5UJ, ☎ 01248 713177, E: llanfairpwll@nwtic.com

Mold, Library, Museum & Art Gallery, Earl Road, Mold, CH7 1AP, ☎ 01352 759331, E: mold@ nwtic.com

Porthmadog, High Street, Porthmadog, LL49 9LD, ☎ 01766 512981, E: porthmadog.tic@ gwynedd.gov.uk

Prestatyn, Offa's Dyke Interpretation Centre, Central Beach, Prestatyn, LL19 7EY, ☎ 01745 889092, E: rhyl.tic@ denbighshire.gov.uk

Pwllheli, Min y Don, Station Square, Pwllheli, LL53 5HG, ☎ 01758 613000, E: pwllheli.tic@ gwynedd.gov.uk

Rhyl, Rhyl Children's Village, West Parade, Rhyl, LL18 1HZ, ☎ 01745 355068, E: rhyl.tic@ denbighshire.gov.uk

Wrexham, Lambpit Street, Wrexham, LL11 1WN, ☎ 01978 292015, E: tic@wrexham.gov.uk

Areas in Brief

For many people, especially those from northern England, the north coast *is* North Wales, a place they've visited and holidayed in from an early age. The classic seaside fun of Rhyl and Llandudno is relentless, but you only have to drive a few miles west to find the quiet backwater of Anglesey, and drop a few miles down the west coast to the pretty Llyn Peninsula to find surfer resorts and casually smart hotels.

In some spots the Snowdonia National Park comes right down to the shore, but it's always a backdrop. Inland, the towns on the English border might not be holiday destinations, but are still worth dropping in on.

Getting Around

By car It's not absolutely essential to have a car, but unless you're going to one resort and staying there for a week without wheels you'll find your choices limited. Driving is easy and fast along the north coast, less so elsewhere.

By bus Buses link the main towns and cities. A Freedom of Wales North & Mid Wales Flexi Pass gives almost unlimited local bus use for eight days and unlimited train travel for four (children 5–15 £22.50, under 5s free), with discounts at attractions and youth hostels. ☎ 0845 6061 660, www.walesflexipass.co.uk

By foot Not many families with small children will be hiking up and down mountains, but there are many marked footpaths around lakes and through forests that can be enjoyed either before or after a picnic near the car. Always take jackets, snacks and drinks in a rucksack with you in case the weather changes suddenly, even if you are only on a short walk – and add a map and compass for longer walks with older children.

Top 10 Family Experiences

❶ **Exploring** Portmeirion, running and climbing around the inspirational buildings, climbing trees in the woodland, and playing on the massive beach which appears at low tide.

❷ **Making sandcastles** on the beach at Abersoch and looking for pretty pink shells.

❸ **Walking the town walls** around Conwy with views over the river and the stunning suspension bridge.

❹ **Caernarfon Castle** – it's a truly beautiful building.

❺ **Cycling the coastal Cycle Path** between Rhos-on-Sea and Rhyl.

❻ **Eating Cadwalader's ice cream** from the original cafe at Criccieth, after exploring the cliff-top castle.

❼ **Enjoying the laburnum walk** at Bodnant Garden near Colwyn Bay in May. Even the children said it was brilliant.

❽ **Exploring Greenwood Forest Park** – everything about it is a child-pleaser.

❾ **Taking a boat ride** along the Llangollen Canal to see the amazing Pontcysyllte aqueduct.

❿ **Whizzing around the horse shoe bends** on the Ffestiniog Railway trip.

Family-friendly Festivals

Conwy River Festival

Various venues; Harbour Office, Conwy Quay, LL32 8BB, ☎ 01492 596253, www.conwyriverfestival. org

Over eight days there are hundreds of races featuring yachts, working boats and cruisers in this yachting festival aimed at the whole family. On Conwy Quay Day there are skills tests and rowing competitions in front of the castle, with music and entertainment including a torch-lit procession for children. *Mid August.*

St David's Festival Week

Various venues, Colwyn Bay, LL29 7RU, ☎ 01493 530478, www. colwyn-bay-tourism.co.uk

Don't forget to wear a leek or daffodil on March 1 for St David's Day celebrating the patron saint of Wales. In Colwyn Bay the festivities last a week, with a St David's Day concert, sport, arts and crafts, and drop-in Welsh language lessons. There's also a Welsh singing festival (Gymanfa Ganu) and a traditional Welsh party night (Noson Lawen) with music and dancing. *Late February–early March.*

Gwyl Caernarfon Festival

Ty Gwyb Bach, Llanfaglan, Caernarfon, LL54 5RG, ☎ 01286 678800, www.gwylcaernarfon. co.uk

It's a weekend of free family entertainment on the stage in front of fabulous Caernarfon

Castle, along with live music and theatre at other venues in town.

Late July.

Llangollen International Musical Eisteddfod

Abbey Road, Llangollen, LL20 8SW, 📞 *01978 862007, www. international-eisteddfod.co.uk*

Musically-minded 10-plus youngsters should enjoy at least some of the programme, which includes music and dance to promote world peace and cultural understanding.

Mid July.

The North Coast

Prestatyn

As gateway to the North Wales coast, Prestatyn was the first of the string of seaside resorts to be established once the railway from Chester to Holyhead opened in 1848 – and it's still going strong, with its six and a half kilometres of sandy beaches. Central Beach offers the usual seaside attractions, Barkby Beach to the east is backed by sand dunes, and Ffrith Beach is the site for the as yet unfinished Festival Gardens. Prestatyn has a quieter atmosphere than its raunchy neighbour Rhyl, and its beautiful surrounding countryside is equally attractive to visitors – not least because Prestatyn is the northern end of the long-distance path Offa's Dyke. The path begins – or ends – at Central Beach, where there's an Offa's Dyke Information Centre and the town's tourist office. The

285km National Trail finishes at Chepstow, but if you want a more leisurely stroll try the boardwalks through the last natural sand dunes in Denbighshire at Gronant Dunes.

Prestatyn Nova Centre ALL AGES

Central Beach, LL19 7EY, 📞 *01745 888021, www.prestatynnova.co.uk*

If the weather turns chilly you can always warm up in the tropical environment of Neptune's Pool. It's shallow at both ends, so ideal for young children, and there are slides and children's KidZone sessions with inflatable toys as well as lanes for serious swimming.

Open daily, KidZone 11.15am–12.15pm, general swimming 12.15–7pm Mon–Fri, 12.15–5pm Sat and Sun. Admission adults £2.90, children/OAPs £2.10, families £9 (for five £10.50). Credit MC, V. Amenities waterslides, KidZone, lane swimming, aquafit sessions, family restaurant, bar.

Greenfield Valley ☆
YOUNGER CHILDREN **VALUE**

Greenfield, Holywell, Flintshire, CH8 7GH 7EY, 📞 *01352 714172, www.greenfieldvalley.com*

There are 70 acres of country park to explore here, with woodland walks and a free visitor centre, plus fishing and bird watching. There's no charge to see the ruins of Basingwerk Abbey and 19th-century cotton mill buildings in the valley, but you have to pay to get into the museum and Victorian farm, which includes original and reconstructed local buildings to create an old-fashioned farmyard, which young children will love. There are pigs, sheep and chickens to see, and an adventure playground to enjoy, plus special children's activities.

Open daily. Museum/farm 10am–4.30pm, late March–early November. Admission adults £3.20, children £1.95, families £9.40, disabled £2.60. Amenities car park and café in country park.

Rhyl

A kiss-me-quick seaside resort and easy to get to by car along the A55 expressway, which links to the M56 and M6, or by rail – the spruced up railway station being in the middle of town and only minutes from the sea. Although some of the amusement arcades – and the funfair – along the front look tired, there have been creditable efforts to modernise the resort with landscaping along the promenade. There's a new play area and giant new paddling pool and water play area – both given a contemporary look with large sculpture-like boulders and swaying coastal grasses in the flower beds. Much of the front has been bricked over, making it a duelling ground for youngsters on bikes and mums with buggies, and there are lots of walls which, depending how you look at it, either spoil the sea view or hide the sight of rundown buildings along the busy road. But the most fascinating part is the open air auditorium which features evocative old photos of Rhyl from as far back as 1794, transferred to ceramic tiles and set into the curving wall. This newly refurbished west promenade is next to a busy section of family attractions but if you walk west along the promenade you'll reach the quiet and pretty Foryd Harbour, with a nature reserve across the harbour. The beach is mostly three miles of sand, although the western part has more stones. Donkey rides cost £1.50, as do deckchairs. There's also a marine lake, miniature railway, tennis, bowling and the Pavilion Theatre. In short, it's a traditional British seaside resort – with all the good and bad points that that implies. So if you love busy places with fish and chips, ice creams and slot machines then give it a whirl. If you like peace and quiet, give it a miss. The children? Henry attempted a kick-about on the stony beach, gave up and joined the cyclists and buggies up top. Biggest amusement value was the fancy-dress character handing out goodie bags promoting the Wimpy Bar.

Rhyl Sun Centre ALL AGES

East Parade, LL18 3AQ, ☎ 01745 344433, www.rhylsuncentre.co.uk

You don't have to worry about the weather in Rhyl – here's a tropical setting where children of all ages can enjoy splashing into the warm water from the giant waterslides – including the 60m-long Dragon Slide. There's a surfing pool with white rollers, tropical rainstorms, and roof-top monorail. It's great fun, very noisy and very popular when it rains.

Open most days during school holidays, 10.30am–5.15pm; Friday (4–

8.15pm) and weekends (10.30am–5.15pm) outside holidays, late March–October. *Closed* late October until late March. *Admission* £6.95, day-time; £3, evening. Credit MC, V. *Amenities* waterslides, surf pool, monorail, lagoons, burger bar, café.

SeaQuarium ⭐ ALL AGES

East Parade, Rhyl, LL18 3AF, ☎ 01745 344660, www.seaquariume.co.uk

The first walk-through aquarium in Wales is a real favourite with our family. There are 30 displays of sea life from around the world but by far the best experience is walking through the acrylic tunnels with fish swimming above and all around you. During the fish feeding sessions you really do learn something about the fish – such as how to stroke a ray – and you see the types of sharks that swim off the Welsh coastline. Once you've bought a ticket you can come and go all day.

Open daily, 10am. Closing times and winter opening times vary. *Admission* adults £6.50, children £5.25, families £24.99, under 4s free, OAPs £5.25, students/disabled £5.15. Credit MC, V. *Amenities* café, shop.

Rhuddlan Castle ALL AGES

Castle Street, Rhuddlan, Rhyl, LL18 5AD, ☎ 01745 590777, www.cadw.wales.gov.uk

Rhuddlan was a Welsh princely seat until William the Conqueror ordered the building nearby of a stronghold – Twthill, now just an earth mound. The impressive Rhuddlan was the second castle in Edward I's ring of steel around Wales, with the added benefit of sea access – hence the canal next to it. The castle was finished in 1282, and played an important role in the peace between Wales and England. Nowadays it's a placid place to stroll, with lots of spots for children to run, hide and all the other things children do in castles. The town of Rhuddlan is quietly unassuming, but Edward I held a parliament here – hence Old Parliament House in the High Street.

Open daily, 10am–5pm, Apr–Sept. *Closed* Oct–Mar. *Admission* adults £2.90, children £2.50, family £8.30,

Rhuddlan Castle

under 5s free, concessions £2.50.
Amenities *free parking, gift shop,
baby changing, toilets.*

Colwyn Bay/Rhos-on-Sea

With one of the longest proms
in Britain, Colwyn Bay is a busy
seaside resort – although not as
frenetic as its neighbour Rhyl.
That's possibly because the railway and A55 cut the beach off
from the rest of the town (which
you get to from a road under a
railway arch) creating a more
detached seaside atmosphere.
But it does mean there's plenty
of parking near the beach, and
picnic areas on the grassy banks
that overlook the road beside the
prom. The bay itself is over three
kilometres of sandy beach,
which sweeps round to the small
but lovely Rhos-on-Sea, popular
for watersports and sea angling.
There's also a Rhos-on-Sea heritage trail which takes in St
Trillo's Chapel, thought to be
the smallest church in Britain
with room for only six people.
The beach here is rockier than at
Colwyn, but it's a small price to
pay for the peaceful atmosphere
of small shops and a few quiet
pubs. Colwyn Bay town has a
new shopping centre and several
cafes and restaurants. Eirias Park
has a leisure centre among 50
acres, which include picnic areas,
tennis, pitch and putt, crown
green bowls, skateboard park,
boating lake and yacht lake.
Colwyn Bay has a nine-hole golf
course, and there's an 18-hole
course at Rhos.

You can cycle from Rhos-on-Sea
through several North Wales seaside resorts to Prestatyn on the
Coastal Cycle Track. The 26km
route is almost all traffic-free and
forms part of the National Cycle
Network. You can also cycle five
kilometres inland from Rhos-on-
Sea to Llandudno. *www.national
cyclenetwork.org.uk.*

Welsh Mountain Zoo ★
ALL AGES

*Old Highway, Colwyn Bay, LL28 5UY,
📞 01492 532938, www.welsh
mountainzoo.org. Off A55
Expressway, J20, then follow signs.*

This amazing little woodland
zoo has grown from one man's
pipedream in 1963 to one of the
most respected wildlife centres
in Wales. Now run by the
Zoological Society of Wales, it is
home to a select list of exotic
mammals including monkeys,
bears, snow leopards and
Sumatran tigers, as well as more
down to earth species such as
otters. There are also many birds
and reptiles – as well as a children's farm of rabbits, ducks,
chickens and goats.

Open *daily, Mar–Oct 9.30am–5pm;
Nov–Feb 9.30am–4pm. Closed Dec
25.* **Admission** *adults £7.95, child
£5.80, family £24.95, under 3s free,
OAP £6.90, students £5.80. Credit
MC, V.* **Amenities** *restaurant, café,
picnic areas, shops, adventure playground, baby changing, parking.*

Harlequin Puppet Theatre
ALL AGES

*Promenade, Rhos-on-Sea, LL28 4EP,
📞 01492 548166, www.puppet
magic.co.uk*

Britain's first permanent puppet theatre is a delight for both adults and children. This beautiful miniature theatre is decorated with Italianate frescoes and ornate plasterwork, and is built of wood, glass and local stone, in gardens only metres from the sea. Although the programme varies, it includes string puppets that are 100 years old. The 8pm performances are aimed at older children and adults.

Open school holidays, Mon, Tue, Fri, 3pm; Wed 3pm and 8pm. *Admission* adults £5, children/OAPs £4.50.

Tir Prince Leisure Park ALL AGES

Towyn Road, Towyn, LL22 9NW, ℓ *01745 345123, www.tirprincee. co.uk*

There really is something for just about everybody here: an eclectic mix of funfair, go-kart racing and, extraordinarily, American-style harness racing – not to mention the largest outdoor market and car boot sale in North Wales. The fairground offers everything from a kiddie coaster to the Z40 Zyclon rollercoaster. You can pay as you go, or choose from a selection of passes with separate charge for go-karting. Harness racing season runs from May until September. The market runs from February until Christmas, and has 400 stalls and parking for 1,000 cars.

Open fairground: daily during school holidays; Sat and Sun April–Oct; Fri, Sat, Sun May, June, Sept; go-karts: daily, April–Oct; market: Sat–Sun, Feb–Christmas; also Wed–Fri, July–Aug. Closing times and winter opening times vary. *Admission* fairground: day pass £10, evening £6, weekly £30 (or pay as you go £1 per ride). Go-kart: £3.50. Market, free. Harness racing £3, under 18s free. *Amenities* car parking, bars, cafes, restaurants.

Llandudno

The long sweep of tall Victorian villas along St George's Crescent is one of Llandudno's best-known sights, but there's more to this still-elegant seaside resort than well-heeled hotels and boarding houses. For a start there's the wide promenade and award-winning North Shore – stony at high tide but sandy once the sea goes out and just right for donkey rides. This is the busiest side of town with the Venue Cymru theatre and arts centre an year-round attraction in Wales's largest seaside resort. On the promenade itself there's a bandstand, with daily summer Punch & Judy shows near the pier. You'll also find the main shopping streets here, with wrought iron-decorated shop fronts. Over in the quieter side of town is the West Shore, another award-winning sandy beach, with children's play area and yacht pond – plus magnificent views across the Conwy estuary to Snowdonia. Then there's Great Orme and Little Orme – headlands at either end of the North Shore's Llandudno Bay. Great Orme is home to several attractions including the tramway to the top and the cable lift that starts at the bottom of the Happy Valley gardens. You can also drive to the top, along the eight kilometre toll road Marine Drive, which will take you to the country park where there's free parking (included in the £2.50 toll) and wonderful views. Back down Great Orme is a miniature golf course, putting green, dry ski slope and toboggan run and several cafes.

One of the best times to visit Llandudno is during the May Day Bank Holiday weekend, when the town hosts a Victorian Extravaganza featuring steam-driven vehicles and fairground attractions. That said, Bank Holidays can be busy – as you'll find out when you've fought your way through the traffic jams.

Great Orme Mines ☆ ALL AGES

Great Orme, Llandudno, LL30 2XG, ☏ 01492 870447, www.greatorme mines.info

These copper mines were discovered in 1987 and include tunnels dug nearly 4,000 years ago during the Bronze Age. It is now thought to be the largest prehistoric mine in the world, and archaeologists are still excavating. The tour includes a Bronze Age cavern dug out with bone and stone tools. There are also tunnels to walk through and exhibitions of some of the artefacts.

Open daily, 9.30–5pm (4pm off-peak), mid-March–Oct. Admission adults £6, children £4, family £16, under 5s free. Credit MC, V. Amenities visitor centre, shop, second-hand book shop, tea room open to non-mine visitors.

Great Orme Tramway ALL AGES

Victoria Station, Church Walks, Llandudno, LL30 1AZ, ☏ 01492 879306, www.greatormetramway. com

Britain's only cable-hauled tramway still operating on British public roads provides a fascinating taste of nostalgia and the museum at the Halfway Station shows how holidaymakers and

Llandudno beach goes on forever and is sandy when the tide's out

locals have enjoyed the spectacular ride for the last 100 years. But the real stars of the show are the beautifully restored trams – and, of course, the views from Great Orme.

Open daily, 10am–6pm (5pm March and Oct), lateMarch–late Oct; Tickets adults £5, children £3.50, under 3s free. Amenities museum.

INSIDER TIP
Look out for the Codman family's Punch and Judy show on the North Shore promenade near the pier. It runs daily during the summer, as it has since Professor Codman first hit town in 1860.

Alice in Wonderland Centre
YOUNGER CHILDREN

3-4 Trinity Square, Llandudno, LL30 2PY, ☎ 01492 860082, www.wonderland.co.uk

Young children will enjoy this journey through a rabbit hole to see life-sized animated displays of scenes from Alice in Wonderland, with excerpts from the story narrated on personal stereos. Older children may not be quite so enchanted though, and anybody with a serious interest in writer Lewis Carroll may be disappointed. Llandudno is where the real-life Alice spent her summer holidays, but Lewis Carroll wasn't a visitor to the family holiday home, Penmorfa, near West Shore. That said, the centre has one of the best-stocked shops for Alice toys and collectables.

Open Mon–Sat, 10am–5pm, Dec–Easter; Mon–Sat, 10am–5pm, Sun 10am–4pm Easter–Christmas. Closed two weeks in November. Admission adults £3.25, children £2.50, OAPs £2.95. *Amenities Alice Curio Shop.*

INSIDER TIP
The Centre also provides free guided walks around Llandudno's Alice Trail, taking in the house where Alice Liddell spent her childhood holidays, the church she attended, and the West Shore's White Rabbit statue – all much more interesting than the displays.

of course, the views from Great Orme.

Open daily, 10am–6pm (5pm March and Oct), lateMarch–late Oct; Tickets adults £5, children £3.50, under 3s free. Amenities museum.

Look out for the Codman family's Punch and Judy show on the North Shore promenade near the pier. It runs daily during the summer, as it has since Professor Codman first hit town in 1860.

Alice in Wonderland Centre

3-4 Trinity Square, Llandudno, LL30 2PY, ☎ 01492 860082, www.wonderland.co.uk

Young children will enjoy this journey through a rabbit hole to see life-sized animated displays of scenes from Alice in Wonderland, with excerpts from the story narrated on personal stereos. Older children may not be quite so enchanted though, and anybody with a serious interest in writer Lewis Carroll may be disappointed. Llandudno is where the real-life Alice spent her summer holidays, but Lewis Carroll wasn't a visitor to the family holiday home, Penmorfa, near West Shore. That said, the centre has

9.30am (closed Dec 24–26, Jan 1), June-Aug until 6pm, April, May, Oct 5.30pm, Nov–March, 4pm, Sun 11am–4pm, adults £4.50, children £4, families £14, *www.cadw.wales.gov.uk*) is a giant masterpiece with eight towers looming over the riverside. Lots of tunnels, tiny rooms and lofty views make a great place for youngsters to explore. They also like running along the town wall outside, and the feeling of flying as you cross the stately suspension bridge, now pedestrian-only, built in iron by Thomas Telford in 1826 to reflect the castle design.

Children of all ages can have fun on the Conwy Valley Cycle Route, a 40km circular trail, and there are boat trips up the river.

Plas Mawr is the best-preserved Elizabethan town house in Britain (📞 *01492 580167; www. cadw.wales.gov.uk*) and you must see Britain's smallest house (📞 *01492 593429*), a quayside fisherman's cottage that our children recognised from the Guinness Book of Records.

Penmaenmawr

Victorian Prime Minister Ewart William Gladstone often spent his holidays at this tiny seaside resort with its huge sandy beach at low tide and views out to Anglesey and Puffin Island. Like other seaside towns along the north coast, the railway and A55 Expressway cut the town off from its seafront, leaving the beach area in almost traffic-free peacefulness.

The mountains behind Penmaenmawr are still quarried for stone, giving the town a slightly grim industrial look, but you won't see that while you're sitting on the beach, and if your children are old enough to tackle walks up the mountain there is one of Wales's best-known stone circles. They might, however, prefer the skateboarding park on the prom, which also has a paddling pool, café and shops.

Llanfairfechan

Another quiet seaside town with a huge sandy beach at low tide, Popular with walkers and also anglers – it's one of the best sea bass beaches in Wales. Among the most popular walks is up into the wooded hillside to see the spectacular Aber Falls.

Bangor

The red-brick Victorian city on the Menai Strait peers across at Anglesey, with its 472m pier all but poking it in the ribs. It's a jolly place, a university town, but the cathedral – the Cathedral Church of St Deiniol – does its best to introduce a sense of decorum. It unites a 15th-century tower with a Victorian reinvention of a medieval original and comes up with a place laden with strange carvings which children find bewitching.

Gwynedd Museum & Art Gallery (📞 *01248 353368,* free) has a grab-bag collection – Roman sword, Neolithic weapons, medieval tiles – along with a Welsh theme involving furniture and clothes.

Penrhyn Castle (*www.national trust.org.uk*, ☎ *01248 353084;* Wed–Mon; 11am–5pm July–Aug; noon–5pm, March–June, Sept, Oct; grounds/café open one hour earlier; adults £8, children £4, family £20; garden and stable block exhibitions only: £5.40/£2.70) is a 19th-century fantasyland.

Caernarfon

It's tempting to drive past Caernarfon rather than get involved with the complicated roundabouts and intersections on the outskirts of town, but if you manage to get in and get parked then the one thing you should see is Caernarfon Castle. For the past 100 years or so it has been the stage for the investiture of each Prince of Wales – the last one being Prince Charles, in 1969. The castle is open daily, year round (☎ *01286 677617, www.cadw.wales.gov.uk*, family ticket £15, 9.30am–6pm in summer, 9.30am–5pm spring/ autumn, 9.30am–4pm winter). It's one of Edward I's finest Welsh castles – built as a royal palace and seat of government, as well as a military stronghold. The result is a fairytale look in contrast to, say, rugged Harlech Castle.

If the children have had enough of castles they might pre-fer the Welsh Highland Railway (☎ *01286 677018; www.whr.bangor. ac.uk*), which leaves from its

station in St Helen's Road and currently goes to Rhyd Ddu, at the foot of Snowdon – useful if you're planning a walk up the mountain. The railway is being gradually extended and will meet with another section of the line which leaves from Porthmadog.

Inigo Jones Slateworks
OLDER CHILDREN

Y Groeslon, Caernarfon, LL54 7UE, ☎ 01286 830242, www.inigojones. co.uk

Not a grubby cave but a place where they've been making slate products since 1861, starting with school slates. Nowadays there's a lot of garden slabs, floor-ing and fireplaces alongside bird-baths, clocks and the like. Go on, treat yourself to a rockery. The self-guided tour (with taped commentary) takes you past skilled workers. Children get to engrave their name on a piece of slate and take part in a quiz, so they're happy enough. Rather surreal is the Welsh Rock Café which features a history of Welsh music rather than what you were thinking.

Open daily, 10am–5pm, except Dec 25, 26, Jan 1. Admission showroom free, tours £4.50, children/conces- sions £4, family £15. Credit MC, V, AE. Amenities showroom, workshop, café, picnic area, parking, disabled access.

Greenwood Forest Park ★
YOUNGER CHILDREN GREEN

Y Felinheli, LL56 4QN, ☎ 01248 671493, www.greenwoodforest park.co.uk. Between Bangor and Caernarfon, off B4366 Bethel Road, near A55 Expressway (follow brown signs).

Beautifully crafted, but deep down a glorified adventure playground, this is the best we have ever been to. You want to spend the day here to get the most for the entrance fee, although as parents you get little more than that familiar feeling of sitting in a park watching your children climbing on things. Definitely not a theme park, and with lots of beautifully-crafted things to clamber across, the emphasis is on the environment rather than thrills and spills. Nevertheless, there were plenty of shrieks from the toboggan-like Great Green Run, and the Green Dragon Coaster really is the world's first environmentally-friendly (small) rollercoaster – powered by the weight of passengers in a funicular rather than the

Greenwood Forest Park

National Grid. However, the queue can be mind-numbingly slow. The children liked the Treetop Towers rope walks and slides, the crocodile maze and jungle boats although you could tell that Georgia, at 10, felt it a bit beneath her. There is plenty for the very young to enjoy, including Toddlers' Village, Rabbit Village and Mini Tractors. As a parent, take a book.

Open March–Sept, daily, 10am–5.30pm; Sept–Nov, Feb half-term daily, 11am–5pm. **Admission** depending on season (low/mid/high) adult £6.85–9.80, child £5.75–8.95, OAPs £6.10–9.20, families £22.50–33.60. Under 3s free. **Credit** MC, V. **Amenities** cafes, gift shop.

Anglesey

This is an island, although the children questioned this when they saw the river-sized Menai Strait, which separates Anglesey from the mainland. Thomas Telford's striking Menai Bridge leads you to a surprisingly flat landscape of largely cultivated fields – a complete contrast to the mountains of Snowdonia. There are some good sandy beaches and plenty of rocks to scramble around – plus that village with the long name (Llanfairpwllgwyn-gyllgogerych-wyrndrobwllllantysiliogogogoch – or Llanfair PG for short, see p 204).

Beaumaris

The picturesque Georgian town and port gazing across to

Snowdonia offers a lovely waterfront to wander. There's also Beaumaris Castle (daily, 9.30am, except Dec 24–26, Jan 1, June–Aug until 6pm, April, May, Oct 5.30, Nov–March, 4pm, Sun 11am–4pm, adults £3.50, children/OAPs £3, family £10, ☎ 01248 810361, www.cadw. wales.gov.uk) the last, and some say the best, of Edward I's chain around Wales. It's quite beautiful in its windswept spot and offers children plenty of passages to creep through and stairs to climb. The Museum of Childhood Memories opposite (☎ 01248 712498) is a collection from rocking horse days.

Llanfairpwllgwyn-gyllgogerych-wyrndrobwllllantysiliogogogoch Yes, this is the one. Longest place name ever, invented to pull in tourists. It translates as *The Church of St Mary by the pool with the white hazel near the rapid whirlpool by St Tysilio's church and the red cave.* Take a photo of the sign then move on (it's on the A5 just over the Britannia Bridge).

Holyhead

Ferry port to Ireland pretty much sums up this little town, though it's surrounded by a lovely rocky coastline with its old South Stack lighthouse and seabird colonies. Holyhead Mountain is the island's highest point at 219m so has the views along with Caer-y-Twr a prehistoric hill fort (open access) which is walkable for older children from the free

lighthouse car park. There's also an exceptionally good youth hostel at Trearddur Bay which is a dedicated activity centre. Anglesey Outdoors (☎ 01407 769351, www.yha.org.yk) can arrange rock climbing, sea kayaking, cycling, sea fishing, wind or kite surfing, sailing, diving and horse riding, and has tepees to rent as well as family rooms.

Llyn Peninsula

This finger of land points west for 39km of meandering coastline – little beaches, bays, small fishing villages and the like – quite charming and often surprisingly upmarket.

Criccieth

A small but lovely little seaside town with two sand and shingle beaches and a medieval castle towering over the sea, Criccieth has been a holiday spot since the Cambrian Coast line reached the town in Victorian times, and still has a regular rail service. A Criccieth Heritage Walk leaflet is available from the summer Tourist Office but walk past the stylish Cadwalader's Ice cream Café and all else is forgotten. This was the original spot, and the queues outside it on a wet Sunday morning in April tell their own story. Criccieth Castle (www.cadw. wales.gov.uk) has nicely steep steps and high grassy banks on which youngsters can unnerve their parents. And the top, with its almost sheer, tumbling cliffs down to the sea is not the place to play football. It's a 15-minute visit, with a few more spent looking at the colourful boards in the shop/visitor centre.

Pwllheli

The largest town on the peninsula, the centre with its Wednes-day market is a walk away from the long, straight stretch of beach with decidedly unattractive flats and houses – although the two are separated by some attractive dunes.

Abersoch

This once tiny village with wonderful horseshoe-shaped beach a goodly walk from the high street is one of Wales's hip new spots, at least among youths with wild hair and surfboards, who are a complete contrast to the yachting types from the marina. As such, it's a colourful place, if busy. It was one of our favourite beaches for an early evening stroll, with groynes to jump over and shells to gather. The shops sell mostly wetsuits and bodyboards, and the restaurants are crammed of an evening. We tried a couple of pizza-plus places at 6pm, but they were booked out.

At the tip of the peninsula is Aberdaron, a tiny windswept place with a one and a half kilometre-long sandy beach (pay car park). On the north coast is Porthor beach (National Trust car park), another desolate spot, with walks up to the lookout point of Mynydd Carreg.

Criccieth Castle towers over the crashing sea

West Coast

Porthmadog

A busy little town – as you'll realise if you're sitting in a summer traffic jam trying to drive in – but worth the effort if you like steam trains. Porthmadog is the terminal for the Cambrian Coast Express, a steam train running on the main line from Machynlleth. The narrow gauge Ffestiniog Railway will get you to Blaenau Ffestiniog and the West Highland Railway will take you to Traeth Mawr. The Ffestiniog Railway once carried slate to Porthmadog docks, so it's handy for the pretty harbour – full of yachts and fishing boats and with a view of mountains and sea. Porthmadog Maritime Museum (*www.tremadog.org.uk*) is housed in an old slate shed on the harbour and illustrates Porthmadog's importance as a port and ship-building area. Madog Car & Motorcycle Museum (📞 07789 063030), near the town centre, has more than 100 vintage British vehicles from the 1930s and 1950s, plus a display of vintage toys. Although there are kilometres of sand when the tide goes out, they can be dangerous, and the town only has a small usable beach at the tiny village of Borth-y-Gest, which you can get to from a footpath at the end of Porthmadog Quay. It's picturesque with some waterfront eating places. Best beach is Black Rock Sands, at Morfa Bychan, five kilometres west, with views of Harlech and Snowdonia.

There is also a beach at Portmeirion, although you have to pay to get into this Italianate village resort, then walk around the coast path. The rest of Porthmadog is not wildly interesting – despite being packed in high season.

Portmeirion ★ ★ ★ ALL AGES FIND

Gwynned, LL48 6ET, 📞 01766 770000, www.portmeirion-village. com. Just off A487, 3.2km south of Porthmadog.

This faux Italian resort boasts two hotels and a number of apartments, but is an attraction as much as a place to stay. With restaurants, shops (including one devoted to souvenirs of '60s TV show *The Prisoner* which was filmed here), gardens and beach it's like a fantasy land and more fun than you could ever imagine – see p 208.

Open daily, 9.30am–5.30pm. Admission adults £7, children £3.50, concessions £5.50, under 4s free, family £17. Amenities cafés, bars, beaches.

> **INSIDER TIP**
>
> Look out for a Portmeirion discount leaflet (shops, tourist offices, etc) – vouchers get you a three-course lunch at the hotel plus village entry for £17.50, and a two-course dinner (including a glass of wine) at Castell Deudraeth for £13.50. Combine them with bargain children's menus and it's a great deal.

Ffestiniog Railway ALL AGES

Harbour Station, Porthmadog, LL49 9NF, 📞 01766 516000, www.festrail. co.uk

Portmeirion is picture-postcard perfect, and great fun too

Narrow-gauge steam trains hauling carriages from 1860 climb 210m through forests and meadows on the 21km between Porthmadog and Blaenau Ffestiniog. You pass lakes and waterfalls and twist around the side of Snowdon in the 70-minute journey. Best bits are the incredible horseshoe bends, when you feel compelled to hold tight as you whizz around the mountain. The world's oldest independent railway company, founded by Act of Parliament in 1832 to transport slate from mine to Porthmadog's port, it also owns the West Highland Railway in Porthmadog which, once fully restored, will provide a link all the way to Caernarfon.

Open daily, April–Oct; first train 10.15am, last 4pm. In Aug and occasional other dates, trains may run from 8.40am–6.20pm. Also open some dates Nov–March, phone for details. Day Rover tickets adults £16.95, children £8.50, OAPs £15.30, under 3s free. Amenities café, shop, bar, on-train refreshments.

INSIDER TIP »

To avoid crowds and traffic, board the Ffestiniog Railway at Tan-y-Bwlch, in Snowdonia National Park, where there is a small car park and licensed café. Or, if you want to break your journey there, the car park is next to Coed Llyn Mair National Nature Reserve, which has a half-hour nature trail through oak woodlands. The path leads to the lake – Llyn Mair – and there is a picnic site on the shore.

Welsh Highland Railway ☆
ALL AGES

Tremadog Road, Porthmadog, LL49 9DY, ☎ 01766 513402, www.whr. co.uk

Children are encouraged to clamber over the locomotive in the Big Shed at Gelert's Farm Halt and press the buttons and switches inside a diesel shunter – great if they're into railways. Then there's the stepping back in time at the 1920s-style railway station at Pen-y-Mount where there's a network of footpaths for

Portmeirion

Forget *The Prisoner*, and the Italian architecture. Within minutes of checking into our apartment in this iconic seaside village the children had spotted a little girl splashing in one of the imposing fountains. They climbed through the French windows and on to the little path outside and were soon soaked but having the time of their lives. We sat on the benches in the fairytale surroundings, pastel buildings atop rocky out-crops, perfectly-tended gardens, and waited for someone to sweep over and tell them to stop. But no one did, which says a great deal about Portmeirion as a family spot. It might be packed with style and history, but it's a playland, whether you're here as a day visitor or are staying in either of two hotels or in an apartment.

The place was designed and built by architect Clough Williams-Ellis between 1925 and 1973, and it featured as the village in '60s TV cult *The Prisoner*, all giant bouncing balloons, Mini Mokes and glowering Patrick McGoohan (a show that captured our children's attention, beamed into every room at 6pm each evening).

But the important thing is the feel of friendliness as you wander around the grounds, visit the shops (*Prisoner* and other TV memorabilia, upmarket cookware, Portmeirion pottery) and eat in the cafes that (cer-tainly when the sun shines) have an Italian feel with their flower-strewn terraces and pizzas.

The resort, something like a National Trust property crossed with an upper crust holiday village, sits just outside Porthmadog on the banks of its own private peninsula with its huge tidal flow turning it quickly from deep sea to desert-like beach. It tends to be muddy near the resort, but you can take a stroll along the quayside. The children love climbing on what at first appears to be a yacht but is actually a stone extension of the quay, and climbing up the lighthouse, past which is a vast but secluded stretch of beach. You can walk back via the extravagantly planted 70 acres of sub-tropical woodland, through a gulley with trick-ling brook, where the children can climb arching trees.

It's all magical. Georgia wanted to live here, and bring her friends to live in adjoining villas, away from the world, in the wonderful accommodation that gives you a chance to wander when the crowds have thinned. Georgia was entranced standing under a full moon watching the enor-mous tidal flow roll in. Like watching paint spill, was how she described it in a postcard. That evening we ate in the '20s cruise-style setting of the restaurant at the quayside Portmeirion Hotel, a bit too glitzy for young-sters, and with generic children's food, including a pretty unpalatable pizza, to suggest they shouldn't be there. At Castell Deudraeth hotel, still in the grounds but set back in the woods, the brasserie was elegantly relaxed with food that suited elegantly relaxed 10-year-olds.

It's not cheap to stay, but it's a treat for children and adults alike.

the really active family – as well as the wonderful views of Snowdon and surrounding countryside. The track has now been extended to Traeth Mawr Loop, and is growing all the time.

Open daily, April–Sept, first train 10.30am, last train 4.30pm (3.30pm in Sept, Oct and Feb); some weekends in Feb and Oct, plus Oct school half term. *Day Rover tickets* adults £5.50, children £3, OAPs £4.50, family £15, under 5s free. *Amenities* free parking, picnic areas, café, shop.

For Active Families

Tal y Foel Riding Centre
ALL AGES

Dwyran, Anglesey LL61 6LQ, 01248 430377, www.tal-y-foel. co.uk. Several kilometres southwest of Llanfair, just off the A4080.

In a delightful coastal position with amazing views over the Menai Straits towards Caernafon Castle, this is a place where you ride – or learn to ride – along empty beaches and pretty grass tracks – a great family experience. Youngsters (age 7 up) also enjoy the summer holiday whole or half-day riding experiences, including horse care. The centre also has its own farmhouse B&B.

Open year-round. *Prices* group lesson £18.Children's half day £35, whole day £55. *Amenities* free parking.

Border Towns

Ruthin

This is a lovely, medieval market town with interesting independent shops and a good craft centre, plus the excellent Ruthin

Produce Market (last Saturday each month). But while children may find the half-timbered buildings picturesque – including Nantclwyd House, the oldest house in Wales – it's the Old Gaol they'll enjoy best. They can visit the Pentonville cell block and find out how prisoners lived, what they ate, and how they spent their day. There's even a gift shop. Open daily, March–October, 10am–5pm and on weekends and school holidays, November-February (01824 708281, www.ruthingaol.co.uk).

Wrexham

The town has been smartened up in the past few years and now provides good shopping facilities and three markets – including the largest covered market in North Wales and a farmers market (third Friday each month). For children there's Waterworld (01978 297300, www.wrexham. gov.uk), a swimming pool with flume and rapid river ride. There's also Techniquest@NEWI (01978 293400, www.tqnewi. org); £4, under 4s free, 4 people £14) with more than 60 interactive games. Our children are not big fans of Techniquest but others are, particularly younger children who love the bright colours.

In Holt, just outside Wrexham, is Bellis Country Market (01829 270302), a friendly farm complex selling local veg, bread, free-range eggs and more, plus pick-your-own berries, currants, runner beans and courgettes. There's a garden centre, tea rooms, play area and countryside walks.

Erddig ⭐

Wrexham, LL13 0YT, ☏ 01978 355314, www.nationaltrust.org.uk. Two miles south of Wrexham.

A particularly interesting stately home for children because so much of it is untouched – including the fascinating servants' quarters such as the laundry, kitchen and bakehouse and – more unusually – estate buildings such as the blacksmith, saw mill, cart sheds and stables, which display carriages and vintage cycles and cars. The walled garden is also lovely and the grounds a perfect place for hide and seek.

Open July/Aug, Sat–Thur, 10am–6pm (garden), 12–5pm (house); Sept, Sat–Wed, 11am–6pm (garden), 12–5pm (house); Oct, Sat–Wed, 11am–5pm (garden), 12–4pm (house); Nov–mid Dec, garden only, Sat and Sun, 11am–4pm; March/April, Sat–Wed, 11am–5pm (garden), 12–4pm (house); April–June, Sat–Wed, 11am–6pm (garden), 12–5pm (house) Closed garden: mid-Dec, house: Nov–March. Admission adults £8.80 (£5.50 garden only), children £4.40 (£2.75 garden only), family £22 (£13.75 garden only) Amenities restaurant, shop, second-hand bookshop, free parking.

Llangollen

This is a busy little place in summer with plenty to see – not least the annual International Musical Eisteddfod (not to be confused with the National Eisteddfod, which alternates between a different venue in north and south Wales each year). The six days of music, singing and dancing attract participants from all over the world – but there are plenty of other attractions. The River Dee tumbles through the town centre, and if you cross over the old bridge – a wonderful four-arch affair dating back to 1347 – you get to Abbey Road and Llangollen Wharf. Here you can take horse-drawn barge trips (☏ 01978 860702; www.horse drawnboats.co.uk) along the Llangollen Canal, or a narrow-boat trip to the incredible Pontcysyllte Aqueduct, which takes the canal 38m above the Dee. You can also walk 6.4km of towpath to the aqueduct from Llangollen – and even walk along the 300m aqueduct itself. Llangollen Motor Museum is a mile out of town and home to 60 vehicles – some quite stunning. It's open from March to October, Tuesday to Sunday, 1am–5pm (☏ 01978 860324, llangollen motormuseum.co.uk).

Llangollen Railway

Abbey Road, Llangollen, LL20 8SN, ☏ 01978 860979, www.llangollen-railway.co.uk. In Llangollen, between the bridge over the River Dee and the A542.

The 11km journey along the picturesque River Dee to the village of Carrog is a hard climb. You can do the whole journey, perhaps hopping off at the lovely little riverside station of Berwyn, next to the arched stone river bridge, or Glyndyfrdwy, for a spell, or a shorter return trip. The service is mostly steam, with railcars (not quite so historic but with their own rattling charm) and diesels at times. There are

Thomas the Tank Engine days, Santa specials and other events.

Open *daily May–September with other services at weekends, Bank and school holidays all year.* **Tickets** *adults £8, OAPs £6, children £4 (full journey return, less for part journey).* *Family £18. Dogs £1. Unlimited day ticket, adults £16, children £8.* **Amenities** *café, shop, toilets, free parking.*

Plas Newydd

Abbey Road, Llangollen, LL20 8SN, 01978 861314, www.llangollen. com

You can't come to Llangollen and not visit the black and white mock Gothic home of The Ladies of Llangollen. Anglo-Irish aristocrats Lady Eleanor Butler and Sarah Ponsonby were hosts to an endless stream of society at the end of the 18th century, with guests including novelist Walter Scott and poet William Wordsworth. Inside are elaborately-carved oak panels and stained glass windows, and the wonderful grounds includes a knot garden, riverside walks and topiary, which children will enjoy exploring.

Open *daily, April–Oct, 10am–5pm.* **Admission** *adults £3.50, children/ OAPs £2.50, family £10.* **Amenities** *café, shop, toilets, free parking, arts events.*

FAMILY-FRIENDLY ACCOMMODATION

An area where there are some top-quality family hotels as well as increasingly-imaginative places to stay.

EXPENSIVE

Portmeirion ★★★

Portmeirion, Gwynned, LL48 6ET, 01766 770000, www.portmeirion-village.com. Two miles south of Portmadog on A487.

See Portmeirion box for full details. The quayside, ocean liner-themed Hotel Portmeirion has 14 rooms in the main building and 28 rooms and suites in the surrounding village. Castell Deudraeth, set in the woods, has 11 smart, very modern hotel rooms and suites. There are also 17 self-catering cottages, sleeping 2 *www.portmeirion-village. co.uk* 8. There's a delightful quayside open-air swimming pool in a private garden on the waterfront, reserved for guests.

From £188 double HB in Portmeirion Hotel or Castell Deudraeth; cottages from £260 (two nights, self-catering). Extra beds and cots free. **Amenities** *2 restaurants, bar, car park. Resort has further cafes and shops during the day.* **In room** *satellite TV, tea maker, sherry decanter.*

Porth Tocyn Country Hotel ★★★

Abersoch, LL53 7BU, 01758 713303, www.porth-tocyn-hotel. co.uk. Drive south through Abersoch, then turn left following signs after a couple of kilometres.

A charmingly quirky country house-style hotel in a row of converted fishermen's cottages on a hillside with fabulous sea views. There is also a six-bed cottage to let. Family-run for several generations in cheery upper-class anything-goes manner, elderly visitors potter about while children play barefoot football matches in the field. The hotel is set in acres of meadows, with lots of gardens where you can have tea and cake, and use the heated swimming pool (late April–end Sept). Very accommodating, with double rooms, lots of them connecting, and a desire to talk through the various options before you book. Very child-friendly with dedicated comfy room with TV, PlayStation, table-tennis, table football, books and games, but adult-friendly, too, featuring in the *Good Food Guide* for 51 years. Children are encouraged to have high tea (£8), a worthy selection of decent food, or if under 14s insist on joining parents for later dinner with the feel of a dinner party (a £39, three-course with coffee and petit fours delight) they pay £20. Excellent cooked breakfasts are £6. A gorse-lined path takes you down to the quiet beach with Abersoch at the other end – a delightful 25 minute walk.

*Open just before Easter–early Nov. 17 rooms. From £90 double. Extra beds and cots free with children sharing room paying flat rate of £25 (inc continental breakfast). Cottage available all year, from £450 a week. **Amenities** restaurant, bar, car park. **In room** satellite TV, modem point in superior rooms. **Open** March–November.*

Escape ★★

48 Church Walks, Llandudno, LL30 2HL, ☎ 0845 034 0700, www.escape bandb.co.uk

A couple of streets back from the Promenade is this Victorian villa, recreated as a stylish modern B&B. Contemporary styling meets timeless elegance – white minimalism with soft leather and rich wood panelling. Rooms have views of the sea and the mountains behind in a great position, away from the seafront frenzy but close to all the action. Escape takes children from age 10 only, and you'll have to get them their own rooms – but it's worth it. Lavish luxury, hi tech, and big breakfasts.

*9 rooms. From £80 double. No child reductions. **Amenities** lounge with 42in plasma TV and DVD library, honesty bar, landscaped gardens. **In room** TV/DVD, PlayStations, free WiFi, tea maker.*

MODERATE

Tros Yr Afon ★★

Penmon, Beaumaris, Anglesey, ☎ 0845 604 3919, www.eng-cc.co.uk

This gorgeous stone-built manor house plus converted cottages and stables round a courtyard is set in six acres of trees and gardens. It's also only a stone's throw from the rocky shores of the Menai Strait and miles of surrounding beaches, and just a walk from the centre of the pretty town of Beaumaris. The main house sleeps up to 18 and has a huge dining room and lounge, both with open fires. Two cottages across the courtyard sleep five and four. One of many stylish properties around Wales from English Country Cottages.

*Main house, 8 bedrooms, from around £1,450 for 7 nights. **Amenities** lounge, TV room, full kitchen with washing machine and tumble drier, large gardens.*

The Talardy

The Roe, St Asaph, Denbighshire LL17 0HY, ☎ *01745 584957, www. talardy.co.uk. 180m into town from the A55 Expressway, Jct 27, just inland from Rhyl.*

Unassuming from the outside, the Talardy is a little boutique world to itself on the inside. In a good, quiet base for frenetic Rhyl and Llandudno, many of the 16 rooms offer stylish world themes such as the African room, awash with animal prints. That includes a soft double bed for adults, plus bunks round a partition wall, or there are free cots and z-beds in other rooms. Downstairs (apart from the smart Cellars wine bar) is Chestnut Tree gastro pub (finalist in UK Family Pub of the Year) and the colourful Jelly Beans, a child-friendly restaurant with a similar menu plus lots of paper, crayons and soft play area. Food is excellent whether the adult fare – lots of local lamb, venison, etc – or the children's meals. There's also an outdoor play area with sandpit, and a family beer garden.

16 rooms. From £85 double B&B. Extra beds and cots free of charge, babysitting available. Children under 15 stay free. Amenities restaurant, wine bar, family pub, bar, play garden, car park. In room A/C, TV, internet access, tea maker.

INEXPENSIVE

Bangor Youth Hostel

Tan-y-Bryn, Bangor, LL57 1PZ, ☎ *0870 770 5686, wwwyha.org.uk. From town centre, take A5 (Beach Road) and hostel is a right turn (signposted) just over the brow of hill.*

Perfectly placed for exploring the mountains of Snowdonia and the beaches of Anglesey. The hostel is very popular with families as it's only a few minutes walk from Bangor town centre. It offers three four-bed rooms and six six-bed rooms.

Nightly rate £12.95, under 18s £9.95. Free cots available. Amenities restaurant, self-catering kitchen, games room, TV lounge, garden, parking, cycle store, laundry room.

Coed Helen Caravan Club Site

Coed Helen Road, Caernarfon, LL54 5RS, ☎ *01286 676770, www.caravan club.co.uk. From town centre, take A487 (Porthmadog) and after crossing river bridge turn right (Llanfaglan), then right into Coed Helen Road. Site to left at T-junction.*

In a fabulous position with views of Snowdonia National Park, yet only a 10-minute walk from Caernarfon and its castle and steam railway, this site has shower, toilet and laundry facilities, and there's a swimming pool nearby open from May to September – plus sandy beaches a few kilometres away. There's also a small lounge bar.

45 pitches. Open March–Oct. Peak season: adult £4.60, child £2, (pp, per night), pitch £6.20 (per pitch, per night); value season: adult £3.80, child £1.50, pitch £4.10; low season: adult £3.60, child £1.30, pitch £4.

FAMILY-FRIENDLY DINING

While the main resorts of Llandudno and Rhyl might not

be over-endowed with good restaurants, there are other places to savour the flavour around the region.

MODERATE

Castell Deudraeth Bar & Grill ★★★

Portmeirion, Gwynedd, LL48 6ET, 📞 *01286 872135, www.portmeirion-village.com*

The main restaurant at Hotel Portmeirion is family friendly, up to a point (a generic children's menu of nuggets and sloppy pizza), but there are a lot of perms and flouncy frocks. We (and the children) much preferred this relaxed place at the castle-like hotel in the grounds. For a start the staff were happy to come up with an off-menu special cod, chips and peas, a perfectly downsized version of what an adult might expect. And the children's menu was all nicely-presented stuff, including a Welsh lamb burger, home-made chips and beans for a creditable £3.50. The big, airy room opened on to a lawn, so lots of youngsters were frolicking between courses. The brasserie-style menu let us start with moules marinere and continue with Welsh lamb shank (£8.50) and Welsh rib-eye steak (£12.50) – local produce simply prepared and not costing the earth. If only eating out with children could always be like this.

Open *8am–8pm (10.30pm high summer).* ***Main courses*** *£2.40–10.* ***Credit*** *MC, V, AE.*

Ye Olde Bulls Head Inn

Castle Street, Beaumaris, Anglesey, LL58 8AP, 📞 *01248 810329, www.bullsheadinn.co.uk*

A 15th-century inn – Charles Dickens and Samuel Johnson have stayed – with accommodation that is not ideal for families, there's a posh restaurant up in the eaves, and a relaxed brasserie – modern but in a rustic wood and stone way. There's lots of local produce like lamb and beef in stylish dishes such as pan-fried fillet of sea bass, charred asparagus and spring onion orange sauce and a good children's menu includes fish and chips and grilled chicken for little over £5.

Open *daily, noon–2pm, 6–9pm (last orders).* ***Main courses*** *£8.25–14.60.* ***Credit*** *MC, V, AE.*

INEXPENSIVE

Badgers Tearooms

The Victoria Centre, Mostyn Street, Llandudno, LL30 2NG, 📞 *01492 871649, www.badgersgroup.co.uk*

In this classic old-fashioned tearoom flouncily-dressed waitresses push heaving cake trolleys bearing meringues, éclairs and Belgian chocolate cake – all stuff to make the children's eyes goggle. There's a large selection of teas (all served in china teapots) and speciality coffees. Light lunches include homemade soup, Welsh Rarebit, and the Badgers Sett, a toasted bun with lettuce, tomato and bacon finished topped with homemade mayonnaise.

Open *Mon–Sat, 9.30am–5pm, Sun, 11am–4pm.* ***Credit*** *MC, V.*

9 Snowdonia

SNOWDONIA

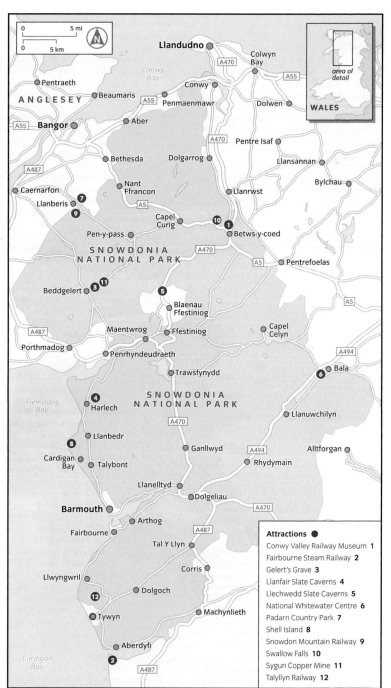

Llandudno

Colwyn Bay

A470

A55

area of detail

WALES

Pentraeth

Beaumaris

ANGLESEY

A55

Conwy

Penmaenmawr

Dolwen

Bangor

A55

Aber

A470

Pentre Isaf

Bethesda

Dolgarrog

Llansannan

A487

Nant Ffrancon

Bylchau

Caernarfon

Llanrwst

Llanberis

7

9

A5

Capel Curig

10 **1**

Betws-y-coed

Pen-y-pass

SNOWDONIA NATIONAL PARK

A470

A5

Pentrefoelas

A5

Beddgelert

3 **11**

5

Blaenau Ffestiniog

Maentwrog

Ffestiniog

Capel Celyn

A487

A494

Porthmadog

Penrhyndeudraeth

Bala

6

Trawsfynydd

Tremadog Bay

4

Harlech

SNOWDONIA NATIONAL PARK

Llanuwchilyn

A470

Llanbedr

8

Ganllwyd

A494

Alltforgan

Cardigan Bay

Talybont

Rhydymain

Llanelltyd

Barmouth

Dolgeliau

A470

Arthog

Fairbourne

A487

Tal Y Llyn

Corris

Llwyngwril

12

Dolgoch

Machynlleth

Tywyn

Aberdyfi

2

Cardigan Bay

A487

Attractions ●
Conwy Valley Railway Museum **1**
Fairbourne Steam Railway **2**
Gelert's Grave **3**
Llanfair Slate Caverns **4**
Llechwedd Slate Caverns **5**
National Whitewater Centre **6**
Padarn Country Park **7**
Shell Island **8**
Snowdon Mountain Railway **9**
Swallow Falls **10**
Sygun Copper Mine **11**
Talyllyn Railway **12**

A confusing place, Snowdonia; there's Snowdon the mountain, Snowdonia National Park, covering 1324km², and Snowdonia, a vague term used to describe parts of north Wales by those who simply want to be included in the tourist frenzy. The park, created in 1951, touches parts of the north coast as well as a stretch of the north-west coast down as far as the River Dyfi estuary on the edge of Cardiganshire (Ceredigion). It also reaches the Conwy Valley in the east. But Snowdon – the highest mountain in England and Wales at 1085m – is the image at the centre of things.

That said, going to Snowdon and going to Snowdonia National Park aren't necessarily the same. The former is an attraction you can head to for a day out, the latter a vast region of bleakly beautiful scrub-covered mountains and foothills. There are more than 90 summits over 600m, and 15 topping 900m, along with more than 100 decent-sized lakes. It's a landscape of steep river gorges, waterfalls, lofty passes and green valleys. Remnants of oak, ash, rowan and hazel woodlands are scattered throughout. It's a region awash with serious hikers and bikers – along with holidaymakers who flock to beautiful beaches in seaside towns like Barmouth, on its 37km of north-west coast.

For the purposes of this book we'll try to stick to the National Park, but the region is so intrinsically linked to the north that overlaps are inevitable.

But if you're going, you're sure to start with Snowdon. Despite the crowds it's magical. We'll never forget the children running and cavorting at the top with the most beautiful views in every direction. Coming here is something every child should do.

VISITOR INFORMATION

Aberdovey The Wharf Gardens, Aberdovey, LL35OED, 01654 767321, E: Tic.aberdyfi@eryri-npa.gov.uk

Bala Penllyn, Pensarn Road, Bala, LL23 7SR, 01678 521021, E: bala.tic@gwynedd.gov.uk

Barmouth The Station, Station Road, Barmouth, LL42 1LU, 01341 280787, E: barmouth.tic@gwynedd.gov.uk

Beddgelert Canolfan Hebog, Beddgelert, LL55 4YD, 01766 890615, E: tic.beddgelert@eryri-npa.gov.uk

Betws-y-Coed Royal Oak Stables, Betws-y-Coed, LL24 0AH, 01690 710426, E: tic.byc@eryri-npa.gov.uk

Blaenau Ffestiniog Unit 3, High Street, Blaennau Ffestiniog, LL41 3ES, 01766 830360, tic.blaenau@eryri-npa.gov.uk

Dolgellau Ty Meirion, Eldon Square, Dolgellau, LL40 1PU, 01341 422888, E: tic.dolgellau@eryri-npa.gov.uk

Harlech Llys y Graig, High Street, Harlech, LL46 2YE,

📞 01766 780658, E: tic.herlech@
eryri-npa.gov.uk

Llanberis 41b High Street,
Llanberis, LL55 4EU, 📞 01286
870765, E: llanberis.tic@gwynedd.
co.uk

Llangollen Y Chapel, Castle
Street, Llangollen, LL20 8NU,
📞 01978 860828, E: llangollen@
nwtic.com

Tywyn High Street, Tywyn,
LL36 9AD, 📞 01654 710070,
E: tywyn.tic@gwynedd.gov.uk

Getting Around

As for North Wales (see
Chapter 8).

WHAT TO SEE & DO

Top 10 Family Experiences

❶ **Glorying in Snowdon** during the ride up the mountain on
the Snowdon Mountain Railway.

❷ **Skimming stones** on Padarn
Lake after visiting the National
Slate Museum Llanberis and
walking through Padarn Country
Park.

❸ **Exploring the caves** at
Sygun Copper Mine then
panning for gold.

❹ **Walking to the waterfall** at
Dolgoch, one of the stops on the
beautiful Talyllyn Railway.

❺ **Searching for shells** on the
beach at amazing Shell Island.

❻ **Taking in Harlech Castle's
view –** over sand dunes and out

to sea one way, up to the mountains the other way.

❼ **Exploring Mawdach estuary** and the most beautiful drive
along the valley road from
Barmouth to Dolgellau.

❽ **Playing rounders on the
beach** at sandy, and practically
deserted, Tywyn.

❾ **Eating ice cream** during a
gentle stroll around pretty
Beddgelert.

❿ **Relaxing in the café garden** at Electric Mountain after a
tour of the James Bond-style
power station.

Family-friendly Festivals

Aberdovey Fun Fest

Various venues, Aberdovey, 📞 *01654
767816, www.aberdyfi.org*

Children will love this festival,
held through most of August.
There are puppet shows, beach
games and street theatre, along
with a grand lantern parade and
huge firework display.

August.

Victorian Festival

High Street, Tywyn, LL36 9AD,
📞 *01654 710070, www.victorian
week.co.uk*

Tywyn turns the clock back for a
whole week with people from all
over Britain taking part in this
fund-raising event in aid of
Talyllyn Railway. Join the fun by
dressing as Victorians and give
your offspring the chance to be
real live Railway Children.

Early August.

The Snowdon Area

The high point of Wales, literally, with Mt Snowdon the country's highest peak (and higher than anything in England too). The scenery is stunning – enough to make our children look up from the portable DVD player as we cruised through it. As an attraction it's a curious blend of charming and rugged outdoors stuff, and manic old-time Brit tourist spot. The railway up the mountain is one of those things everyone should do – and, trust us, everyone does. Llanberis is the engagingly eccentric centrepoint of touristy goings-on, albeit on the edge of the Park. Everyone stays in B&Bs and wanders from attraction to attraction, or simply wanders around in boots, shorts and long socks.

Considering how busy it gets, some restaurants still operate surprisingly old-time hours (9pm closing). On arrival one quiet but mid-summer evening after a long drive, we were directed to the fish and chip shop with enthusiasm. But an hour before its 10pm close the girl behind the counter told us we couldn't have fish – as they'd run out of batter. Ah, the British tourism industry. Henry made do with a sausage while Georgia enjoyed the ever-reliable delights of a Chinese takeaway across the road.

Llanberis

Tourists have been visiting Llanberis to get a closer view of Snowdonia for more than 100 years, but this little mountain town also has a wealth of industrial heritage to explore as well as a ruined medieval castle and unspoilt countryside all around. But it was walkers and climbers who really put Llanberis on the map and there's a path up Snowdon that starts opposite the Royal Victoria Hotel. This 16km walk is one of the easiest routes up the mountain and takes around three hours to reach the summit – OK for energetic teenagers, though suitable footwear, protective clothing, food, drink and a map are essential. Increasingly, Llanberis is also known as a centre for water sports, cycling, paragliding and pony trekking. As well as tourist attractions and specialist climbing shops, Llanberis also has the beautiful **Padarn Country Park**. Wildflower meadows surround one side of Lake Padarn, home to the rare Arctic char – a fish species that has survived there since the Ice Age. There are pay car parks in town next to the Electric Mountain visitor centre, and at the other side of the lake beside the National Slate Museum. Nearby is the **Quarry Hospital Museum** where you can have tea on the terrace overlooking the lake after viewing the original operating theatre and medical equipment. Older children and adults might like the instructor-led **Ropes & Ladders** adventure centre (*www.ropesandladders.co.uk*, ☎ *01286 872310*) and for the more sedate there is the **Llanberis**

Lake Cruise (📞 *01248 671156*) from May to October. The **Vivian Diving Centre** is also based here and **Dolbardarn Castle** is nearby. Llanberis is one of the country's centres for family adventure holidays often for children as young as eight. **Canolfan Tryweryn** is Britain's oldest and biggest whitewater rafting operation, **Surf Lines** is an innovative rocks and water specialist (see Active Families section) while **Boulder Adventures** (*www.boulderadventures.co.uk*, 📞 *01286 870556*) and **Bach Ventures** (*www.bachventures.co.uk*, 📞 *01286 650643*) offer everything from half-day tasters to multi-day multi-activity breaks (kayaking, canyoning, climbing, etc), the former in their own bunkhouse accommodation, the latter on their camp site with camping barn just outside town.

Woodland paths lead to 800-year-old **Dolbardarn Castle** –

built by the Welsh Princes to keep out English invaders – and entrance is free. The town has a number of small hotels, a handful of restaurants and shops such as the Saffron deli, delectable Giorgio's ice cream – mango and ginger, tiramisu, banoffi – and a Spar supermarket.

Snowdon Mountain Railway ★★★ ALL AGES

Llanberis, LL55 4TY, 📞 *0870 458003, www.snowdoniarailway.co.uk*

Exploring the majesty of Mount Snowdon is an absolute must – but if you can't face the climb to the 1085m top then no one will blame you for taking the little red mountain train instead. It's an unforgettable experience – and just as well because it's not cheap. We were incredibly lucky to have clear blue skies and sunshine when we climbed aboard the lovely old carriage to be pushed

Snowdon Mountain Railway

up the mountain by Enid, one of the original little locomotives that have taken visitors to within 21m of the summit since 1896. It's Britain's only rack and pinion railway and the track was carved out of the mountainside with picks, shovels and dynamite.

On the journey up you pass a waterfall and river, then take in views of the glaciated valley and neighbouring mountains Glyder Fawr and Glyder Fach. If you've got older children you might enjoy walking back down the mountain instead of taking the return train – but make sure you have enough time to get down safely.

The new £9million visitor centre at the summit (replacing a trusty 1930s café) is a stunning creation of stone, steel and glass. Christened Hafod Eryri, it offers views in the warm, whether in the café or among the interpretive displays.

Open Daily, late March to early Nov, 9am–5pm in peak season. **Tickets** adults £22 return, £15 single, children £15/£12. £3.50 charge for advance credit/debit card bookings. **Amenities** café, gift shop, toilets.

> **INSIDER TIP**
>
> Book half-price tickets for Snowdon Mountain Railway's 9am departure on the ticket hotline (0870 458 0033) at least one day in advance. Just do it. It's a gamble with the weather (and tickets are non-refundable) but you're unlikely to have the time to hang around for days waiting for the sky to clear. And sunny summer days are chaos – we arrived at 10.30am and had to queue 30

minutes for seats on the earliest train available which was 2pm. Other departures are bookable on the day by phone, for a small fee.

National Slate Museum ★
VALUE ALL AGES

Padarn Country Park, Llanberis, Gwynedd, LL55 4TY, 01286 870630, www.museumwales.ac.uk

You wouldn't put a slate museum down as a place for children to have fun, but they loved it. They sat and watched slates being split, stared open-mouthed at the huge buzz saws used to cut up trees for railway sleepers, ran past the historic workers' houses, climbed on slate walls, and looked at slate things in the gift shop. The slate once quarried at Dinorwig in Llanberis was exported all over the world and, at its peak – 1850–1910 – employed 3,000 men. You can still imagine them hard at work in the impressive Victorian-built engineering workshops that now house the National Slate Museum. Their spirit lives on in the workshops where you can still see the machinery used to cut whole trees into logs, the blacksmiths' forges, slate rail locomotive, iron and brass foundry and much more. There are regular slate splitting demos, which really bring home the skills of the slate workers and the harsh conditions under which they worked. There are also guided quarry walks. A row of four slate miners' cottages has been re-erected

National Slate Museum, Llanberis, is much more entertaining than it sounds

behind the workshops and furnished to illustrate the differences in lifestyle from 1861 – when Dinorwig opened – until 1969 – when it closed. It really is an interesting place, with a good café and small play area on site. Best of all – it's free.

Open *Easter–Oct, daily, 10am–5pm. Nov–Easter, Sun–Fri, 10am–4pm. Closed Dec 24, 25, 26, Jan 1.* **Admission** *free.* **Amenities** *café, gift shop, play area, children's activities during school holidays.*

Electric Mountain & Dinorwig Power Station OLDER CHILDREN

Llanberis, LL55 4UR, 📞 *01286 870636, www.electricmountain. co.uk*

Electric Mountain is the evocative name used to describe Dinorwig Power Station, an extraordinary feat of engineering deep inside Elidir Fawr mountain, where slate was once mined. The Electric Mountain adventure begins at its visitor centre in Llanberis, next to Padarn Country Park. It's from here that the expedition buses take visitors over to the power station and into one of the biggest man-made caverns in Europe for a close-up look at one of the world's fastest response turbine generators (meaning flick a switch and it can be heating your kettle within minutes). It's a tour which may appeal more to machine-obsessed dads and lads – although the facts and figures really are impressive. The bus then takes everybody back to the visitor centre, where children may enjoy playing with the science-based games in the Techniquest room. When we visited, this was free of charge and kept the children entertained while we queued to see the film shown before boarding the bus. There's also a small children's area next to Connections Café where the children can do colouring for free while you enjoy a Fairtrade coffee. The café is a nice airy place, with mountain views, and a garden, and there's Welsh rarebit and Welsh cheese ploughman's on the menu. The Den soft play area is £2.50–4 depending on age.

*Open June, July, Aug, school/bank holidays, daily, 9.30am–5.30pm; Feb–May and Sept–Jan, daily, 10am–4.30pm. Closed Dec 24, 25, 26. **Admission** adults £7, children £3.50; various family tickets. Entrance to visitor centre free. **Credit** V, MC. **Amenities** Café, gift shop, Techniquest play area, soft play area, exhibitions.*

Llanberis Lake Railway
ALL AGES

Padarn Country Park, Llanberis, LL55 4TY, ☎ 01286 870549, www.lake-railway.co.uk

The little steam trains pulling these lovely old carriages once transported slate from the engineering workshops that are now the National Slate Museum Llanberis. The start of the Llanberis Lake Railway experience is a few yards away at Gilfach Ddu station, within Padarn Country Park. Confusingly, the railway first takes you to Llanberis, then back out again to the country park and around Padarn Lake to Penllyn. But the advantage of this is that having parked your car near the slate museum you can jump off at Llanberis to have a look around the town, then get back on for a picnic at the lakeside Cei Llydan station before catching another train to the end of the line at Penllyn where the train simply turns around to take you back to Gilfach Ddu. Children tire quickly of train rides (a way of getting somewhere rather than enjoyment for its own sake) but this one is useful as swift transport for a nice half-day out.

Llanberis Lake Railway is a great way to go for a picnic

Open *June, July, Aug, daily, 9.30am–5.30pm; April, May, Sept Sun–Fri with occasional Sundays; Feb-March, Oct–Dec, intermittently. Closed Jan.* **Admission** *adults £6.50, children £4.50; family £19.* **Amenities** *café, gift shop.*

Beddgelert

A magical place in more ways than one, Beddgelert is one of the prettiest villages in Wales, with its old stone bridge over the bubbling Rivers Colwyn and Glaslyn, and its cafes, pubs and craft shops decorated with window boxes full of flowers. It's the ideal place for mooching about, eating ice cream, or wandering along the river bank for a gentle stroll in the sunshine. Beautiful **Aberglaslyn Pass** and **Nant Gwynant Valley** provide exhilarating walks for those with older children, but many people are content to limit themselves to the short walk along **the Glaslyn River** to **Gelert's Grave** – a monument to Prince Llewelyn the Great's faithful dog, Gelert. Legend has it that Llewelyn killed the dog because he thought it had savaged his baby son – but the dog had saved the baby from a wolf and Llewelyn only realised his mistake when he found his son hiding. Spoilsports say the legend was made up by a local innkeeper who built a cairn to mark the grave as a tourist attraction, but where's the romance in that? Another ideal family stroll along the River Glaslyn is to **Cae Gel** wild flower meadow and picnic spot, which has been planted with shrubs and trees in memory of Alfred Edmeades Bestall, who illustrated the *Rupert Bear* stories for the *Daily Express* and once lived in Beddgelert.

Sygun Copper Mine ★
OLDER CHILDREN

Beddgelert, Gwynedd, LL55 4NE, 📞 *01766 890595, www.sygun coppermine.co.uk. On A498, just west of Beddgelert.*

It's not very often you get to go down a copper mine, and this one is especially interesting because of its beautiful location in Gwynant Valley, in the heart of Snowdonia. The list of activities available makes it even more beguiling. Our children couldn't get in fast enough, (partly because of the swirling, misty rain), and enjoyed the clambering, ladder-climbing self-guided tour along and up tunnels. They listened to the recorded accounts of conditions down the mine, abandoned in 1903, and loved the bit where all the lights go out. There are no huge caverns, which is a little disappointing, but the few stalagmites and stalactites are beautiful burnished copper colours. The tour ends much higher up the mountain than where you start, and the walk back down is stunningly beautiful through shoulder-high gorse. A huge success on our visit was the panning for (fools') gold, for a small extra charge – the children still have their little bottles of loot on display. There's also the chance to paint pottery or go metal detecting for coins –

all for a small charge. The nature trails are free.

Open *Easter–Oct, daily, 9.30am–5pm; Dec 26, Jan1 and Feb half term, 9.30am–5pm.* **Admission** *adults £7.95, children £5.95, OAPs £6.95.* **Amenities** *museum, nature trails, gift shop, play area.*

Betws-y-Coed

A tourist retreat since Victorian times, this is a town that retains some of its original rugged grandeur alongside an influx of outdoors shops and more. It's a nice place to walk through and there's a bit of history to throw at the children – the gorgeous 14th-century St Michael's Church, one of the county's oldest, and Thomas Telford's 1815 iron Waterloo Bridge (taking the A5 over the River Conwy), which carries the inscription *This arch was constructed in the same year the battle of Waterloo was fought.* **Conwy Valley Railway Museum** (*www.conwy railwaymuseum.co.uk*) operates fun daily miniature steam trains for rides next to the town's real station. Under-10s can drive Toby the miniature tram, and there are exhibits and a shop. **Betws-y-coed Motor Museum** (📞 *01690 710760;* daily April–Oct, 10am–6pm) at an old farm near the station, is a private collection of cars from a Model T Ford to classic Aston Martin.

Along one side of town is the charming Gwydr Forest and **Gwydr Forest Park** with walks and cycle paths. **Swallow Falls**, where the River Llugwy thunders

down into a narrow chasm, are quite spectacular. Also worth a look are **Conwy Falls**, off the road to Pentrefoelas, and **Fairy Glen** off the A470 where the River Conwy flows through a narrow gorge.

Blaenau Ffestiniog

A fascinating but grim town, worth visiting if only to see the mountains of slate waste left behind by the almost defunct slate industry. In fact Blaenau Ffestiniog was regarded as such an eyesore that it isn't officially included in Snowdonia National Park, although it's surrounded by it on all sides. Ironically, the slate mounds have a gloomy beauty in the springtime when they're a riot of colour, covered in wild rhododendrons. However most people come simply to ride the **Ffestiniog Railway** (see Porthmadog) or visit a slate mine. There are also some good walks into the Vale of Ffestiniog.

Llechwedd Slate Caverns
OLDER CHILDREN

Blaenau Ffestiniog, LL41 3NB, 📞 *01766 830306, www.llechwedd-slate-caverns.co.uk*

More dark and dirty history with one of Wales's most important slate mines, but done in a very smart way. Above ground you've got the Victorian village, with an old-fashioned sweet shop and lots of people in costume, as well as the Miner's Arms – an original pub that plays its part serving family lunches in the garden. Underground you've got two fabulous attractions in one. The Deep Mine tour takes you on Britain's steepest passenger railway, which drops 30m leaving you, with the addition of some steps, 137m below the mountain summit, where you can walk through huge caverns. The Miners' Tramway is a small battery-electric train which goes through an 1846 tunnel, again with walks and exhibits.

Open daily, 10am; last tour 5.15pm March–Sept, 4.15pm Oct–Feb. *Admission* both rides, adult £14.75, OAP £12.50, child, child £11.25; one ride, £9.25£7.75/£7. *Amenities* museum, nature trails, gift shop, play area

Bala

This pretty little place is no more than a single, Georgian-style main street, here because of **Llyn Tegid** – Lake Bala – the biggest natural lake in Wales. The lake is six and a half kilometres long, over one and a half kilometres wide, and well over 30m deep in places. The town gets packed with tourists, and the lake, home to the **National Whitewater Centre** (see p 230), becomes awash with kayakers and other water-sports types. **Bala Lake Railway** has splendid views as it runs along the lake from a station just south of town.

Capel Curig

More of a walking headquarters than a tourist destination, children might enjoy visiting the

Ugly House here (☎ 01690 720287), a tiny Seven Dwarfs-like cottage said to have been built in the 15th century. It's now the office for the Snowdonia Society but there's an exhibition room and four acres of gardens and woodland to explore for just £1. The town has plenty of cafes and outdoor equipment shops, but many people are drawn by the internationally-renowned **Plas Y Brenin – The National Mountain Centre** (see p 231).

INSIDER TIP »

Sleepy Llanrwst has one of the most picturesque tea rooms you've ever seen. Ty Hwnt I'r Bont was once a courthouse but is now owned by the National Trust and serves splendid cream teas on the banks of the River Conwy.

Harlech

This is a pleasant town, with Snowdonia on one side and the might of the castle on the other, the splendid backdrop of Tremadog Bay fighting to get a look in. **Harlech Castle** (☎ 01766 780552; www.cadw.wales.gov.uk open daily, 9.30am (closed Dec 24–26, Jan 1), June–Aug until 6pm, April, May, Oct 5pm, Nov–March, 4pm, Sun 11am–4pm, adults £3.50, concessions £3, families £10,) is one of those perfect, film set castles built by Edward I as one of a string designed to keep the Welsh in check. Ironically, it was captured by Welsh warrior Owain Glyndwr in 1404, who used it for a Welsh parliament. Interestingly, a long siege at the

Why Slate Still Rocks

In a world of PlayStations and *The Simpsons*, a small nation's mining history might not seem an obvious attraction for children. But the Welsh manage to make it appealing with a combination of dark caverns and chunky machinery. Slate is the backbone of Snowdonia – its colour forming the overwhelming backdrop of the area. Slate also made Snowdonia wealthy in the 19th century as it covered the roofs of homes across Britain and the world. Today it features in a number of tourist attractions that please youngsters as well as their parents. The National Slate Museum in Llanberis is the place to start, with its steam trains, sheds, chainsaws and big hammers. This is where watching a dusty workman splitting slate into wafer-thin sheets somehow transfers its magical appeal to youngsters.

Blaenau Ffestiniog is at the heart of the slate-producing region and is surrounded by mountains of strangely-beautiful rubble. Just outside town are the Llechwedd Slate Caverns, with a choice of underground tours.

Llanfair Slate Caverns near Harlech are gorgeous in their echoey, cathedral-like scope; they're old, and roofed many an industrial town with their slate, some of the world's oldest.

And if you want to take some home with you, try the Inigo Jones Slateworks near Caernarfon which has been making things from slate since 1861, starting with school boards and now trendy stuff like floors and fireplaces alongside things you can actually get in the car such as clocks and place mats. Take a workshop tour and see your holiday gifts being made.

castle during the Wars of the Roses between the houses of Lancaster and York, resulted in the Welsh song Men of Harlech. The castle is almost as invincible now as it was in the 13th century, and with views from the towers out to sea and inland to Snowdonia and the Llyn Peninsular it is one of the most dramatic of Welsh castles. The town is backed by a network of sand dunes and the golden sweep of Harlech beach, and the Cambrian coast line train calls here. There are also walks into the surrounding hills and valleys.

Llanfair Slate Caverns and Children's Farm Park ALL AGES

Harlech, LL46 2SA, ✆ *01766 780247,* ***www.llanfairslatecaverns.co.uk.*** *One and a half kilometres south of Harlech on A496.*

The slate here is among the oldest in the world and caverns are impressively cathedral-like, though they'll probably be more interesting for older children than under 8s, who are catered for at the Farm Park. Here you'll see some of the cuddlier varieties of farm animals, and there are other amusements such as crazy golf and water blasters. The beauty of the farm is that your ticket lasts seven days so you can really get your money's worth.

Open *daily, Easter–Sept, 10am–5pm (caverns 11am–4pm).* **Admission** *caverns: adult £4.30, child £3.20, OAP £3.70, family £14–16; farm: adult £4.20, child £, OAP £3.70, family.* **Amenities** *café, gift shop, picnic areas.*

Shell Island

This is the ultimate place for beachcombing. It's not so much an island as a peninsula cut off by the sea at high tide, and it's absolute heaven for any child intent on collecting shells and pretty pebbles, or spending the day rockpooling. The beach is littered with shells washed up by winter storms – about 200 varieties – and the best time to collect them is between January and April. However, this is private land and you have to pay to cross the causeway £6 per car June–Aug, £5 March, May, Sept, Oct, £4 weekends in Nov/Dec) and use the three beaches, which

includes a nine and a half kilometre sandy beach backed by dunes. You can stay at the 45-acre tents-only camp site, where tents must be at least 18m apart for privacy, or in three holiday flats. The island has its own Tavern bar, reasonably-priced café (with children's menu), and a restaurant in a converted barn, which opens for Sunday lunch. Shell Island (*www.shellisland.co.uk*) is two miles west of Llanbedr on the A496.

Barmouth

Driving in past the fairground rides and bucket and spade shops, then crossing the seafront railway line (there are trains down from Porthmadog) amid holiday crowds, we didn't hold out too much hope on our first visit to Barmouth. But what we found was a big, fun, sandy beach with masses of space for everyone. The expanse gives over to dunes at one end, where we ate our lunch looking at the mountain backdrop

Barmouth

and the people hiking up **Dinas Oleu**, where Snowdonia tumbles into the sea. This was the first property given to the National Trust when it was formed in 1895, and you can follow Panorama Walk to the top where you'll have fantastic views of the town and the incredibly beautiful Mawddach estuary. At the estuary end of the beach the road curves round and the quayside part of town becomes quite attractive with ice cream shops, cafes, pubs and a place selling seafood. From here you can see the Fairbourne and Barmouth steam train puffing on the other side of the estuary, and making its way across the bridge – which you can also walk across. Leaving town along the A496 towards Dolgellau you'll experience the full beauty of the Mawddach estuary – it's breathtaking.

Dolgellau

A dark, handsome market town with enticing shops and cafes, and an excellent farmers market (third Sunday each month) doesn't offer much to interest the average child. Not far away, however, is Fairbourne, starting point of the **Fairbourne Steam Railway** (01341 250362, *www.fairbourne railway.com*) with its museum, nature centre and station tea room. The railway is only a few kilometres long and runs between Fairbourne, which has a sandy beach (although not much else), and Penrhyn Point, where you can catch the ferry to Barmouth.

A family ticket costs £18 return. Thirteen kilometres north of Dolgellau on the A470 is **Coed y Brenin** (0845 6040845, *www. forestry.gov.uk*), a mountain bike mecca and a great place for outdoor families, too. It's run by the Forestry Commission Wales and as well as mountain bike trails, walks and an orienteering course suitable for children, there is also an adventure playground, visitor centre and café – with stunning views up to the Cadair Idris mountain range. There's a bike hire and repair shop and riverside picnic spot, too.

Tywyn

This is a quiet seaside town with five glorious miles of golden, sandy beach that never gets crowded. But most people come to Tywyn for the **Talyllyn Railway** (*www.talyllyn.co.uk*), which winds its way through the delightful green and tree-lined **Tywyn Valley**. The railway was built to transport slate from the mines, and passengers to isolated farms, but it was near to closure in 1950 until the world's first railway preservation society was formed to save it. The group of volunteers ran their first service in 1951, and trains have run ever since. Buy a Day Rover ticket (adults £11, accompanied children £2, under 5s free) and you can ride all day. Many people stop at **Dolgoch**, a short walk from waterfalls, and at **Abergynolwyn** where there are picnic tables and an adventure playground. There's also a good network of paths near the final stop, **Nant Gwernol**. Back at Tywyn Wharf you can explore the **Narrow Gauge Railway Museum,** and see locomotives plus memorabilia from nearly 80 British narrow gauge railways.

Aberdyfi (Aberdovey)

Equally well known by its Welsh name – Aberdyfi – as by the English Aberdovey version, this is a town popular with those who like watersports, thanks to the beautiful River Dyfi (Dovey). The river is a broad, peaceful estuary by the time it reaches here, and makes its way the last few kilometres to the sea. Once an important port, the town is now a quiet but colourful village, full of specialist shops. It's particularly linked with the **Outward Bound** organisation, which has a centre here. If you want a rather more relaxing time, the estuary is also good for just digging in the sand, paddling and crabbing off the jetty in the calm, salty waters.

For Active Families

Canolfan Tryweryn National Whitewater Centre ★
AGES 12 AND UP

Frongoch, Bala, Gwynedd LL23 7NU, 📞 *01678 521083, www.ukrafting. co.uk. Just northwest of Bala, on the A2412.*

This is a serious rafting operation in Snowdonia National Park on Afon Tryweryn, covering eight kilometres of classic whitewater, fed by releases from the Llyn Celyn reservoir, so able to operate almost year-round. Minimum age is 12 (able to swim 25 metres). There are also Orcas, two-man inflatables like a cross between rafts and kayaks (from age 16), with a guide paddling alongside.

Open variable, but most of the year. ***Prices*** *40-minute raft taster £28, wetsuit £2. Midweek £228 per raft (seats 7), wetsuit £5. No child reductions. Half-day Orca £70pp (including guide), wetsuit £5.* ***Amenities*** *free parking, picnic areas, café, shop, showers, lockers.*

Surf Lines AGES 8 AND UP

Unit 2, Y Glyn, Llanberis, LL55 4EL, 📞 *01286 879001, www.surf-lines. co.uk. 100m off the main road at the north end of the village.*

This is run by adventure activity gurus who offer watery and rocky fun, with family options among the school parties and corporate bonding, with day and half-day sessions climbing and kayaking around Llanberis. There's also coasteering (scrambling around) and kayaking off the coast. If as a family you want to try other things such as a day hiking in the mountains, they're open to suggestions. On organised trips they can take unaccompanied children from age 8, but as parents you're free to bring younger ones, and adrenaline levels are geared to match.

Open whenever there are bookings, although summer is regarded as family time. ***Prices*** *Family packages (2X2), £140 (half day), £220 (day), £430 (two days).* ***Amenities*** *free parking, picnic areas, café, shop.*

The National Mountain Centre AGES 8 AND UP

Plas y Brenin, Capel Curig, LL24 OET, 📞 *01690 720214,* **www.pyb.co.uk**

This is a top-class adventure outfit, which also caters for children and families with taster days. Two hours of climbing, canoeing or skiing costs £12 – or all three in one day cost £30. The courses are open for children from the age of eight, and over 10s can be left there to get on with it – though adults can join in too. There are also residential courses at the smart, comfortable centre.

Amenities Accommodation, bar, restaurant, car park, climbing wall, dry ski slope.

Outward Bound AGES 8 AND UP

Aberdovey, 📞 *01931 740000,* **www. outwardbound.org.uk**

Outward Bound has galvanised generations of teenagers into taking up outdoor pursuits, and now families can get a piece of the action here with weekend courses in water sports (from their own wharf) and mountaineering. There are forest cabins for overnight expeditions. Two-day courses (on Bank Holiday weekends) cost £150 (£75 children) and include accommodation and food. The far more serious three-week Welsh Expedition, age 16–24, is £1,300. Download a brochure from the website.

FAMILY-FRIENDLY ACCOMMODATION

Being a very traditional holiday area, there are all the guest houses, B&Bs and self-catering accommodation you'd expect. Much of it is very good, and there are increasing numbers of stylish places.

EXPENSIVE

Ffynnon ★★★

Brynffynnon, Love Lane, Dolgellau, LL40 1RR, 📞 *01341 421774,* **www. ffynnontownhouse.com**

This townhouse at the foot of Cader Idris is not only a luxury guesthouse with just three sublime suites, it's also as child-friendly as they come. Each bedroom is a welter of Egyptian cotton and goosedown, one with a king-size brass bedstead. Rates include breakfast, afternoon tea on arrival, use of the exquisite lounge with honesty bar and butler's pantry (where you can prepare snacks), and library and gardens. Each suite can take an extra bed – a proper job, not fold-up – and there are free cots, high chairs, baby monitor, steriliser and child friendly crockery and cutlery. Children's high tea is about £5 depending on requirements. There are board games, DVDs, PlayStation 2, and swings and trampoline in the heady garden – which also has a barbecue for a relaxed family evening, as well as a hot tub (which children can use if they're with parents).

3 suites. From £120. Extra child in a bed £25, baby in cot free. **Amenities** lounge with TV, DVDs. *In room TV/DVD, free WiFi.*

Plas Coch Guest House ★

High Street, Llanberis, LL55 4HB, 📞 *01286 872122, www.plas-coch. co.uk*

This big, relaxed B&B in a cosy 19th-century stone house in the village centre is just along from the mountain railway. Family-run by Frank and Jane Gibson along with their friendly dog, it's a children's favourite offering comfortable rooms, double, twin, or family, with extra beds for youngsters. A big lounge provides games and books, and excellent breakfasts feature kippers, kedgeree, and local top-quality bacon and sausages. The owners fall over themselves to cater to children's wishes.

8 rooms. From £56 double. Free cots. Children under 6, £10 regardless of length of stay; 6–10 £5 per night, min charge £10; 11–13 £10 per night. Amenities lounge, restaurant, car park. In room TV, tea maker.

Glan-y-Bala

Llanberis, LL55 4TY, 📞 *01286 871097, www.glanybala.com*

A delightfully restored complex on a hillside overlooks the town and lakes, with three self-catering options. Set in seven acres of land that cries out for muddy-kneed exploring, there are still the remains of pigsties, chicken coops and other treasures from the farm that dated back to the 17th century, though the main residence was built in the mid

19th century for the Dinorwig slate quarry manager. Here there are two apartments, one which sleeps two or three, the other sleeps eight, plus two children in bunks, along with a single futon in the lounge. Cots are free, along with high chairs and playpens. In some places the solid slate flooring and Victorian pine woodwork still exist.

The neighbouring Coach House has been converted by local craftsmen into a holiday cottage sleeping six. It includes a 9m lounge with cathedral ceiling, suntrap courtyard and barbecue. It's a bit of a walk from the busy High Street, but all the better for it – and the children can charge around in safety.

From £280pw for 2. Cots (up to age 2) and high chairs free. Extra bed £25pw. Dogs £10pw. Cycle store, drying room, coin-operated laundry. In room TV, video, stereo, kitchen.

Cadair View Lodge

Trawsfynydd Holiday Village, Bronaber, Trawsfynydd, LL41 4YB, 📞 *01978 759603, www.cadairviewlodge.co. uk. Just off the A470, 16km north of Dolgellau.*

This is the collective name for more than 20 individually-owned log cabins within a sprawling and rural holiday village in Snowdonia National Park. Most sleep six, with two bedrooms and a sofabed, the others catering for two to four. Some also have an extra foldaway bed. Don't think this is roughing it: these are warm, comfy places in a beautiful spot with views of Cadair Idris and only three kilometres from

Coed y Brenin forest and its biking trails for all abilities (mountain bikes can be rented on site). There are also lots of other biking and hiking opportunities, and it's close to Porthmadog-Ffestiniog with the railways and shops.

From £220 for 2 nights, up to £550 for a week high season. Travel cot and high chair for small charge. **Amenities** *general store, off-licence, launderette, pub/restaurant, parking.* **In cabin** *food welcome basket, household essentials, TV, DVD, CD.*

INEXPENSIVE

Bryn Gwynant Youth Hostel ★

Nantgwynant, LL55 4NP, ☎ 0870 770 5732, www.yha.org.uk. On the A498, 6.5km east of Beddgelert.

A lakeside Victorian mansion with views of Mt Snowdon, this is a perfect place for exploring. While there are plenty of the woolly sock brigade, it's comfortable and fine for families, with four rooms with four beds, three with five, and one with three, along with several bunk rooms. The 40 acres of grounds are great for youngsters. It's just one of a handful of hostels around Snowdonia.

£12 per night adults, £9 under 18s. **Credit** *MC, V.* **Amenities** *restaurant, self-catering kitchen, lounge, parking, cycle store, washing machine.*

Nantcol Waterfalls ★

Cefn Uchaf, Llanbedr, LL45 2PL, ☎ 01341 241209, www.nantcol waterfalls.co.uk. From A496 turn inland at Victoria Hotel just north of Barmouth and follow signs.

Well, at least you don't have to worry about trying to get the children to wash – there isn't anywhere for that other than a quick splash in the river. This camp site is a wild place on the edge of the mountains, right by the falls of the same name. And you don't have to worry about whether they allow barbies – the owners will sell you logs for a campfire.

Children love the near-barbaric simplicity of it all and there are great walks that aren't daunting for youngsters – one around a lake with its own island, another through 10 acres of woodland open by Prince Charles in 1995, and another following the river.

Camping/caravans, £5 adult, £2 child (4–16). **Amenities** *portable toilets (Easter–Sept), parking.*

FAMILY-FRIENDLY DINING

In Snowdonia if you dress casual you'll still be too smart for the simple restaurants and tourist staples.

MODERATE

Dovey Inn ★

Sea View Terrace, Aberdovey, LL35 0EF, zzz ☎ 01654 767332, www. doveyinn.com

A friendly, rambling pub with B&B rooms (including two family rooms for four) is at the heart of the Aberdovey social scene, on the banks of the Dyfi estuary with glorious views. Families are catered for with a special (cosy) indoor area, and there are two patios. The menu includes local lamb shank, steak and sea bass,

Pete's Eats, Llanberis

fish and home-cut chips, burgers, lasagne – and pint mugs of hot chocolate (tea, too) that send youngsters into a dream. It's good value – children's menu from £2.05 (egg and chips), plus baked potatoes and other stuff they like, particularly the sticky puddings. Breakfasts are good and they actually sell chip butties. There's now the posher Pete's Bistro across the street, serving varied tapas-style food (although we can't see the children demanding black pudding with red cabbage and sultana coleslaw) with a couple of flats available above, sleeping six.

Open *8am— (10.30pm high summer). Main courses £2.40–10.*

Rhaedr Peris

59 High Street, Llanberis, LL55 4HA, ☎ *01286 871239.*

This friendly and often packed, reasonably-priced child-friendly place includes a tucked away rock-walled garden with tables. Tuesday night is £5 night with queues to get a table for the specials, which include a glass of wine. When we were there they had spag bol, moules mariniere, burger and fries or a big bowl of decidedly perky spicy fish soup – a rather Thai-like affair. The bottle of wine we ordered for a sunny evening drink by the pond was less than £10, and came as 1 litre, which was much needed as they forgot about us in the fray and we only just crept in before the 9pm cut-off.

Open *noon–9pm.* **Main courses** *£5–15.*

along with pizzas. Children's menu includes pizzas and smaller portions of adult meals. There's a Friday evening barbie in July and August.

Open *daily. Food, summer: Mon–Fri noon–2.30pm, 5.30pm–9.30pm, Sat/Sun noon–9pm. Main courses £8–13.* **Credit** *MC, V.*

INEXPENSIVE

Pete's Eats ★

40 High Street, Llanberis, LL55 4EU, ☎ *01286 872135, **www.petes-eats. co.uk***

It's the place where you eat if you've been yomping up and down hillsides, paddling canoes and stuff, a favourite of the active community since 1978. But the friendly, colourful (it's painted bright blue), hippyish combination of caff and café is great for families too. There are

The Insider

USEFUL CONTACTS

Local council websites are a wealth of information about beauty spots and activities, especially in the popular holiday areas. In some regions there are also separate websites for tourist authorities.

Visit Wales is the national tourist organisation that produces a huge selection of informative and attractive brochures on destinations, activities, accommodation and more. Its website (*www.visitwales.com*) also leads you to individual sites dealing with specific activities, such as cycling and golf.

West Wales

Pembrokeshire
www.pembrokeshire.gov.uk
www.visitpembrokeshire.com

Carmathenshire
www.carmarthenshire.gov.uk,
www.visit-carmarthenshire.co.uk

Neath
www.neath-porttalbot.gov.uk

South Wales

Southern Wales is a tourist organisation uniting 10 regions from the Seven to the Vale of Glamorgan and up to the Brecon Beacons: *www.southernwales.com*

Cardiff
www.cardiff.gov.uk
www.visitcardiff.com

Swansea
www.swansea.gov.uk
visitswanseabay.com

Monmouthshire
www.monmouthshire.gov.uk
www.visitmonmouthshire.co.uk

Bridgend
www.bridgend.gov.uk

Glamorgan
www.valeofglamorgan.gov.uk

North Wales

North Wales Tourism (*www.nwt.co.uk*) covers Snowdonia, the Borderlands, Anglesey and the north coast.

Anglesey
www.anglesey.gov.uk
www.visitanglesey.com

Snowdonia
www.snowdonia-npa.gov.uk

The website of Snowdonia National Park Authority.
www.snowdonia.org.uk

The tourist authority.
www.star-attractions.co.uk
Group representing many of the region's top attractions.

Conwy
www.conwy.gov.uk
vititconwy.org.uk

Denbighshire
www.denbighshire.gov.uk

Flintshire
www.flintshire.gov.uk

Wrexham
www.wrexham.gov.uk

North Wales Borderlands (*www.borderlands.co.uk*) is the tourist board for Flintshire, Denbighshire and Wrexham.

Mid Wales

Cardiganshire

www.ceredigion.gov.uk
www.tourism.ceredigion.gov.uk
www.visitcardigan.com
www.gomidwales.co.uk unites a number of tourist organisations, *www.breconbeaconstourism.co.uk*, is tourist groups in and around the park, while *www.brecon beacons.org* is the National Park itself.

Powys

www.powys.gov.uk
www.tourism.powys.gov.uk

ACCOMMODATION

There are dozens, if not hundreds, of firms specialising in cottages and apartments for rent. It's impossible to list them all but here are some of the bigger ones.

www.stayinwales.co.uk is a commercial site but a good place to look for accommodation from camp sites upward.

For camping gear, we'd recommend Blacks (*www.blacks.co. uk*) for the latest in high tech but reasonably-priced family tents which make life a whole lot easier – simple to assemble with separate bedrooms, hanging space and even strings of LED lights which work off a tiny battery. Millets (*www.millets.co.uk*) also has a selection of good stuff.

English Country Cottages

Despite the name, a huge array of stylish cottages and homes across the country, even places that will take 20-plus for a major family get together. *www.eng-cc. co.uk*, ☏ 08700 781100

West Wales Cottages A selection of self-catering properties in and around New Quay, on the coast and inland, with some ideal properties for families. *www.westwales-cottages.com*, ☏ 01545 580496

Coastal Cottages of Pembrokeshire

Massive selection of properties in the southwest throughout the year, even Christmas get-togethers, with clusters of cottages sleeping up to 45. *www.coastalcottages.co. uk*, ☏ 01437 765765

Youth Hostels Association

With around 30 properties in Wales, from the very edge of the sea to half way up mountains, this is the way to see Wales at a bargain price. *www.yha.org.uk*, ☏ 0870 770 6113 *reservations)*

Caravan Club Several club sites (some open to non-members) and many associated sites for caravans, camper vans and tents. *www.caravanclub.co.uk*

Camping and Caravanning Club

Club sites (some open to non-members and dozens of certified sites for tents, caravans and camper vans. *www.campingand caravanningclub.co.uk*

A Smattering of Useful Words

Aber	river mouth	**ffordd**	road
Afon	river	**gorsaf**	station
Araf	slow	**gwesty**	hotel
bach/fach	small	**heddlu**	police
bont/pont	bridge	**llan**	church lands
bwlch	gap, pass	**llyn**	lake
carreg	stone	**llwybr**	public
cefn	ridge	**cyhoeddus**	footpath
coed	wood	**lôn**	lane
croes/groes	cross	**marched**	ladies
cwm	valley	**mynydd**	mountain
dim mynediad	no entry	**pen**	top
dim	no	**rhyd**	ford
dinas	fort, city	**siôp**	shop
dynion	gentlemen	**Swyddfa'r Post**	Post Office
eglwys	church	**Toiledau**	toilets
fawr/mawr	big	**Traeth**	beach
felin/melin	mill	**Ysbyty**	hospital

ACTIVITY INFORMATION

The British Activity Holiday Association details a number of quality options, including family breaks. *www.baha.org.uk*, 📞 *01244 301342*

National Cycle Network A whole array of pedal power ideas throughout Wales, from cycle trails to cycle hire. *www.national cyclenetwork.co.uk*, 📞 *0845 113 0065*

Activitypembrokeshire.com County Council website with an in-depth listing of activities, with links to individual sites such as its own *www. cyclepembrokeshire.com*.

Walesdirectory.co.uk Directory with extensive information of tourist spots, accommodation and towns throughout Wales.

Goodbeachguide.co.uk Directory of beaches by the Marine Conservation Society, from major resorts to remote spots, with details of sand and water quality, along with access, parking and facilities.

FARMERS' MARKETS

The co-operative FARMAcymru (*www. farmacymru.org.uk*) co-ordinates farmers' markets at more than 40 locations, farm shops and pick-your-own farms. Its website has a list of all farmers' markets. The website *www.organicwales.com* is also a useful reference for markets, produce and events. Markets around the country include:

Cardiff Riverside Farmers' Market (Sundays, 10am–2pm) Fitzhamon Embankment, *www.riversidemarket.org.uk*

Celyn Farmers' Markets Mold, Flintshire (St Mary's Church Hall, King Street, first Saturday of the month, 9am–2pm).
Northop, Flintshire (Welsh College of Horticulture, third Sunday of the month, 9am–1pm). *www.celynfarmersmarket.co.uk*

Chepstow Farmers' Market (Senior Citizens Centre, Cormeilles Square, first Tuesday of each month, 9am–1pm.
📞 *01291 650672*

Colwyn Bay Farmers' Market (Bayview Shopping Centre car park, every Thursday, 9am–3pm. 📞 *01492 680209*)

Mumbles Farmers' Market (Dairy Car Park, on the Seafront, Swansea, 2nd Saturday of the month, 9am–1pm. *www.mumblesmatters.org.uk*)

The Welsh Assembly actually has what amounts to a good eating department, whose website, *www.foodwales.com*, is a treasure trove of info on farmers' markets and shops, festivals and regional food, along with recipes and news on its annual True Taste Wales Food & Drink Awards.

OTHER USEFUL CONTACTS

CADW The guardian of many historic buildings and sites in Wales and the Welsh equivalent of English Heritage. English Heritage members of more than one year can get free entry to Cadw sites (and vice versa). In case you need to know – it's pronounced cadew. *www.cadw.wales.gov.uk*

The National Trust The organisation looks after a large number of historic properties throughout Wales, as well as large tracts of coastline, *www.nationaltrust.org.uk*

Railways in Wales Quirkily enthusiastic website that has more information than you'll ever need about both historic train services and the modern network. *www.walesrails.co.uk*

Boating

It's possible to hire boats on Welsh waterways, although the choice is small by UK standards. Ukboathire.com has narrow boats available from Goytre Wharf on the Monmouth and Brecon Canal. From Goytre you head north through the Brecon Beacons National Park to Brecon, one of the longest lock-free stretches of waterway in the UK. Brecon Park Boats (*www.beaconparkboats.com*) also has longboats on the canal, from Llanfoist Wharf, a third of the way along. Hoseasons (*www.hoseasons.co.uk*), Maestermyn (*www.maestermyn. co.uk*), Anglo Welsh Waterway Holidays (*www.anglowelsh.co.uk*) and boatingholidaysdirect.com have boats on the Llangollen Canal which heads into north Wales, from Shropshire where you pick up your craft. Waterways UK (*www.waterways-uk. com*) has more general information. For a more active holiday it is possible to charter yachts from various harbours. *euphoriasailing. com* has a number of stylish vessels based at Swansea Marina. Charter Boat Wales (*www.charter boatwales.co.uk*) has a motor cruiser based at Deganwy, near Colwyn Bay, North Wales, for hire with skipper, for an unusual day out for groups of up to 10.

yachtcharterguide.com has a list of yachts, fishing boats and diving charters on offer around Wales.

Responsible Tourism

It's difficult to argue that holidays to Wales are completely innocent when it comes to carbon footprints, given the driving that can be involved, but for most of us they still offer a getaway without air travel. If you decide on a trip to a resort served by rail, all the better, although as we'd said before, Wales isn't an easy place if you don't have your own vehicle.

The Welsh Assembly (*www. new.wales.gov.uk*) has extensive details on sustainable tourism and current environmental initiatives. Many companies are working towards a greener world, whether it's in careful management or simply using local produce and materials. The eco-friendly Bluestone resort in Pembrokeshire (*www.bluestone wales.com*, and p 134) is a good example. Swansea Valley Holiday Cottages (*www.welshholiday cottages.com*, *01792 864611)* specialises in rentals from the Gower to the Brecon Beacons and boasts a strong environmental stance, from low-energy light bulbs to recycling bins. There's even a Carbon Neutral Cottage Holiday Scheme with climate-friendly projects such as tree planting at the company's farm HQ in the Swansea Valley.

responsibletravel.com has a selection of Welsh offerings on its site, from campsites and cottages to cycling tours and other low-emission activities.

ecotravelling.co.uk also has a number of different suggestions, including cycling and boat hire.

Index

See also Accommodations and Restaurant indexes, below.

General

A

Abbey Mill (Tintern), 61
Aberaeron, 165
Aberaeron Seafood Festival, 159
Abercastle, 140
Aberdaron, 205
Aberdovey Fun Fest, 218
Aberdyfi (Aberdovey), 230
Abereiddy, 140
Abergavenny, 107–108
Abergavenny Food Festival, 95
Aberglaslyn Pass, 224
Abergynolwyn, 229–230
Abermawr, 140
Aberporth, 162
Abersoch, 205
Aberystwyth, 165–167
Accommodations. *See also*
  Accommodations Index
  best, 5–7
  Brecon Beacons, 114–118
  Cardiff, 46–49
  information, 237–238
  Mid Wales, 184–187
  North Wales, 211–214
  Snowdonia, 231–233
  South Wales, 86–89
  West Wales, 147–150
Adventures Outdoor Activity Centre
  (Porthcawl), 86
Air travel, 15
Alice in Wonderland Centre (Llandudno),
  200
Amroth, 128
Anglesey, 203–204
Anglesey Outdoors, 204
Arthur, King, 113
Artisans Craft Shop (Lake Vyrnwy), 173

B

Bach Ventures (Llanberis), 220
The Bailey Walk, 110
Bala, 226
Bala, Lake, 226
Bala Lake Railway, 18, 226
Bangor, 201–202
Barafundle Bay, 132
Barmout, 228–229
Barry Island, 45–46
Barry Island Funfair, 46
Barry Island Railway, 19
Barry Island Railway Heritage Centre, 46
Beaches. *See also specific beaches*
  best, 3
  Cardiganshire (Ceredigion), 182
  Porthcawl, 71–72
Beacons Reservoir, 101
Beacons Way, 112

Beaumaris, 203–204
Beaumaris Castle, 204
Beddarthur (Arthur's Grave), 143
Beddgelert, 224
Bedford Park & Ironworks, 71
Bellis Country Market (Holt), 209–210
Bethania Adventure (Lake Vyrnwy), 173
Betws-y-Coed, 225
Betws-y-coed Motor Museum, 225
Big Pit (Blaenavon), 66
Biking and mountain biking, 8
  Coed y Brenin, 229
  Conwy Valley Cycle Route, 201
  Llys Y Fran cycle route
    (Haverfordwest), 145
  Machynlleth, 170
  Vale of Rheidol, 174
Bird Rock (Craig Yr Adar), 164
Bird-watching, 17
  Red Kite Feeding Station (Rhayader),
    170
  Skomer Island, 138
Black Mountain (Llyn-y-Fan Fach), 104
Black Mountain Activities (Brecon), 114
The Black Mountains, 106–107
Black Tar, 135
Blaenau Ffestiniog, 225, 227
Blaenavon, 55
Blaenavon World Heritage Site, 65–66
Bluestone, 134
Boating, 239–240
Boat trips. *See also specific destinations*
  best, 4
  Whitesands Bay, 139–140, 147
Bodnant Garden (Colwyn Bay), 200
Borth, 167–168
Borth Animalarium, 168
Borth-y-Gest, 206
Boulder Adventures (Llanberis), 220
Bracelet Bay, 80
Brandy Cove, 81
Brecknock Museum and Art Gallery
  (Brecon), 97
Brecon, 96–97
Brecon Beacons, 91–118
  accommodations, 114–118
  areas in brief, 93
  festivals, 95–96
  getting around, 94
  legends about, 113
  outdoor activities, 110–114
  restaurants, 118
  sights and activities, 96–110
  top 10 family experiences, 94–95
  visitor information, 93
Brecon Beacons Food Festival, 95
Brecon Beacons National Park, 93
Brecon Beacons National Park Llandovery
  Heritage Centre, 102
Brecon Beacons National Park Mountain
  Centre, 96–97
Brecon Cathedral, 96

Accommodations

Restaurants